Grade Aid

for

Kosslyn and Rosenberg

Fundamentals of Psychology in Context

Third Edition

prepared by

Marcia J. McKinley
Mount St. Mary's College

PEARSON

Boston   New York   San Francisco
Mexico City   Montreal   Toronto   London   Madrid   Munich   Paris
Hong Kong   Singapore   Tokyo   Cape Town   Sydney

ISBN-13: 978-0-205-54315-1
ISBN-10: 0-205-54315-4

Printed in the United States of America

10 9 8 7 6 5 4 3 2 1   10 09 08 07 06

Preface

This Grade Aid is designed to help you find your way in the new world you have just entered: Psychology. Through studying Psychology, you will learn about yourself and others. How do people think? How can you learn to remember people's names better? Why do some people develop psychological disorders and others don't? The Grade Aid will help you to better understand, conceptualize, and integrate the material in the text.

In the Grade Aid, you will find:

- **Before you read sections**, which contain a short summary of each chapter to help you understand its overall organization.

- **Chapter objectives**, or what you should learn from the chapter.

- **As you read sections**, including
  - A list of key terms, which you are encouraged to put on note cards for studying.
  - A collection of exercises designed to engage you in the active learning process, including tables to be completed, essay questions, and Web activities. These activities will allow you to understand the material in different ways. No answer keys have been provided for these exercises, and that's no mistake! The idea is for you to complete these exercises as you are reading the text – the answers are clear-cut, and can either be found directly in the textbook or require you to apply course content to your own life.

- **After you read sections**, including
  - "Thinking Back" questions, which ask you to integrate material from this chapter with material from previous chapters.
  - "Thinking Ahead" questions, which ask you to consider how the material you learned in the chapter may relate to future topics in the course.
  - "Practice Tests" that will allow you to check your comprehension of chapter material.

- **After you are finished sections** containing crossword puzzles that test your knowledge of the chapter material in a fun way!

Table of Contents

Chapter 1
Psychology: Yesterday and Today

Before You Read . . .

In this chapter, you will learn what psychology is and what psychologists do. The chapter also presents a theme that runs throughout the book: "levels of analysis." Basically, this means that we can understand most psychological concepts at the levels of the brain, the person, and the group. You will learn how psychology has evolved. Be sure you take note of the various schools of thought in psychology and the famous people in these schools, because you will be seeing these names again and again throughout the book! In addition, you will learn about the benefits of using the scientific method and how the scientific method is applied to psychology.

Hollywood might lead you to believe that most psychologists practice therapy (often badly), and that many of them behave unethically (e.g., in *Mumford* and *Prince of Tides*). In this chapter, you will learn the facts: Psychologists do lots of different things, and all psychologists are bound by ethical principles, both in research and clinical practice.

Chapter Objectives

- After reading this chapter, you should be able to:

- Define psychology.

- Describe the concept of "levels of analysis," and explain how it can be used to better understand psychology.

- Describe how psychology has evolved over time.

- Define the different fields of psychology.

- Discuss what the different types of psychologists do.

- Discuss each of the six steps of the scientific method and describe the benefits of using the scientific method to gain knowledge.

- Describe the differences among experimental, correlational, and descriptive research, and discuss when you would want to use each kind

- Discuss proper ethics in research with humans and animals and in clinical practice.

As You Read . . . Term Identification

Make flashcards using the following terms as you go. Use the definitions in the margins of this chapter for help. If you write the definitions in your own words, though, you will remember them better!

Academic psychologist
Applied psychologist
Behavior
Behaviorism
Bias
Clinical psychologist
Cognitive neuroscience
Cognitive psychology
Confound
Control condition
Control group
Correlation coefficient
Counseling psychologist
Data
Debriefing
Dependent variable
Double-blind design
Effect
Evolutionary psychology
Experimental condition
Experimental group
Experimenter expectancy effects
Functionalism
Gestalt psychology
Humanistic psychology
Hypothesis
Independent variable
Informed consent

Introspection
Level of the brain
Level of the group
Level of the person
Mental processes
Meta-analysis
Operational definition
Population
Prediction
Pseudopsychology
Psychiatric nurse
Psychiatrist
Psychodynamic theory
Psychology
Psychotherapy
Random assignment
Reliability
Replication
Response bias
Sample
Sampling bias
Scientific method
Social worker
Structuralism
Survey
Theory
Unconscious
Validity
Variable

As You Read . . . Questions and Exercises

The Science of Psychology: Getting to Know You

What is Psychology?

Kosslyn and Rosenberg define **psychology** as the _____ of _____ and _____.
Look at each part of this definition:

Part 1: Science

Which of your classes this semester are **sciences**? _____
_____

Which of your classes this semester are non-**sciences**? _____
_____

How do your **science** and non-**science** classes differ? _____
_____

Because it is a **science,** psychology requires ideas to be tested by collecting additional facts. Some questions can be answered through science; others can't. In the table on the top of the next page, decide whether you could answer the question with scientific methods. Explain why or why not.

Question	Answer with Science?	Why or Why Not?
Is there a God?	YES NO	
Should marijuana be legalized?	YES NO	
What makes people angry?	YES NO	
How does stress affect health?	YES NO	
What happens after we die?	YES NO	

Part 2: Mental Processes

Name some **mental processes** that you are using as you answer these questions. _____
_____

Part 3: Behaviors

Name some **behaviors** that you are doing as you answer these questions. _____
_____

Which usually come first: **mental processes** or **behaviors**? Why? _____
_____

Kosslyn and Rosenberg describe the four **goals** of psychologists as follows:

Goal 1: To DESCRIBE mental processes and behavior.
How could you use research that *describes* mental processes and/or behavior in your own life?

_____

_____

Goal 2: To EXPLAIN mental processes and behavior.
How could you use research that *explains* mental processes and/or behavior in your own life?

_____

_____

Goal 3: To PREDICT mental processes and behavior.
How could you use research that *predicts* mental processes and/or behavior in your own life?

_____

_____

Goal 4: To CONTROL mental processes and behavior.
How could you use research about *how to control* mental processes or behavior in your own life?

_____

_____

Name _____

Why Should I Study Psychology?

Ideally, you are taking this class because you really want to, not just because it fits into your schedule, you like the professor (although I hope you do!), or your friends are taking it. But, if not, take a moment to see how much you can really learn from the field of psychology.

Look at the *skills* you can learn in a psychology course as well as the *material*. List some of the things you hope to learn here. To get some ideas, you may want to flip through your textbook (to look at all the different topics that you will be covering) or visit one of the many school Web sites that lists the benefits of studying psychology.

GO SURFING...

Skills I will learn in psychology:

1. _____

2. _____

3. _____

4. _____

5. _____

Material I hope to learn in psychology:

1. _____

2. _____

3. _____

4. _____

5. _____

Levels of Analysis: The Complete Psychology

We can study phenomena at various **levels:** the **brain,** the **person,** and the **group.** Identify a question that can be asked at each level in the following situations:

Phenomenon	Brain	Person	Group
Fighting with your roommate			
Falling in love			
Drinking too much			
Acing a test			
Wrecking your car			

Looking at Levels

Your textbook explains how the levels of analysis can help us to understand human behavior. Complete the following chart to explain the computer and human analogies at each level.

Computer Component	Level of Analysis in Psychology
Mechanism, or the machine itself	
	Level of the person, or mental processes including beliefs, desires, and feelings
Computer network, or how different computers affect each other and the network itself	

Throughout the Grade Aid, you will be asked to consider the events that occur at the levels of the brain, the person, and the world to influence various psychological phenomena. You should list the factors in the charts provided. Below is an example of a completed chart, using the information contained in "Examining Racial Prejudice" on pages 8–9. Use this as a model for the other Looking at Levels charts in this Grade Aid.

The Brain	The Person	The Group
Activation of the amygdala in response to unfamiliar Black faces	Conscious attitudes Unconscious attitudes Behaviors - Verbal friendliness - Nonverbal friendliness	Social conventions, including politeness

On September 11, 2001, al-Qaeda terrorists flew planes into the World Trade Centers and the Pentagon. Name some of the factors at each of the **three levels that** may have influenced the terrorists' decision to take this action. Draw arrows indicating how events at the different levels may interact.

The Brain	The Person	The Group

Name some of the factors at each of the **three levels that** influenced your decision to attend college. Draw arrows indicating how events at the different levels may have interacted to influence your decision.

The Brain	The Person	The Group

Psychology Then and Now: The Evolution of a Science

The Evolution of a Science

Fill in the following. Who are the key people and what are the key ideas of each **school of psychology?** Which level(s) does each theory concentrate on most?

School of Thought	Key People	Key Ideas	Levels of Analysis (Brain, Person, World)
Structuralism			
Functionalism			
Gestalt psychology			
Psychodynamic theory			
Behaviorism			
Humanistic psychology			
Cognitive psychology			
Cognitive neuroscience			
Evolutionary psychology			

After Saddam Hussein's Iraqi regime fell, the Abu Ghraib prison became a U.S. facility. During the following years, Abu Ghraib housed several thousand prisoners, including some members of Hussein's regime and many common criminals. Recently, several U.S. Army personnel have been charged with abusing these prisoners. How would each of the following theorists explain these abuses?

Psychologist	Explanations
Psychodynamic theorist	
Behaviorist	

Psychologist	Explanations
Humanistic psychologist	
Cognitive psychologist	
Cognitive neuroscientist	
Evolutionary psychologist	

GO SURFING...

...to put faces with the names and to find out more about your favorite psychologists.
Here are some places to start:

- **The History of Psychology Web Site:**
  http://elvers.stjoe.udayton.edu/history/welcome.htm
  This site allows you to search by birthdays (do you have the same birthday as any famous psychologist?), people, and categories. Although some of the trivia questions aren't covered in this chapter, others are. Test yourself!

- **The History of Psychology:**
  http://www.ship.edu/~cgboeree/historyofpsych.html
  This site is an e-book, written by Dr. C. George Boeree of Shippensburg University. It tells more about the early days of psychology. Scroll down for more recent happenings.

- **Today in the History of Psychology:**
  http://www.cwu.edu/~warren/today.html
  With more than 3,100 events included, chances are good that something important happened today in the history of psychology. Find out!

- **Centre for Psychology Resources:**
  http://psych.athabascau.ca/html/aupr/history.shtml
  This site, sponsored by Athabasca University, has tons of links for various schools of psychology and famous psychologists.

What Kind of Psychologist Are You?

1. Human beings are driven by _____.
   a. irrational passions
   b. external events
   c. brain-based mental processes
   d. their desire to be the best they can be
   e. instincts

2. We can learn more about humankind by studying _____.
   a. people's dreams
   b. people's behaviors
   c. people's brains
   d. model humans
   e. their predecessors, animals

3. How do parents most influence their children?
   a. By causing pain which becomes hidden and will be uncovered later.
   b. By rewarding and punishing their children.
   c. By providing a model for future relationships.
   d. By providing a good environment to help them develop to their fullest potential.
   e. By passing on their genetics.

4. Humans _____.
   a. are basically aggressive
   b. can be bad or good, depending on their environments
   c. are basically rational, reasoning beings
   d. are basically good, although some may be corrupted by bad experiences in life
   e. are basically selfish and are driven to reproduce

5. Mental illness _____.
   a. results from repressed pain
   b. results from negative experiences
   c. results from negative thoughts
   d. results from a person not being valued unconditionally
   e. is inborn, a result of bad genetics

6. What kind of evidence is needed to prove a psychological fact?
   a. Anecdotal evidence from cases of people seeing psychologists.
   b. Behaviors, observed in lab settings.
   c. Evidence of brain functioning (e.g., from a brain scan).
   d. Anecdotal evidence from cases of exceptional human beings.
   e. Evidence that a certain phenomenon exists in multiple cultures.

Compare your answers with those at the end of the book to find out what kind of psychologist you are. (Although you could probably take a good guess as to which theory is represented by each letter!) Do you agree with these results?

Early Days

When did the interest in **mental processes** and **behavior** start? Who started it? _____

_____

_____

Was this the same time that the field of **psychology** started? Why or why not? _____

_____

_____

What was the primary tool of **structuralism**? _____

What was the problem with this tool? _____

_____

_____

How did the schools of **structuralism** and **functionalism** differ? _____

_____

_____

Has **functionalism** made any contributions to psychology that have endured until today? If so, what
are they? _____

_____

_____

_____

How are **structuralism** and **Gestalt psychology** similar and different? _____

_____

_____

How is **Gestalt psychology** related to current psychological research? _____

_____

_____

Psychodynamic Theory

What are the drawbacks to **psychodynamic theory** (as proposed by Freud)? _____

_____

_____

List some of the positive consequences of **psychodynamic theory**:

1. _____
2. _____
3. _____
4. _____

Behaviorism

Behaviorists pointed out that the consequences of a person's behavior influence whether that behavior is repeated. If the consequences are good, then the person will be more likely to repeat the behavior. If the consequences are bad, then the person will be less likely to repeat it.

Describe a situation in which you were more or less likely to do something because you had previously experienced the consequences of that behavior. _____
_____
_____

Humanistic Psychology

How do you think **humanistic psychology** has influenced many of the therapies now used? (You can check your answers in Chapter 15.) _____
_____
_____

Cognitive Revolution

The **cognitive revolution** led to a tremendous change in American psychology. Before this revolution, the predominant theory within the field had been **behaviorism.** Afterward, it became **cognitive psychology.**

How are cognitive psychology and behaviorism different? _____
_____
_____

How did computers influence the **cognitive revolution**? _____
_____
_____

How has **cognitive psychology** changed the field of psychology in general? _____
_____
_____

What effects have new technologies, such as brain-scanning equipment, had on the field? _____
_____
_____

Evolutionary Psychology

How is **evolutionary psychology** similar to **functionalism**? _____
_____
_____

How does **evolutionary psychology** differ from **functionalism**? _____
_____
_____

What evidence do **evolutionary psychologists** look for? Why? _____
_____
_____

What is the fundamental limitation of **evolutionary psychology**? _____
_____

What is the current state of psychology? _____
_____
_____
_____
_____

The Psychological Way:
What Today's Psychologists Do

Do you know any **psychologists**? If so, what do they do? _____
_____

Kosslyn & Rosenberg identify three main types of psychologists: **clinical/counseling psychologists, academic psychologists,** and **applied psychologists.** For each of these types of psychologists, give their job descriptions and what degrees they have.

Type of Psychologist	Job Description	Degree
Clinical/counseling psychologist		
Academic psychologist		
Applied psychologist		

The following are jobs related to **psychology.** Describe the jobs and the degrees these professionals must have.

Job	Job Description	Degree
Psychiatrist		
Psychiatric nurse		
Social worker		

Clinical/Counseling Psychologists

Students often say that they want to be **clinical or counseling psychologists** so they can "help people." What skills do you think a **clinical or counseling psychologist** must have, beyond this motivation? _____

_____

What difficulties do you think **clinical or counseling psychologists** might face? _____

_____

_____

Academic Psychologists

GO SURFING...

...to find out about the many different specialties within psychology. (Your book lists only a few.) The numerous divisions of the American Psychology Association (APA) will give you an idea of all the different subfields. Here is the official APA Web site: http://www.apa.org. Follow the Quick Links to Divisions.

List some of the other subfields that are not mentioned in your text:_____

_____

_____

_____

Do any of them sound especially interesting to you? Which ones? _____

_____

_____

Visit your school's Web site and discover what types of **psychologists** are on your school's faculty. Below, list some of the professors and their specialties. Keep this list for later reference, especially if you are considering a major in psychology!

Professor	Specialty

What do they do? You may wonder what your professors do all day—after all, they just teach a few classes a week and hold a few office hours, right? You might be surprised! Here are just a few of the things that professors do. Take a guess about how many hours a week they spend on each task. Then, ask your psychology professor for his or her estimate.

Task	Your Estimate	Your Professor's Estimate
Teaching (preparing for class, in-class time, grading, consulting with students, holding office hours)		
Research/Scholarly Activity (planning and conducting studies, writing studies for publication, other writing projects—like your textbook!)		
Service (working on university and psychology-related committees, presentations in various venues, service in community organizations		
Advising Students (formally and informally)		

GO SURFING...

...at http://chronicle.com/jobs/blogs.htm for links to professors' blogs. Read some of these blogs.

What are some of the benefits of academic life? _____
_____
_____

What are some of the disadvantages of academic life? _____
_____
_____

Applied Psychologists

How do the jobs of **academic** and **applied psychologists** differ? How are they similar? _____
_____
_____

Where might each of these types of **applied psychologists** look for jobs? What kinds of companies could they work for? What would they be doing?

Type of Applied Psychologist	Job Possibilities	Companies	Job Description
Cognitive psychologist			
Developmental psychologist			
Human factors psychologist			
Industrial/ organizational psychologist			

Type of Applied Psychologist	Job Possibilities	Companies	Job Description
Personality psychologist			
Physiological psychologist			
School (educational) psychologist			
Social psychologist			
Sport psychologist			

GO SURFING...

...to find out what the job outlooks are like for different types of psychologists, holding various degrees. Use this information to fill out the chart on the next page. Here are some places to start:

- **Occupational Outlook Handbook, by the U.S. Department of Labor**
  http://www.bls.gov/oco/home.htm
  Allows you to search by occupation. Be sure to notice all the subspecialties of psychology.
- **O*Net OnLine, by the National O*Net Consortium**
  http://online.onetcenter.org
  Provides information about the working environments and tasks of a variety of jobs, including psychologists.
- **American Psychological Association**
  http://www.apa.org
  Use the APA search engine to find out what recent psychology majors and psychology Ph.D.'s are doing with their degrees.

Type of Psychologist	Working Environment
Clinical/counseling psychologist	
Academic psychologist	
Applied psychologist	

If you were going to be a **psychologist,** what type would you want to be? Why? _____
_____

Would you have a preferred subfield (e.g., developmental, social, personality)? _____
_____

What is the outlook like for this type of psychologist? _____
_____

What type of degree would you need to be this type of psychologist? _____

What could you do with a bachelor's degree in psychology? _____
_____
_____

The Research Process: How We Find Things Out

The Scientific Method

Step 1: Specifying a Problem

What does "problem" mean, in this context? _____
_____
_____

Where do you think scientists get their problems? _____
_____
_____
_____
_____

Name some problems or questions that you have that would be suitable for psychological research:

Problem 1: _____

Problem 2: _____

Problem 3: _____

Problem 4: _____

Step 2: Observing Events

What does it mean for a scientist to **replicate** a study? _____

_____

_____

Why do psychologists prefer to use numerical measurements? _____

_____

_____

What are the two kinds of events in which psychologists are interested? _____

_____

Look at the problems you listed in Step 1. What kind of **data** could you collect for each of these problems?

Problem 1: _____

Problem 2: _____

Problem 3: _____

Problem 4: _____

Step 3: Forming a Hypothesis

What would the opposite of a **variable** be? _____

Can you think of an example? _____

What is a **hypothesis**? _____

_____

_____

_____

_____

_____

Look at the questions you listed in Step 1. Do you have hypotheses about each of these problems?

Problem 1: _____

Problem 2: _____

Problem 3: _____

Problem 4: _____

Step 4: Testing the Hypothesis

What is an **operational definition**? _____

_____

_____

_____

_____

How is an **operational definition** different from any other type of definition? _____

_____

_____

Offer an **operational definition** for one of the variables in your previously identified problems:

Problem 1: _____

Problem 2: _____

Problem 3: _____

Problem 4: _____

Step 5: Formulating a Theory

Compare and contrast hypotheses and theories in the table below.

	Hypotheses	Theories
Similarities		
Differences		

Step 6: Testing the Theory

How can a **theory** be supported? _____
_____
_____

What happens when a **theory** is supported? _____
_____

What leads to a **theory** being rejected? _____
_____
_____
_____

What does it mean for a theory to be *falsifiable?* _____
_____

The Psychologist's Toolbox: Techniques of Scientific Research

Descriptive Research: Just the Facts, Ma'am

What does descriptive research do? _____
_____
_____

What are the benefits of using **naturalistic observation?** _____
_____
_____

What are the disadvantages of using **naturalistic observation?** _____
_____
_____

Can you think of another person, or type of person, about whom a **case study** might be meaningful or informative (besides those described in the book)? _____
_____
_____

Under what circumstances might a **case study** be particularly useful? _____
_____
_____

What are the benefits of using **surveys** to collect data? _____
_____
_____

What topics are frequently studied using **surveys?**_____
_____
_____

What are some of the difficulties with using **surveys** to collect data? _____
_____
_____
_____
_____

Correlational Research: Do Birds of a Feather Flock Together?

A correlation coefficient will be a number between _____ and _____. The sign of the correlation indicates _____, and the number indicates _____.

In the space below, draw scatter plots showing the following correlations:

- −.70
- −1.0
- +.30
- +.90

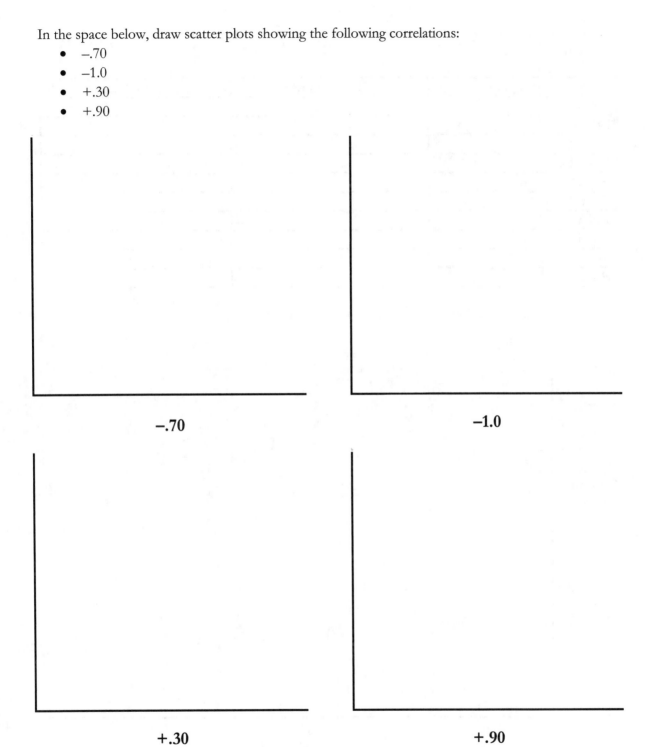

−.70

−1.0

+.30

+.90

Find ten adult friends (or family members) and ask them for their birthweights and current weights. Record the data in the chart below.

Participant	Birthweight	Current Weight
Friend 1		
Friend 2		
Friend 3		
Friend 4		
Friend 5		
Friend 6		
Friend 7		
Friend 8		
Friend 9		
Friend 10		

Now, draw a scatter plot. Record your data on this scatter plot.

Current Weight

Birthweight

Based on this scatter plot, does it appear that there is a correlation between birthweight and current weight? _____. What size and direction would you estimate the correlation to be? _____.

GO SURFING...

...at one of the following sites and calculate the correlation coefficient for these data, following the directions at the sites.

- http://faculty.vassar.edu/lowry/VassarStats.html
    (Choose the "direct-entry method" of basic linear correlation and regression, then enter 10 for the pop-up screen. The correlation coefficient will be abbreviated as *r* in the results.)
- http://calculators.stat.ucla.edu/correlation.php

What **correlation** coefficient did you obtain at one of these sites? _____

How accurate was your prediction? _____

What factors influenced the size of the **correlation?** _____

_____

What is the main advantage of correlational research? _____

_____

_____

What is the main disadvantage of correlational research? _____

_____

_____

Experimental Research: Manipulating and Measuring

For each of the following hypotheses, indicate the **independent variable** (IV) and the **dependent variable** (DV); also identify one possible confound. If you have trouble remembering which variable is the IV and which is the DV, try using the following sentence to help:

> The ___*(dependent variable)*___ is dependent on the ___*(independent variable)*___.

- Children who are abused during childhood will have lower self-esteem in adulthood than will children who were not abused.

    IV = _____

    DV = _____

    Possible confound = _____

- Seniors have better study skills than do freshmen.
  IV = _____
  DV = _____
  Possible confound = _____

- The more children watch TV, the less intelligent they are.
  IV = _____
  DV = _____
  Possible confound = _____

- Lawyers are more devious than psychologists.
  IV = _____
  DV = _____
  Possible confound = _____

- Lawyers make more money than psychologists.
  IV = _____
  DV = _____
  Possible confound = _____

- The happier people are with their jobs, the more hours they will work.
  IV = _____
  DV = _____
  Possible confound = _____

- Catholics are more likely to vote Republican than are non-Catholics.
  IV = _____
  DV = _____
  Possible confound = _____

- The more religious people are, the less they will be afraid of death.
  IV = _____
  DV = _____
  Possible confound = _____

- People who are underweight live longer than people who are overweight.
  IV = _____
  DV = _____
  Possible confound = _____

- People who have more than twelve years of education are less likely to get Alzheimer's disease than others.
  IV = _____
  DV = _____
  Possible confound = _____

Describe two ways that researchers can avoid **confounds** in experimental research.

- _____
  _____
  _____
  _____
  _____

- _____
  _____
  _____
  _____
  _____
  _____

How is a **quasi-experimental design** similar to an **experiment?** _____
_____
_____

How is a **quasi-experimental design** different from an **experiment?** _____
_____
_____

Name one advantage and one disadvantage for each of the following types of **research:**

Technique	Advantage	Disadvantage
Experimentation		
Quasi-experimentation		
Correlational research		
Naturalistic observation		
Case studies		
Surveys		

Be a Critical Consumer of Psychology

Provide an example of a measure that is **reliable** and a measure that is **unreliable.**

- **Reliable:** _____
  _____

- **Unreliable:** _____
  _____

Name and describe, in your own words, two sources of **bias** in a study:

▪ _____
  _____
  _____
  _____

▪ _____
  _____
  _____
  _____
  _____

How can a researcher unintentionally affect the results of a study? _____
_____
_____
_____

What can a researcher do to ensure that he or she *doesn't* affect the results of a study? _____
_____
_____
_____

Go to the health or science section of a newspaper and find a brief (one- to two-paragraph) article about a research study. Obviously, the study was summarized for inclusion in the newspaper. What questions about the study does the article leave you with? What is the significance of each of these unanswered questions?

● **Question:** _____
  _____
  Importance: _____
  _____

● **Question:** _____
  _____
  Importance: _____
  _____

● **Question:** _____
  _____
  Importance: _____
  _____

What is **pseudopsychology?** _____
_____
_____
_____

Why is ESP not necessarily **pseudopsychology?** _____
_____
_____

Ethics: Doing It Right

GO SURFING...

...to find out more about the controversy about whether Nazi research should be used. Here is a starting point: "The Ethics of Using Medical Data from Nazi Experiments," by Baruch Cohen, at http://www.jlaw.com/Articles/NaziMedEx.html.

The Nazis conducted horrific studies on Holocaust victims. List some of those studies here:

_____

_____

Some people argue that the results of these studies should be used, if appropriate. Again, surf the Web. Then, summarize this position. What do *you* think? Should data collected in an unethical way ever be used? Under what conditions? Why or why not?

_____

_____

What guidelines are now in place to avoid ethical violations in research? _____

_____

_____

_____

_____

How are animals protected in research studies? _____

_____

_____

Name three specific things that it would be unethical for a clinical psychologist to do:

1. _____

2. _____

3. _____

After You Read . . . Thinking Back

1. Early philosophers shared some of psychologists' interests. What makes philosophy and a psychology different? _____

_____

_____

_____

_____

2. What type of data did the structuralists collect? What were some of the problems with that type of data? _____

_____

_____

_____

_____

3. What type of data do you think Freud collected? What are the problems with that method of data collection? How has this issue affected the status of Freud's theory?

_____

_____

_____

_____

_____

4. Why is humanism considered a "nonscientific approach"? Discuss. _____

_____

_____

_____

_____

5. Given that many clinical and counseling psychologists do not engage in research, why is it important for them to know about research? Give an example. Why are they still called "psychologists" if they do not conduct research? _____

_____

_____

_____

_____

After You Read . . . Thinking Ahead

The theories that you learned in this chapter will reappear again and again throughout the textbook. Can you imagine what some of these theorists would say about these topics? Take a shot! Check your answers as they come up.

Theory	Emotion	Personality	Psychological Disorders	Therapy
Psychodynamic theorist				
Behaviorist				
Humanistic psychologist				
Cognitive psychologist				
Cognitive neuroscientist				
Evolutionary psychologist				

1. Flip through the table of contents of your textbook. Which topics that you will be considering are more likely to use survey methods? Why? _____
   _____
   _____
   _____
   _____
   _____

2. Which topics might lend themselves more easily to experimental methods? Why?

_____

_____

_____

_____

_____

3. Are there some topics for which it might be impossible to use an experimental technique? Why?

_____

_____

_____

_____

_____

4. How might a researcher's stereotypes affect the results of his or her studies? What would this be called? _____

_____

_____

_____

_____

_____

5. Can you think of situations in which it would be difficult to collect numerical data? Describe.

_____

_____

_____

_____

_____

6. Which topics might lend themselves well to case study research? Why? _____

_____

_____

_____

_____

_____

After You Read . . . Practice Tests

PRACTICE TEST #1:

Multiple-Choice Questions

For each question, circle the best answer from the choices given.

1. The three major ideas in the definition of psychology are: (p. 4)
   a. behavior, cognition, and emotion.
   b. cognition, emotion, and science.
   c. behavior, emotion, and mental processes.
   d. behavior, mental processes, and science.

2. All of the following are associated with mental processes EXCEPT: (p. 5)
   a. thinking
   b. dreaming
   c. listening
   d. None of the above.

3. All of the following are true about the term "science" EXCEPT: (p. 4)
   a. Science avoids mere opinions and intuitions.
   b. Science avoids mere intuitions and guesses.
   c. Science values subjective evidence.
   d. Science values objective evidence.

4. Explaining aggressive behavior in terms of an excess of testosterone would illustrate which level of analysis? (p. 6)
   a. brain
   b. person
   c. group
   d. environment

5. The four goals of psychology are to: (pp. 5 - 6)
   a. predict, describe, explain, control.
   b. predict, contribute, describe, answer.
   c. theorize, control, describe, explain.
   d. describe, explain, hypothesize, answer.

6. Which of the following questions would be least likely to be answered by a psychologist? (pp. 4-5)
   a. How do people store memories?
   b. Are there basic human rights?
   c. Are personalities more influenced by genetics or the environment?
   d. How would damage to the frontal lobes affect a person's thinking?

7. At the level of the person, psychologists focus on which of the following? (p. 7)
   a. activity of neurons
   b. activity of the brain
   c. content of mental processes
   d. influences of one's surroundings

8. Social norms would most likely fall into which level of analysis? (pp. 7-8)
   a. brain
   b. person
   c. group
   d. environment

9. Which of the following types of psychologists would be most likely the one to treat a person with anorexia nervosa based on the example case provided in the text? (p. 19)
   a. clinical psychologist
   b. clinical neuropsychologist
   c. counseling psychologist
   d. developmental psychologist

10. A psychiatrist has a(n) _____, whereas a psychologist has a(n) _____. (p. 20)
   a. Ed.D.; M.D.
   b. Psy.D.; Ph.D.
   c. Ph.D.; Psy.D.
   d. M.D.; Ph.D.

11. Which of the following psychologists would be most interested in how groups influence individuals' behavior? (p. 21)
   a. cognitive psychologist
   b. developmental psychologist
   c. personality psychologist
   d. social psychologist

12. How are academic and applied psychology different? (p. 21-22)
   a. There are many sub-specialties of academic psychology (e.g., developmental, social, etc., whereas there are not with applied psychology.
   b. Applied psychologists do research whereas academic psychologists do not.
   c. Academic psychologists do research whereas applied psychologists do not.
   d. By definition, applied psychologists help to solve specific practical problems, whereas academic psychologists may study practical or theoretical problems.

13. Social psychology and industrial-organizational psychology are alike in that they both: (pp. 21-22)
   a. focus on the level of the person.
   b. focus on the level of the brain
   c. study people in a group context.
   d. work in applied settings.

PRACTICE TEST #2:

Multiple-Choice Questions

For each question, circle the best answer from the choices given.

1. Which of the following selections most accurately represents the parent disciplines of psychology? (p. 10)
   a. physiology, biology
   b. physiology, sociology
   c. philosophy, sociology
   d. philosophy, physiology

2. The idea that we only know the world by the way in which it is represented in our minds stems from which of the following historical figures? (p. 10)
   a. Plato
   b. Hippocrates
   c. Descartes
   d. Locke

3. Which historical figure is associated with functionalism, one of the earlier schools of psychology? (p. 10)
   a. James
   b. Skinner
   c. Titchener
   d. Wundt

4. Charles Darwin's theory of evolution influenced which early school of psychology? (pp. 11-12)
   a. Structuralism
   b. Functionalism
   c. Gestalt Psychology
   d. Psychodynamic Psychology

5. One serious criticism of psychodynamic theory stated in the text was that (p.13)
   a. it stresses the role of feelings of inferiority.
   b. it addresses all levels of analysis.
   c. it deals with unconscious thoughts.
   d. it is nearly impossible to evaluate.

6. According to behaviorists, people behave in certain ways because: (pp. 13-14)
   a. They are reinforced for their behaviors.
   b. They want to.
   c. It is part of the basic human desire to self-actualize.
   d. They unconsciously wish to be successful.

7. Self-actualization is representative of _____ psychology. (p. 15)
   a. Behavioral
   b. Cognitive
   c. Gestalt
   d. Humanistic

8. How are behaviorism and cognitive psychology different? (pp. 13 - 15)
   a. Behaviorism relies on the scientific method, whereas cognitive psychology does not.
   b. Mental processes are irrelevant in behaviorism, whereas they are central to cognitive psychology.
   c. Behaviorists do not believe that there is such a thing as mental illness, whereas cognitive psychologists do.
   d. Cognitive psychologists attach no importance to social experiences, whereas behaviorists do.

9. Evolutionary psychology is most closely associated with which early school of psychology? (pp. 16-17)
   a. Structuralism
   b. Functionalism
   c. Gestalt psychology
   d. Psychodynamic psychology

10. Which of the following statements is consistent with the authors' summary of the history of psychology? (pp. 18 - 19)
    a. The early schools of psychology have gradually been replaced by their descendents, which are increasingly both biological and philosophical in nature.
    b. The early schools of psychology had no descendents and most have faded away.
    c. The early schools of psychology are decreasingly productive, but they have given rise to two major new schools of psychology, which dominate the field today.
    d. The early schools of psychology gave rise to many new schools of psychology while continuing to be productive themselves, and many schools have influenced one another.

PRACTICE TEST #3:

Multiple-Choice Questions

For each question, circle the best answer from the choices given.

1. The third step of the scientific method is: (p. 25)
   a. specifying a problem.
   b. systematically observing events.
   c. collecting new observations to test a hypothesis.
   d. forming a hypothesis.

2. Amy has just read about a study that she finds very interesting. Unfortunately, the researchers do not provide many details about how they collected their data. As a result, Amy is unable to _____ the study. (p. 25)
   a. Validate
   b. Copy
   c. Replicate
   d. Repeat

3. Which of the following best represents an operational definition for the variable caffeine? (p. 26)
   a. coffee was served to half the participants in an experiment
   b. half the participants received one caffeine pill
   c. half the participants ingested a beverage containing 100 mg of caffeine
   d. half the participants received a solution consisting of eight ounces of water mixed with 100 mg of caffeine

4. In discussing the scientific method, the authors reviewed a total of _____ steps. (p. 24-26)
   a. four
   b. five
   c. six
   d. seven

5. A psychologist interested in the social behavior of the cheetah investigates such behavior in the cheetahs' natural habitat. This type of research most likely represents: (p. 28)
   a. naturalistic observation.
   b. a case study.
   c. survey research.
   d. naturalistic research.

Scenario 1: Please read the following scenario and use it to answer questions 6 through 9. Pete was interested in whether training students in memory techniques really improved their memory. He randomly assigned students in his class to one of two groups. One group received memory training and the other did not. A week later, Pete tested the students' memory.

6. This is an example of: (pp. 28-33)
   a. An experiment.
   b. A quasi-experiment.
   c. A correlation.
   d. A case study.

7. In Scenario 1 above, the independent variable is: (p. 31)
   a. Memory
   b. The presence of memory training
   c. Pete
   d. Subjects' intelligence

8. A possible confounding variable in the study described in Scenario 1 above is: (p. 31)
   a. Amount of sleep the subjects have had recently.
   b. Their memory.
   c. Their memory training.
   d. Pete.

9. The group that did not receive training in Scenario 1 above would be called: (p. 32)
   a. the control group.
   b. the control condition.
   c. the experimental group.
   d. confounding subjects.

10. A researcher investigates whether age of groups (adolescents, young adults, middle-aged adults, and senior citizens) affects performance on a test of short-term memory. Because the researcher cannot randomly assign participants into the various age groups, this research is referred to as _____research. (p. 32)
   a. experimental
   b. quasi-experimental
   c. semi-experimental
   d. naturalistic

11. What historical event led to the establishment of ethics for conducting research? (p. 39)
   a. War trials in Nuremberg following World War II
   b. Civil Rights movement
   c. Experiments performed on humans during World War I
   d. Ghastly events that took place during the Civil War

12. Before participating in research, participants must first provide experimenters with: (p. 40)
    a. informed consent.
    b. consent.
    c. informed approval.
    d. debriefing form.

13. In California (and most other states), if a client threatens the life of another individual, his/her therapist must: (p. 42)
    a. inform the individual of the threat.
    b. do nothing—it would be a breech of confidentiality.
    c. place the client under house arrest.
    d. discontinue treatment with the client.

14. All of the following would be included in an informed consent EXCEPT: (p. 40)
    a. information about the risks of the study
    b. information about the benefits of the study
    c. notice that participants can withdraw from the study at any time
    d. information about what journal will publish the results of the study

15. Who may serve on an IRB? (p. 40)
    a. Psychologists
    b. Representatives from the local community
    c. Clergy
    d. All of the above

COMPREHENSIVE PRACTICE TEST

True/False Questions

Circle TRUE or FALSE for each of the following statements.

1. TRUE   FALSE   The goals of psychology are simply to describe and explain mental processes and behavior. (pp.5-6)

2. TRUE   FALSE   Events at different levels of analysis are constantly influencing one another. (pp. 7-8)

3. TRUE   FALSE   The first psychology lab was established in approximately 1700. (p. 10)

4. TRUE   FALSE   The founder of scientific psychology was Sigmund Freud. (p. 10)

5. TRUE   FALSE   Relative to graduate training to become a Clinical psychologist with a Ph.D., a graduate student earning a Psy. D. is more likely to have training that emphasized practicing therapy over conducting research. (p. 20)

6. TRUE   FALSE   In some states, clinical psychologists can prescribe medicine. (p. 20)

7. TRUE   FALSE   A hypothesis is a tentative idea that might explain a set of observations. (p. 39)

8. TRUE   FALSE   Correlational research involves the researcher controlling the situation. (p. 44)

9. TRUE   FALSE   If results of a study have been replicated, then you can have greater confidence that the measurements were reliable. (p. 49)

10. TRUE   FALSE   Validity means that a finding has been replicated. (p. 49)

11. TRUE   FALSE   Sampling bias refers to the tendency of people to respond in a particular way regardless of their actual knowledge or beliefs. (p. 50-51)

12. TRUE   FALSE   Research is conducted using animals to help better understand the workings of the brain. (p. 40)

13. TRUE   FALSE   Neuroethics is a relatively new branch of ethics that addresses the dangers and benefits of research investigating the brain. (p. 42)

Multiple-Choice Questions

For each question, circle the best answer from the choices given.

1. A psychologist who investigates the effects of caffeine on problem solving is most likely studying events at the level of the _____. (pp. 6-7)
    a. brain
    b. person
    c. group
    d. environment

2. The first formal psychological movement in America was _____. (p. 10)
    a. Structuralism
    b. Functionalsim
    c. Gestalt Psychology
    d. Psychoanalysis

3. The problem with the research method of introspection was that: (p. 11)
    a. it couldn't be verified.
    b. it relied on expensive equipment most psychologists couldn't afford.
    c. it ignored the level of the group.
    d. it didn't focus on mental processes.

4. Descartes was interested in the: (p. 10)
    a. question of how we learn.
    b. question of how come to know the world around us.
    c. question of how we develop over time.
    d. question of how the mind and body relate to one another.

5. It was the _____ who led us to realize that the observation of animals could provide clues to human behavior. (p. 12)
    a. Structuralists
    b. Functionalists
    c. Psychoanalysts
    d. Behaviorists

6. According to _____ psychology, people have positive values, free will, and a deep inner creativity, which in combination allow us to choose life-fulfilling paths to personal growth. (p. 15)
    a. Cognitive
    b. Developmental
    c. Humanistic
    d. Psychoanalytic

7. The cognitive neuroscience approach considers events at the three levels of analysis, but with a primary focus on the: (p. 16)
    a. brain.
    b. group.
    c. person.
    d. interactions among individuals.

8. Which of the following is the most recent development in psychology? (p. 16)
    a. Structuralism
    b. Behaviorism
    c. Cognitive Psychology
    d. Evolutionary Psychology

9. Modern psychology is grounded in all previous schools of psychology. Which of the following is a false statement about the roots of modern psychology? (pp. 13-14)
    a. The scientific standards set by behaviorists are still used today.
    b. Gestalt psychology has influenced the modern study of perception.
    c. Research in cognitive psychology addresses some questions initially proposed by functionalists.
    d. The behaviorists' view that behavior is driven by mental processes is still applicable today.

10. If a mental health practitioner holds a M.S.W. degree, then he/she is definitely a (p. 20)
    a. clinical psychologist.
    b. counseling psychologist.
    c. psychiatric nurse.
    d. social worker.

11. In addition to a C.S. (clinical specialization), a psychiatric nurse is most likely to hold which of the following degrees? (p. 20)
    a. M.S.N.
    b. M.S.W.
    c. Ph.D.
    d. Psy.D.

12. Which type of psychologist is most likely to be interested in studying individual differences in preferences and inclinations? (p. 21)
    a. cognitive
    b. developmental
    c. personality
    d. social

13. According to the text authors, the second step of the scientific method involves: (p. 38)
    a. observing events
    b. forming a hypothesis
    c. testing a prediction
    d. brainstorming ideas

14. Dr. Altmay indicated in her study that aggression was measured as the number of times children threw stuffed animals in a 10 minute period. The description of aggression is considered a(n): (p. 39)
    a. variable
    b. hypothesis
    c. operational definition
    d. operational description

15. All of the following are true about testing theories EXCEPT: (p. 40-41)
    a. Researchers evaluate a theory by testing its predictions.
    b. A theory plays a key role in the process of formulating hypotheses, which in turn allows for testing of the theory.
    c. Each prediction stemming from a theory is a hypothesis to be tested.
    d. A good theory is very unlikely to be falsifiable.

16. The process of describing things as they are is a major goal for: (p. 42)
    a. descriptive research
    b. inferential research
    c. experimental research
    d. quasi-experimental research

17. All of the following are examples of descriptive research except: (p. 42-43)
    a. naturalistic observation
    b. case studies
    c. surveys
    d. correlational studies

18. Which of the following correlation coefficients represents the "strongest" relationship between two variables? (p. 44)
    a. -.75
    b. -.50
    c. 0
    d. .60

19. Dr. Russett is interested in the effects of caffeine on memory in lab rats. In setting up an experiment, the independent variable is: (p. 31)
    a. the number rats used in the study
    b. presence of caffeine
    c. memory
    d. the measure of memory used in the study

20. The dependent variable in #7 is: (p. 31)
    a. caffeine
    b. measurements of caffeine used
    c. the number of rats used in the study
    d. memory

21. To test his hypothesis, Dr. Russett decides to inject one group of rats with caffeine every day for a week, but to leave the other group alone. At the end of the week, he will measure the rats' memory for a maze they had previously learned. To avoid a confound, Dr. Russell should probably: (p. 31)
    a. inject all the rats, some with caffeine and some with water.
    b. use a correlational study.
    c. allow only one group of rats to learn the maze before the injections.
    d. groom the rats every day.

22. To get an idea for how students at your university feel about a recent tuition hike, you survey all of your fellow students in your psychology class. The surveyed students represent a: (p. 34)
    a. variable.
    b. population.
    c. parameter.
    d. sample.

23. An individual cannot participate in an experiment until he/she has provided: (p. 29)
    a. informed consent.
    b. papers verifying his/her age.
    c. documents verifying citizenship.
    d. debriefing forms.

24. A therapist may do all of the following EXCEPT: (pp. 41-42)
    a. engage in sexual relations with patients.
    b. physically mistreat patients.
    c. mentally mistreat patients.
    d. all of the above.

Short-Answer Questions
Answer each question in the space provided.

1. What school of psychology is considered to be the first formal movement in psychology? What was a major goal of this school and what was the primary method used to accomplish this goal?

_____
_____
_____
_____
_____
_____
_____
_____
_____

2. Compare and contrast functionalism with evolutionary psychology. _____

_____

_____

_____

_____

_____

_____

3. How might an academic psychologist spend a day at work? Describe at least three different types of activities. _____

_____

_____

_____

_____

_____

_____

_____

_____

4. List the steps involved when using the scientific method. _____

_____

_____

_____

_____

_____

_____

5. Describe the concept of "correlation." How does a positive relationship indicated by a (positive correlation) between two variables differ from a negative relationship (indicated by a negative correlation) between two variables? Describe an example illustrating each type of relationship.

_____

_____

_____

_____

_____

_____

_____

_____

6. What kinds of problems must you be careful to avoid when using surveys? Explain. _____

_____

_____

_____

_____

_____

_____

_____

_____

7. Describe an experiment in which you investigate the effects of sugar consumption on ability to solve math problems. In your description clearly note the following: independent variable, dependent variable, experimental condition or group, and control condition or group.

_____

_____

_____

_____

_____

_____

_____

_____

_____

8. Compare and contrast sample with population. _____

_____

_____

_____

_____

_____

_____

_____

9. Would it be unethical to investigate the effects of shock on human participants' ability to learn? Why? Under what circumstances would it be ethical to run such an experiment? _____

_____

_____

_____

_____

_____

_____

_____

_____

When You Are Finished . . . Puzzle It Out

<table>
<tr><td>

Across

5. Set up first psychology lab in U.S.

7. Can range from −1 to +1

9. Occurs when no random sampling

11. Type of psychology that assumes that certain cognitive strategies and goals are inborn

12. Careful observations or numerical measurement

15. Type of psychologist who provides psychotherapy

16. Behaviorist concerned with the content of the stimulus-stimulus and stimulus-response associations

17. Tentative idea to explain data

18. Subset of the population

19. Getting the same results when an experiment is repeated

20. Entire set of relevant people

21. Founder of scientific psychology

</td><td>

Down

1. Redoing study and getting similar data

2. Variable that depends on another

3. Functionalists were influenced by his theory

4. School of psychology which says a whole is greater than the sum of its parts

6. Combining results from different studies

8. Type of definition indicating how data are measured

9. Questionnaire

10. Father of psychodynamic theory

13. Type of psychologist who works on improving products and procedures and conducts research aimed at solving specific practical problems

14. Means "looking within"

Puzzle created with Puzzlemaker at DiscoverySchool.com.

</td></tr>
</table>

Chapter 2
The Biology of Mind and Behavior:
The Brain in Action

Before You Read . . .

Have you ever known any who has suffered brain damage—perhaps someone who has had a stroke or Alzheimer's disease? How did this damage affect that person's functioning?

In this chapter, you will learn the basics of how the brain works, beginning with the basic cell of the nervous system, the neuron. Communication within the brain and across the nervous system is an electrochemical process that results in neurotransmitters being released into the synapses between neurons. You will also learn how the brain and the nervous system are organized.

The chapter also discusses two other systems of the body that interact with our brains to keep our bodies healthy: the neuroendocrine system and the immune system. You will discover how researchers have learned about the brain, based on neuroimaging and research on lesions and strokes. The chapter ends by considering genetic influences on behavior and exploring the dynamic interaction of genes and the environment.

Chapter Objectives

After reading this chapter, you should be able to:

- Describe how neurons work and why they may die.

- Explain how chemicals allow neurons to communicate.

- Name and describe the major parts of the brain and the nervous system and their functions.

- Understand how the functions of the two sides of the brain differ.

- Name and explain the techniques used to study the brain.

- Describe the role of genes in behavior, and explain how genes and the environment interact as the brain develops and functions.

- Explain what "heritability" means and how evolution shaped the functions of the brain.

As You Read . . . Term Identification

Make flashcards using the following terms as you go. Use the definitions in the margins of this chapter for help. If you write the definitions in your own words, though, you will remember them better!

Action potential	Heritability
Active interaction	Hindbrain
Adaptation	Hippocampus
Adoption study	Hormone
Agonist	Hypothalamic-pituitary-adrenal axis (HPA)
All-or-none law	Hypothalamus
Amygdala	Interneuron
Antagonist	Ion
Autonomic nervous system (ANS)	Lesion
Axon	Limbic system
Basal ganglia	Lobes
Behavioral genetics	Magnetic resonance imaging (MRI)
Brain circuit	Magnetoencephalography (MEG)
Brainstem	Medulla
Cell body	Mendelian inheritance
Cell membrane	Meninges
Central nervous system (CNS)	Microelectrode
Cerebellum	Midbrain
Cerebral cortex	Monozygotic
Cerebral hemisphere	Motor neuron
Complex inheritance	Motor strip
Computer-assisted tomography (CT, formerly CAT)	Mutation
Corpus callosum	Myelin
Cortisol	Natural selection
Dendrite	Neuroendocrine system
Deoxyribonucleic acid (DNA)	Neuroimaging
Dizygotic	Neuromodulator
Electroencephalogram	Neuron
Electroencephalograph (EEG)	Neurotransmitter
Endogenous cannabinoids	Occipital lobe
Estrogen	Parasympathetic nervous system
Evocative (or reactive) interaction	Parietal lobe
Evolution	Passive interaction
Forebrain	Peripheral nervous system (PNS)
Frontal lobe	Phenotype
Functional magnetic resonance imaging (fMRI)	Pituitary gland
Gene	Plasticity
Genotype	Pons
Glial cell	Positron emission tomography (PET)
	Pruning
Gyrus	Receptor

Resting potential
Reticular formation
Reflex
Reuptake
Selective serotonin-reuptake inhibiter (SSRI)
Sensory neuron
Sensory-somatic nervous system (SSNS)
Skeletal system
Somatosensory strip
Spinal cord
Split-brain patient
Stroke

Subcortical structure
Sulcus
Sympathetic nervous system
Synapse
Synaptic cleft
Temporal lobe
Terminal button
Testosterone
Thalamus
Transcranial magnetic stimulation (TMS)
Twin study

As You Read . . . Questions and Exercises

Brain Circuits: Making Connections

The Neuron: A Powerful Computer

For each of the following types of neurons, offer a definition and an example.

Type of Neuron	Definition	Example
Sensory neuron		
Motor neuron		
Interneurons		

What are brain circuits and how do they work? _____

_____

_____

_____

Describe an analogy for brain circuits that will help you to remember them and their functions.

_____

_____

_____

_____

_____

In the space below, draw a picture of two connecting neurons.

Label each part on the previous page to correspond with its number below. Also, complete the following chart to provide the function of each part of the **neuron.**

	Neural Structure	Function
1	Cell membrane	
2	Cell body	
3	Dendrites	
4	Axon	
5	Myelin	
6	Terminal buttons	
7	Synapse	
8	Synaptic cleft	
9	Receptors	
10	Neurotransmitter substances	

Fill in the blanks in the following paragraph.

Ions can be either _____ or _____ charged. When the neuron is at rest, there are more _____ ions inside the neuron and more _____ ions outside the neuron. When the neuron receives enough stimulation from other neurons, so that a _____ is exceeded, some of the _____ in the neuron open. This allows a complex exchange of ions that changes the _____ in the axon. This exchange of ions, or the _____, works its way down the neuron until the _____ release _____. Most axons are covered with _____, which allows impulses to travel down the axon more efficiently.

GO SURFING…

…at http://faculty.washington.edu/chudler/synapse.html or
http://psych.hanover.edu/Krantz/neural/actionpotential.html to read more (and see pictures) of
how an action potential travels.

What is the **all-or-none law?** _____

_____

_____

_____

_____

Neurotransmitters and Neuromodulators: Bridging the Gap

Describe the difference in the functions of **neurotransmitters** and **neuromodulators.**

Neurotransmitters	Neuromodulators

Fill in the blanks in the following paragraph.

Usually, neurotransmitters and neuromodulators flow from the terminal buttons of the
sending neuron *to* the receptor sites of the receiving neurons. However, sometimes these
chemicals flow the opposite way. Specifically, _____ are neuromodulators released by
the *receiving* neuron that _____ the activity of the *sending* neuron. This allows the
chemicals to fine-tune underlying activities such as _____, _____, _____,
and _____. Although marijuana contains cannabinoids, it affects neurons
indiscriminately, overwhelming the neural system.

When neurotransmitters or neuromodulators **bind** to receptors, they can have one of two effects. Explain each.

- **Excitatory:** _____
  _____
  _____

- **Inhibitory:** _____
  _____
  _____

Do **neurotransmitters** and **neuromodulators** always have the same effect? Why or why not?

_____
_____
_____
_____
_____

What happens to any extra **neurotransmitter** that is released by the terminal buttons, but not taken up by receptors? _____

_____
_____
_____
_____

Why do Kosslyn and Rosenberg use the term **neurotransmitter substance** in this textbook?

_____
_____
_____

Name and describe three ways that drugs may affect **neurotransmitters:**

- _____
  _____
  _____

- _____
  _____
  _____

- _____
  _____
  _____

Glial Cells: More than the Neurons' Helpmates

The average human brain contains about 100 billion neurons and ten times as many **glial cells.** According to the traditional view, glial cells perform the following tasks:

- _____
  _____
- _____
  _____
- _____
  _____
- _____
  _____
- _____
  _____

Newer research indicates that glial cells also perform these tasks:

- _____
  _____
- _____
  _____
- _____
  _____
- _____
  _____
- _____
  _____

The Nervous System: An Orchestra with Many Members

The Peripheral Nervous System: A Moving Story

The nervous system has two parts:

1. The **peripheral nervous system (PNS)** which, in turn, has two parts:

   a. _____ **(ANS)** is responsible for _____
   _____
   _____.

There are two branches of the ANS:

- _____ is involved in _____
  _____
  _____ .

- _____ is involved in _____
  _____
  _____ .

b.   The **sensory-somatic nervous system (SSNS)** includes

- Neurons in our _____, which have the following functions:
  _____
  _____

- The **skeletal system,** which consists of _____
  _____
  _____ .

2.   The **central nervous system (CNS)** includes two parts:

a.   The **brain.**

b.   The **spinal cord**, which is involved in

- _____
- _____
- _____
- _____

In the following chart, compare the **autonomic nervous system** and the **skeletal** (or **somatic**) **nervous system** in terms of the muscles they control and the appearance and other characteristics of the muscles controlled.

	Autonomic Nervous System	Skeletal (or Somatic) System
Muscles controlled		
Appearance of muscles controlled		
Other characteristics of muscles controlled		

Provide the following characteristics of the two parts of the autonomic nervous system: the **sympathetic nervous system** and the **parasympathetic nervous system.**

	Sympathetic Nervous System	Parasympathetic Nervous System
What is the purpose of the system?		
What are the effects of activation of the system?		

The Central Nervous System: Reflex and Reflection

If you could see under someone's skull, what would you see (in order)? Name and describe each feature.

- _____
- _____
  _____
  _____

Under all this, you would see two **cerebral hemispheres.**

- Why are these parts named hemispheres? _____
  _____
  _____

- What does each hemisphere do? _____
  _____
  _____

GO SURFING...

...at http://www.pbs.org/wnet/brain/3d/ to see more pictures of the brain.

Each hemisphere is divided into four **lobes.** List the location of each lobe. (An example is given for the **temporal lobes.**)

	Occipital	Temporal	Parietal	Frontal
Location		At the temples		

How are the two hemispheres of the brain connected? _____

Why is the **cerebral cortex** so "crumpled-up"? _____

_____

_____

Spotlight on the Brain: How It Divides and Conquers

The Cerebral Cortex: The Seat of the Mind

	Function	Result of Damage to This Part
Occipital lobes		
Temporal lobes		
Parietal lobes		
Frontal lobes		

The Dual Brain: Thinking with Both Barrels

GO SURFING...

...at http://www.uwm.edu/~johnchay/sb.htm to see a demonstration of the **split-brain syndrome** before answering the following questions.

Who are **split-brain patients?** What information can studies of split-brain patients provide?

_____

_____

_____

Mark an "X" in the "Left" or "Right" column to indicate in which **hemisphere** the following functions typically take place.

Function	Left	Right
Understanding humor		
Determining whether an object is above or below another object		
Making the pitch of a voice rise at the end of a question		

Why must generalizations about the specializations of each **hemisphere** be made cautiously?

_____

_____

_____

_____

_____

If you had to suffer damage to one **hemisphere,** which one would it be? Why? _____

_____

_____

_____

_____

GO SURFING...

...at http://faculty.washington.edu/chudler/rightl.html to determine how strong your hand preference is.

Take one of the Handedness Questionnaires. How strong is your hand preference? _____
_____

What is the relationship between handedness and hemispheric specialization? See
http://faculty.washington.edu/chudler/split.html, and then briefly explain this relationship here.
_____
_____
_____
_____
_____
_____

Beneath the Cortex: The Inner Brain

For each of the following **brain parts,** explain its function and then provide a personal example of when you use this brain part in your life.

Brain Part	Function	Personal Example
Thalamus		
Hypothalamus		
Hippocampus		
Amygdala		

Brain Part	Function	Personal Example
Basal ganglia		
Brainstem		
Cerebellum		

GO SURFING...

...at http://www.gpc.edu/~bbrown/psyc1501/brain/locfunct.htm. Create lesions or stimulate the brain to determine what each of the indicated brain parts is. Complete the chart and the first eight questions on that Web page.

The Neuroendocrine and Neuroimmune Systems: More Brain–Body Connections

How is the **CNS** related to the **neuroendocrine system?** _____

_____

_____

_____

What are **hormones?** Define this term in your own words. _____

_____

_____

What are the effects of the following **hormones?**

Hormone	Effects
Testosterone	
Estrogen	
Cortisol	

In addition to physical effects, sexual hormones (e.g., testosterone and estrogen) may have psychological effects. Can you think of any psychological or behavioral changes you experienced in adolescence that may have resulted from hormonal changes? _____

_____

_____

_____

_____

_____

What role does the **pituitary gland** play in the neuroendocrine system? Explain. _____

_____

_____

_____

_____

Looking at Levels: The Musical Brain

Explain the factors at each of the **three levels** that may be involved in hearing and appreciating music. Draw arrows to indicate how these factors may interact.

The Brain	The Person	The Group

Probing the Brain

The Damaged Brain: What's Missing?

What are **strokes** and **lesions,** and how do they help us to understand the brain's functions?

_____
_____
_____
_____
_____
_____
_____

Recording Techniques: The Music of the Cells

The following techniques record the activity of neurons. Describe how each works.

	Description of Technique
Electroencephalograph (EEG)	
Magnetoencephalography (MEG)	
Single-cell recording	

Neuroimaging: Picturing the Living Brain

How has **neuroimaging** transformed psychology? _____

_____
_____

In the following chart, explain how each technique works.

	Description of Technique
Techniques Allowing Visualization of Brain Structure	
Computer-assisted tomography (CT or CAT)	
Magnetic resonance imaging (MRI)	
Techniques Allowing Visualization of Brain Function	
Positron emission tomography (PET)	
Functional magnetic resonance imaging (fMRI)	

Stimulation: Tickling the Neurons

In your own words, describe the three types of **neural stimulation techniques** and the disadvantages of each.

Technique and Description	Disadvantages

GO SURFING...

...at http://www.pbs.org/wgbh/aso/tryit/brain/or http://www.pbs.org/wgbh/aso/tryit/brain/ to electronically recreate one of Wilder Penfield's studies.

What does this activity tell you about how much of the **motor cortex** is devoted to different brain parts? Discuss. _____

_____

_____

_____

_____

_____

Genes, Brain, and Environment: The Brain in the World

Genes as Blueprints: Born to Be Wild?

What are the two key ideas of **Mendelian inheritance?**

- _____
  _____
  _____

- _____
  _____
  _____

GO SURFING...

...at http://gslc.genetics.utah.edu/units/basics/builddna to build a virtual DNA molecule. You may also want to visit http://gslc.genetics.utah.edu/units/basics/tour and take the "What Is DNA?," "What Is a Gene?," "What Is a Chromosome?," "What Is Heredity?," and "What Is a Trait?" tours to have a visual demonstration of much of the material described in the book.

Name and describe a way that you resemble your parents in terms of your behavior or health.

_____

_____

Do these similarities (in terms of behavior or health) necessarily mean that you inherited these qualities? Can you think of alternative explanations? If so, explain. _____

_____

_____

GO SURFING...

...at the official Web site of the Human Genome Project, http://www.ornl.gov/sci/techresources/Human_Genome/home.shtml.

What are some of the benefits that may be obtained from scientists' attempts to "map the genes"?

_____

_____

_____

Why do some neural connections get **pruned**? _____

_____

_____

Do you think that **pruning** might have any good results? If so, what would they be? _____

_____

_____

When is **plasticity** most evident?

- _____
- _____
- _____
- _____

Give original examples from your own life of **passive interaction, evocative interaction,** and **active interaction.**

Type of Interaction	Example
Passive	
Evocative	
Active	

Behavioral Genetics

What types of questions might someone in **behavioral genetics** ask?

- _____
- _____
- _____
- _____

In your own words, define **heritability**. _____

_____

_____

_____

_____

_____

Describe the following types of studies, which allow researchers to study the relative contributions of genes and environment to a particular trait.

- **Twin studies:** _____

   _____

   _____

- **Adoption studies:** _____

   _____

   _____

   _____

   _____

Evolution and the Brain: The Best of All Possible Brains?

Consider the giraffe, the elephant, and the human. Name a characteristic of each species that may have evolved over time (been reproduced over and over again) because it ensured survival and helped the animals adapt to the environment.

Animal	Characteristic	Reason for Adaptation
Giraffe		
Elephant		
Human		

Natural selection cannot explain all characteristics. Name and describe three other factors that may explain existing characteristics of human beings or other forms of life.

- _____

- _____

- _____

   _____

After You Read . . . _Thinking Back_

1. What must researchers do to ensure that their use of animals in research settings is ethical? Discuss. _____
   _____
   _____
   _____
   _____

2. Of the various theories of psychology discussed in Chapter 1, which ones do you think rely the most on the brain research described in this chapter? Why? _____
   _____
   _____
   _____
   _____
   _____

3. Which theories do you think rely the least on this research? Why? _____
   _____
   _____
   _____
   _____
   _____

4. Explain how a neuropsychologist might use experimental, quasi-experimental, and correlational research designs.
   - Experimental: _____
     _____
     _____
     _____

   - Quasi-experimental: _____
     _____
     _____
     _____

   - Correlational: _____
     _____
     _____
     _____

5. What are some of the difficulties with using case studies to make conclusions about brain functioning? _____
   _____
   _____
   _____

After You Read . . . Thinking Ahead

1. Based on what you have learned about the functions of the parts of the brain, which brain parts might be involved in the following:
   - Depression: _____
   - Anxiety disorders: _____
   - Sleep disorders: _____

2. Which parts of the brain would you think would be undergoing the most development at the following ages? Why?

   - 0–6 months: _____

   _____

   - 18–24 months: _____

   _____

   - Early school-age years: _____

   _____

   - Teenage years: _____

   _____

3. What outcome would you predict for a child who suffered brain damage, as opposed to an older person who suffered the same type of damage? _____

   _____

   _____

   _____

4. How could the research on plasticity explain the fact that it is easier to learn second languages as a child than as an adult? Discuss. _____

   _____

   _____

   _____

5. What do you think the role of the brain is in intelligence? Which brain parts do you think are especially relevant? Why? _____

   _____

   _____

   _____

6. Can you think of ways to use the idea of brain connections, as described in this chapter, to develop better memory techniques? Discuss. _____

   _____

   _____

   _____

After You Read . . . Practice Tests

PRACTICE TEST #1

Multiple-Choice Questions

For each question, circle the best answer from the choices given.

1. Most of the neurons in the brain are: (p. 53)
   a. sensory neurons.
   b. motor neurons.
   c. channel neurons.
   d. interneurons.

2. During an action potential, _____ ions move into the neuron and _____ ions move out. (p. 55)
   a. sodium; potassium
   b. sodium; chloride
   c. potassium; sodium
   d. hydrogen; potassium

3. Reuptake refers to the process of: (p. 59)
   a. absorbing neurotransmitters on the part of the receiving neuron.
   b. recycling of excess neurotransmitters on the part of the receiving neuron.
   c. abolishing neurotransmitters on the part of the sending neuron.
   d. absorbing excess neurotransmitters on the part of the sending neuron.

4. All of the following are SSRIs EXCEPT: (p. 57)
   a. Prozac
   b. Zoloft
   c. L-Dopa
   d. Paxil

5. The nervous system has _____ major parts. (p. 61)
   a. 2
   b. 4
   c. 8
   d. 16

6. The sympathetic nervous system is most closely associated with which of the following? (p. 62)
   a. general nervous system
   b. central nervous system
   c. peripheral nervous system
   d. autonomic nervous system

7. The central nervous system consists of the: (p. 63)
   a. brain
   b. spinal column
   c. spinal cord
   d. brain and spinal cord

8. The creases in the cerebral cortex are called: (p. 64)
   a. sulci
   b. collosi
   c. gyri
   d. ventricles

9. The two cerebral hemispheres are connected by the: (p. 64)
   a. meninges
   b. ventricles
   c. sulci and gyri
   d. corpus callosum

PRACTICE TEST #2

Multiple-Choice Questions

For each question, circle the best answer from the choices given.

1. The somatosensory strip is located in the _____. (p. 68)
   a. frontal
   b. parietal
   c. temporal
   d. occipital

2. The motor strip is located in the _____ lobe. (p. 68)
   a. frontal
   b. parietal
   c. temporal
   d. occipital

3. Split-brain patients have undergone surgery in which: (p. 69)
   a. a region of the temporal lobe has been lesioned.
   b. one of the ventricles has been lesioned.
   c. a region of the parietal lobe has been lesioned.
   d. the corpus callosum has been lesioned.

4. Based on the research of Gazzaniga and Ledoux, the left hemisphere plays a crucial role in: (p. 70)
   a. language.
   b. interpreting the world.
   c. many forms of reasoning.
   d. all of the above.

5. The notion that the left brain is analytical and verbal, whereas the right brain in intuitive and perceptual: (p. 70)
   a. is true for only left-handed individuals.
   b. should actually be stated such that the processes are reversed for each half of the brain.
   c. is actually false when considering right-handed individuals.
   d. is not completely accurate.

6. If you suffered damage to your hippocampus, you would most likely have problems: (p. 72)
   a. involving the retrieval of old memories
   b. involving the regulation of bodily functions
   c. involving the storage of new memories
   d. involving the acquisition of procedural skills

7. Testosterone is to estrogen as: (p. 75)
   a. hormones are to chemicals
   b. neurotransmitters are to hormones
   c. males are to females
   d. females are to males

8. Which of the following is TRUE concerning the role of the brain in processing music? (p. 76)
   a. The left frontal lobe is responsible.
   b. The right parietal lobe is responsible.
   c. The left hemisphere is responsible.
   d. Both hemispheres are responsible.

PRACTICE TEST #3

Multiple-Choice Questions

For each question, circle the best answer from the choices given.

1. The most frequent source of damage to the brain is a(n): (p. 79)
    a. aneurysm.
    b. stroke.
    c. lesion.
    d. EEG.

2. EEG stands for: (p. 80)
    a. Electroencephalograph.
    b. Excitatory encephalogram.
    c. Electric event graphing.
    d. Entrance and exit graphing.

3. Which of the following provides a visual picture of brain structure? (p. 81)
    a. MRI
    b. MEG
    c. EEG
    d. TMS

4. Which of the following is an alternative to using an fMRI for visualizing brain function? (p. 82)
    a. Single-cell recordings
    b. CT scan
    c. MRI scan
    d. Optical imaging

5. The process by which certain neural connections are eliminated is called: (p. 86)
    a. cutting
    b. pruning
    c. lesioning
    d. lablating

6. Plasticity refers to: (p. 86)
    a. The soft spots on an infant's head.
    b. The fact that people are born with few neural connections.
    c. The ability of the brain to change with experience.
    d. The fluid-filled parts at the center of the brain.

7. A famous pianist has a child and introduces her to the piano at the age of two. In terms of how this might affect the child, this would constitute an example of _____ a(n) interaction. (p. 88)
    a. passive
    b. active
    c. evocative
    d. reactive

8. Difficult babies tend to elicit punitive reactions from their caregivers. This is an example of a(n) _____ interaction. (p. 88)
    a. passive
    b. active
    c. evocative
    d. provocative

9. Saying that intelligence is 50% heritable means: (p. 89)
    a. You get 50% of your intelligence from you mom, and 50% from your dad.
    b. You get 50% of your intelligence from your parents, and 50% from the environment.
    c. In a specific environment, 50% of the variability in intelligence among people is due to genetics.
    d. In a specific environment, 50% of people are intelligent and 50% are not.

10. Whose genes would be the most similar? (p. 89)
    a. Parent and child
    b. Monozygotic twins
    c. Siblings born at different times
    d. Dizygotic twins

COMPREHENSIVE PRACTICE TEST

True/False Questions

Circle TRUE or FALSE for each of the following statements.

1. TRUE   FALSE   A neuron can fire at different strengths. (p. 54)

2. TRUE   FALSE   Prozac is an SSRI. (p. 57)

3. TRUE   FALSE   Watching a scary movie would result in the activation of the parasympathetic system. (p. 63)

4. TRUE   FALSE   The hypothalamus controls motor movement. (p. 72)

5. TRUE   FALSE   An EEG allows us to observe brain structure. (p. 80)

6. TRUE   FALSE   Gregor Mendel is credited for discovering basic ideas of inheritance. (p. 84)

Multiple-Choice Questions

For each question, circle the best answer from the choices given.

1. Which of the following is NOT a type of neuron? (p. 53)
    a. sensory neuron
    b. interneuron
    c. motor neuron
    d. glial neuron

2. The part of the neuron responsible for the release of neurotransmitters is/are the: (p. 53)
    a. dendrites
    b. cell body
    c. axon
    d. terminal buttons

3. Sending and receiving neurons: (p. 56)
    a. touch each other.
    b. are separated by the glial cells
    c. are separated by large gaps referred to as cliffs
    d. are separated by a gap referred to as the synaptic cleft.

4. A drug that alters the major neurotransmitter substance, GABA, is: (p. 57)
    a. alcohol
    b. amphetamine
    c. SSRIs
    d. scopolamine

5. The process by which a surplus of neurotransmitter is reabsorbed back into the sending neuron is called: (p. 59)
    a. reuptake
    b. reusage
    c. reabsorption
    d. removal

6. All of the following are examples of SSRIs EXCEPT: (p. 57)
    a. Prozac
    b. Zoloft
    c. Paxil
    d. Advil

7. The peripheral nervous system is composed of the: (p. 61)
    a. brain and spinal cord.
    b. sympathetic and parasympathetic systems.
    c. sensory-somatic nervous system and autonomic nervous system.
    d. midbrain and the hindbrain.

8. The system that is said to prepare us to "rest or digest" is most likely the: (p. 63)
    a. parasympathetic system
    b. skeletal system
    c. reticular formation
    d. sympathetic system

9. Damage to the temporal lobes is most likely to result in which of the following: (p. 67)
    a. breathing difficulties
    b. difficulty in swallowing
    c. difficulty in understanding others
    d. difficulty in talking

10. Damage to the _____ lobes may result in trouble controlling emotions. (pp. 68-69)
    a. occipital
    b. parietal
    c. temporal
    d. frontal

11. Damage to the _____ would most likely result in impaired movement. (pp. 72-73)
    a. cerebral cortex
    b. thalamus
    c. basal ganglia
    d. hippocampus

12. Farah signed up for a sleep study and the neurologist hooked wires up to her head. Most likely, the neurologist plans to keep a running log of the electrical activity in Farah's brain as she descends through the sleep stages. Doing so would require the use of: (p. 79)
    a. transcranial recording
    b. magnetic resonance imaging
    c. electroencephalogram
    d. neuroimage

13. The idea that offspring inherit genes from each parent is most in line with which of the following? (p. 84)
    a. Gregorian inheritance
    b. Mendelian inheritance
    c. complex inheritance
    d. simple inheritance

14. The theory of _____ asserts that inherited characteristics that contribute to survival in a particular environment will come to be widespread in the population. (p. 90)
    a. genetic selection
    b. Darwinism
    c. natural selection
    d. adaptation

Short-Answer/Essay Questions

Answer each question in the space provided.

1. Explain the passage of the electrical signal along the axon._____
_____
_____
_____
_____
_____
_____
_____
_____

2. If an individual is afflicted with Parkinson's disease, what is most likely the problem at the level of neurotransmitters and how is the disease treated?_____
_____
_____
_____
_____
_____
_____
_____

3. Name and briefly describe the two major divisions of the Peripheral Nervous System._____

_____

_____

_____

_____

_____

_____

_____

_____

4. List the four lobes of the cerebral cortex. Which lobe dramatically distinguishes our brain from the brain of a monkey?_____

_____

_____

_____

_____

_____

_____

_____

_____

5. Define plasticity and discuss the four circumstances in which plasticity is most evident._____

_____

_____

_____

_____

_____

_____

_____

_____

_____

When You Are Finished . . . Puzzle It Out

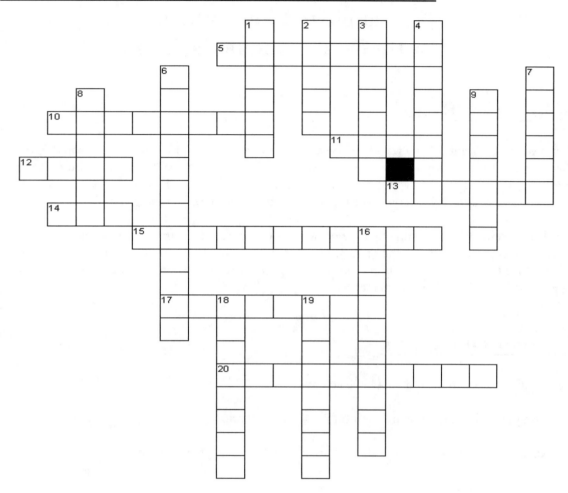

Across

5. Individual's genetic code
10. Neuronal part, from the Greek word for tree
11. Drug that blocks reuptake of serotonin
12. Bulges in the cortex
13. Region of impaired tissue
14. Includes the spinal cord and brain
15. Brain part critical to making new memories
17. Brain part often thought of as switching center
20. Type of cell with name coming from the Greek word for "glue"

Down

1. Automatic response to an event
2. Four parts of each hemisphere
3. Place where two neurons meet
4. Charge of the resting potential
6. Amount of variability due to genetics
7. Helps impulses travel faster down axon
8. The basic unit of the nervous system
9. Elimination of neural connections
16. Molding of brain by experience
18. Brain part involved in emotions like anger
19. Physical change of a gene

Puzzle created with Puzzlemaker at DiscoverySchool.com.

Chapter 3
Sensation and Perception:
How the World Enters the Mind

Before You Read . . .

Why is your significant other always able to spot the deer at the side of the road when you don't? Why does food taste funny when you have a cold? In this chapter, you will learn how you come to understand the world around you through your senses. Understanding the world depends not only on sensation, but also on perception, or the brain's interpretation of incoming stimuli.

The chapter starts with in-depth coverage of two senses: vision and hearing. Less detailed information is presented about the other senses: smell, taste, and the somasthetic senses (those that have to do with sensing your body and position in space). The chapter concludes with discussions of magnetic sense and extrasensory perception.

Chapter Objectives

After reading this chapter, you should be able to:

- Define sensation and explain how it differs from perception.

- Explain how you see, including the sensation of color, shape, and motion.

- Describe how you make sense of what you see.

- Define attention.

- Explain how ears normally register sound.

- Describe how the sense of smell works.

- Describe how the sense of taste works.

- Explain how we sense our bodies.

- Understand the evidence for the existence of magnetic sense and extrasensory perception (ESP).

As You Read . . . Term Identification

Make flashcards using the following terms as you go. Use the definitions in the margins of this chapter for help. If you write the definitions in your own words, though, you will remember them better!

Absolute threshold
Accommodation
Afterimage
Amplitude
Attention
Attentional blink
Bias
Binocular cues
Bottom-up processing
Categorical perception
Chemical senses
Cocktail party phenomenon
Color blindness
Color constancy
Conduction deafness
Cones
Convergence
Cornea
Dark adaptation
Decibel (dB)
Dichotic listening
Double pain
Endorphins
Extrasensory perception (ESP)
Figure
Fovea
Frequency
Frequency theory
Gate control
Gestalt laws of organization
Ground
Hair cells
Iris
Just-noticeable difference (JND)
Kinesthetic sense
Loudness
Monocular static cues

Motion cues
Nerve deafness
Opponent cells
Opponent process theory of color vision
Optic nerve
Paradoxical cold
Perception
Perceptual constancy
Perceptual set
Pheromones
Pitch
Place theory
Placebo
Pop-out
Psychophysics
Pupil
Repetition blindness
Retina
Retinal disparity
Rods
Selective attention
Sensation
Sensitivity
Shape constancy
Signal detection theory
Size constancy
Somasthetic senses
Speech-segmentation problem
Taste buds
Texture gradient
Threshold
Top-down processing
Transduction
Trichromatic theory of color vision
Vestibular sense
Wavelength
Weber's law

As You Read . . . Questions and Exercises

Vision: Window on the World

Phases of Vision

Name and describe the broad two phases of **visual perception.**

- _____
  _____
  _____
  _____

- _____
  _____
  _____
  _____
  _____

What are the two phases of processing within **perception?**

- _____
  _____
  _____
  _____

Visual Sensation: More Than Meets the Eye

GO SURFING...

...at http://dictionary.reference.com.

What does the abbreviation **psycho-** or **psyche-** mean? _____
_____
_____

What does the word **physics** mean? _____
_____
_____

Put **psycho-** and **physics** together to explain what researchers in the field of **psychophysics** study.

_____
_____
_____
_____

Define each of the following terms and give a personal example of why it could be important in your life.

Term	Definition	Personal Example
Threshold		
Absolute threshold		
Just-noticeable difference (JND)		
Weber's law		

What does **signal detection theory** explain? _____
_____
_____
_____
_____

Two key concepts explain why **signals** are detected or missed. First, define each of these concepts. Then, explain how these concepts could be used in ensuring that airport security personnel detect any dangerous materials during screening procedures.

Concept	Definition	Effect on Airport Security Screening
Sensitivity		
Bias		

What is light? _____
_____
_____
_____

Define the following terms:

- **Amplitude:** _____
_____
_____
_____

- **Frequency:** _____
_____
_____
_____

- **Wavelength:** _____
_____
_____
_____

GO SURFING...

...at http://www.keystoneblind.org/wiseweb/intheeye.htm to see how the eye works. Then, explain the steps involved in **transduction,** or the conversion of electromagnetic energy into nerve impulses:

- The **iris:** _____
  _____

- The **pupil:** _____
  _____

- The **cornea:** _____
  _____

- The **lens:** _____
  _____

- The **retina:** _____
  _____

- The **fovea:** _____
  _____
  _____

Complete the following chart to compare **rods** and **cones.**

	Rods	Cones
Number		
Location within the eye		
Purpose		

 Hint! To remember the difference between rods and cones, remember that <u>c</u>ones and <u>c</u>olor both begin with C.

Why does everything look gray at night? Explain. _____
_____
_____
_____
_____
_____
_____

GO SURFING...

...at http://faculty.washington.edu/chudler/chvision.html and do the experiments on finding your **blind spot.**

Why do you have a **blind spot?** Explain. _____
_____
_____
_____
_____
_____
_____
_____

Explain how **dark adaptation works.**

- _____
_____
_____
_____

- _____
_____
_____
_____

What is the third type of cell in the eye that registers light? _____
_____

What is the purpose of these types of cells? _____
_____
_____
_____

Name and briefly describe the three ways that **colors** can vary.

- _____
  _____
  _____
  _____

- _____
  _____
  _____
  _____

- _____
  _____
  _____
  _____

Fill in the missing words in the following paragraph.

Recent research has supported the **trichromatic theory of color vision** with some modifications. This theory says that we can see different hues because we have three types of cones. Each type is _most_ sensitive to a different light in the wavelength. Thus one type is most sensitive to light seen as _____, a second type is most sensitive to light seen as _____, and yet another type is most sensitive to light seen as _____. For each color, at least two different types of cones are sensitive to it, although one type of cone will be _more_ sensitive. The brain registers the **mixture** of the different responses of the three types of cones. However, some materials, such as paint, absorb some light. As a result, not all light is reflected. Only the wavelengths that are _____, meaning "not absorbed," reach your eyes. However, there is more to seeing color than what this theory explains. The **opponent process theory of color vision** provides another factor: It says that the presence of one color of a pair inhibits the perception of the other color. The opponent pairs are: red/_____, yellow/_____, and black/_____.

GO SURFING...

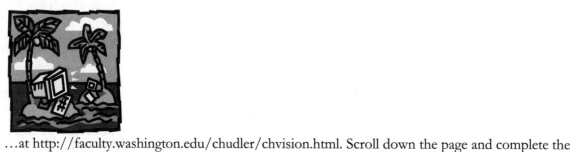

...at http://faculty.washington.edu/chudler/chvision.html. Scroll down the page and complete the activities on **afterimages** in #5 and #6.

Why can't you see the **mixture** of blue and yellow at the same time? _____

_____

_____

_____

_____

_____

_____

_____

GO SURFING...

...at http://colorlab.wickline.org/colorblind/colorlab/ and see what colors would look like if you had different forms of **color blindness.**

Do you know anyone who has **color blindness?** If so, what form does it take? _____

_____

_____

_____

Who is most likely to have **color blindness?** _____

_____

What is the most common form of **color blindness?** _____

_____

What causes **color blindness?**

- _____
  _____
  _____

- _____
  _____
  _____

- _____
  _____
  _____

What implications would it have in your life if you were **color-blind?** (For example, the author of this manual once had a karate instructor who was color-blind and could not identify the different colored belts of his students!) _____
_____
_____
_____
_____

Phase 1 of Visual Perception: Organizing the World

Complete the missing words in the following paragraph.

To distinguish the figure from the ground, your brain must take the tiny fragments of information that it obtains through the senses and organize that information into edges. The first part of the cortex to receive visual information is the _____, which is located in the _____, The neurons there are arranged into _____. Different columns fire in response to edges with different _____. The columns are arranged into _____, which are driven by incoming information from the _____ or _____. The sets are arranged into _____, which respond to incoming information on different spots on the retina. These hypercolumns are _____, meaning that the pattern on the retina is spatially laid out on the _____.

Match each of the following circumstances with the Gestalt law of organization that best explains it.

_____ 1. Closure

A. Seeing the following as three rows of faces or as three columns of faces, even though both sets have the same number of faces:

_____ 2. Proximity

B. Seeing the following as a triangle within a square:

_____ 3. Good form

C. Seeing this as a smiley face, despite the missing part of the circle:

_____ 4. Similarity

D. Seeing the following as a square overlapping a triangle, rather than several more complicated shapes:

_____ 5. Continuity

E. Seeing the following as two intersecting lines rather than two adjacent angles:

How does learning affect your **perception?** _____
_____
_____
_____
_____
_____
_____
_____

Perceptual constancy is the perception of the characteristics of objects as the same even though the sensory information striking the eyes changes. Give a personal example of each of the following types of constancy:

Type of Constancy	Example
Size constancy	
Shape constancy	
Color constancy	

To perceive the world as three-dimensional, the brain uses several types of cues. Briefly describe, and then provide an example of, the following types of **cues:**

Type of Cue	Description	Example
Binocular static cues	Cues about static (unmoving) information obtained from both eyes working together.	
Retinal disparity (binocular disparity)		
Monocular static cues	Cues about distance obtained that can be obtained by one eye.	
Texture gradient		

Linear perspective (foreshortening)		
Atmospheric perspective		
Occlusion cue		
Motion cues	Cues that specify the distance of an object based on its movement.	
Motion parallax		

GO SURFING...

...at http://psych.hanover.edu/Krantz/SizeConstancy/index.html to learn more about size constancy. Be sure to play with the interactive figure. Which three cues do you use to determine whether the sizes of objects are constant? Name and briefly describe them.

■ _____

_____

_____

■ _____

_____

_____

■ _____

_____

_____

Which two cues help you to perceive whether an object is coming closer to you?

■ _____

_____

_____

▪ _____

_____

_____

_____

_____

How does culture influence how cues are portrayed in artwork? _____

_____

_____

_____

_____

_____

_____

_____

GO SURFING...

…at http://faculty.washington.edu/chudler/chvision.html. Scroll down and take a look at the visual illusions there. Here are some other good sites for viewing illusions:

- http://www.sandlotscience.com
- http://www.optillusions.com

Which **illusions** are your favorites? In the chart below, describe them and explain how they work.

Illusion (Name and Draw)	Explanation

<table>
<tr><td></td><td></td></tr>
<tr><td></td><td></td></tr>
</table>

How does motion help people to perceive depth? _____
_____
_____
_____

What evidence is there to suggest that experience or learning affects the ability to perceive motion? _
_____
_____
_____

What evidence is there to suggest that the ability to perceive motion is brain-based? _____
_____
_____
_____

Phase 2 of Visual Perception: Recognition and Identification

What are the two major goals in the second phase of visual perception?

- _____
_____
_____

- _____
_____
_____

Fill in the following chart with information about the two major neural pathways in the brain.

Pathway	Purpose	Brain Mechanisms
"What" pathway		
"Where" pathway		

Where do these two pathways meet? What happens there? _____
_____
_____
_____

Suppose that you see a dog. The first phases of visual processing tell you that it is a four-legged furry animal. What has to happen for you to *recognize* it as a dog? _____
_____
_____
_____

What other information might you have about the dog if you *identified* it? _____
_____
_____
_____

What evidence is there that you see the dog as more than just a triangular head, rectangular body, and rectangular legs? _____
_____
_____
_____

Give the definition and an example of each of the following:

Type of Processing	Description	Example
Bottom-up processing		
Top-down processing		

How do **bottom-up** and **top-down processing** interact? _____

_____

_____

_____

_____

_____

_____

_____

What are **perceptual sets?** _____

_____

_____

_____

_____

_____

What kinds of **perceptual expectancies** do you have of your psychology class? _____

_____

_____

_____

_____

Kosslyn (one of your textbook authors) proposes that the brain uses two different ways to **code space.** Describe each of these two ways and identify the hemisphere that is primarily responsible for these tasks.

Method of Coding Space	Purpose of Coding Method	Hemisphere
Categorical spatial relations		
Coordinate spatial relations		

Kosslyn hypothesized that the left hemisphere is better at _____

_____

_____

and that the right hemisphere is better at _____

_____

_____

Attention: The Gateway to Awareness

Attention is the act of focusing on particular information. Which topics do you pay particular attention to? _____
_____
_____
_____

Give an example of a time that you have used **selective attention.** _____
_____
_____
_____

There are two reasons why people pay attention to something.

Type of Attention	What It Is	How It Works
Pop-out		
Active searching		

How is it possible for blind people to see? _____
_____
_____
_____

GO SURFING...

...at http://serendip.brynmawr.edu/bb/blindsight.html and try the online demonstration of **blindsight** there.

What is **blindsight?** _____
_____
_____
_____

Define the following phenomena and give an example of how they may affect an editor's job.

Phenomena	Explanation	Effect
Repetition blindness		
Attentional blink		

Looking at Levels: The Essential Features of Good Looks

Which body parts do most people find most attractive in others? Analyze your preferences at each of the three levels. Draw arrows to indicate how factors at the different levels may interact.

The Brain	The Person	The Group

Hearing

Auditory Sensation: If a Tree Falls but Nobody Hears It, Is there a Sound?

Why do some people make sounds from their ears, sometimes so loud that others can hear it?

_____
_____
_____

Name and describe the two phases of **auditory processing:**

- _____
  _____
  _____
  _____

- _____
  _____
  _____
  _____

If a tree falls in the forest but nobody hears it, is there a sound? Explain your answer. _____
_____
_____
_____
_____

GO SURFING…

…at http://science.howstuffworks.com/hearing.htm to see how the ear works. Then explain the steps involved in **auditory processing.**

- **Waves:** _____
  _____

- The **eardrum:** _____
  _____

- The **three bones in the middle ear (hammer, anvil, and stirrup):** _____
  _____

- The **basilar membrane** (inside the **cochlea**): _____
  _____

- **Hair cells sticking up from the basilar membrane:** _____
  _____

There are two main theories about how the **basilar membrane** converts pressure waves to sound:
frequency theory and **place theory.** Which of these theories appears to be correct? Explain this
theory. _____
_____
_____
_____
_____
_____
_____

More than twenty-eight million Americans have some sort of **hearing** difficulty. Describe each of
the following problems.

Auditory Problem	Explanation
Nerve deafness	
Conduction deafness	

Phase I of Auditory Perception: Organizing the Auditory World

The first column of the following chart lists some of the ways that **vision** and **hearing** are similar.
In the last two columns, explain how this idea relates specifically to vision and hearing.

What are the two phases of both visual and auditory perception?

- **Phase I:** _____
  _____
  _____

- **Phase 2:** _____
  _____
  _____

Idea	As Applied to Vision	As Applied to Hearing
Gestalt laws		
Identification of individual words		
Categorical perception		
Use of two sensory organs (e.g., two eyes or two ears)		

Phase 2 of Auditory Perception: Recognition and Identification

How do your **expectations** influence your **hearing?**

- _____
_____
_____
_____

- _____
_____
_____
_____

What is the **cocktail party phenomenon?** _____
_____
_____
_____

Describe how **dichotic listening studies** are conducted. _____
_____
_____
_____
_____

What do **dichotic listening studies** indicate? _____
_____
_____
_____
_____

Sensing and Perceiving in Other Ways

Smell: A Nose for News?

What are the two **chemical senses**? _____
_____

Why are they called that? _____
_____
_____
_____

What are are some categories of people who are, on average, better at identifying smells than the rest of the population?

- _____

- _____

- _____

Explain the steps involved in **olfaction.**

- **Molecules:** _____
_____

- **Receptors:** _____
_____

What are the two major neural tracks by which odors can travel into the brain?

- _____

- _____

Do you have a memory associated with a particular odor? Describe it. _____
_____
_____
_____

Why do people have strong memories attached to particular odors? _____
_____
_____
_____

How does olfaction assist in keeping people **safe?** _____
_____
_____
_____

Female **pheromones** can attract men. Women who wore perfume with the pheromone reported more of the following:

- _____

- _____

- _____

- _____

However, these same women did not report an increase in the following:

- _____

- _____

- _____

Would you ever wear a **pheromone?** Why or why not? _____
_____
_____
_____
_____

Taste: The Mouth Has It

Where are **taste buds** found? _____
_____
_____
_____

In addition to the four tastes that are traditionally identified (sweet, sour, bitter, and salty), there is another taste called **umami.** Which foods elicit this taste? _____
_____
_____
_____

What is the relationship between smell and taste? _____
_____
_____
_____

Somasthetic Senses: Not Just Skin Deep

How are the **somasthetic senses** similar? _____
_____
_____
_____

Briefly describe each of the following **somasthetic senses** in the chart below.

Sense	Description/Definition	Source
Kinesthetic sense		
Vestibular sense		
Touch		
Temperature		

What are the two different kinds of **pain?**

- _____

- _____

Research indicates that people differ widely in the amount of pain that they can withstand. Do you think that you have a low or high pain threshold? _____

_____

_____

_____

_____

Other Senses

What effect would it have on the medical field if humans responded to magnetic fields as strongly as birds do? _____

_____

_____

_____

_____

_____

_____

_____

Briefly describe each of the following forms of **extrasensory perception (ESP):**

Form	Description
Anomalous cognition (psi)	
Telepathy	
Clairvoyance	
Precognition	
Psychokinesis (PK)	

What are the four reasons why most psychologists are skeptical about ESP?

- _____

  _____

  _____

  _____

- _____

  _____

  _____

  _____

- _____
  _____
  _____
  _____

- _____
  _____
  _____
  _____

After You Read . . . Thinking Back

1. What is the relationship between the **sense organs** and **neural impulses in the brain?**

_____
_____
_____
_____
_____
_____

2. In Chapter 1, you learned about **evolutionary psychology.** Give some examples of how evolutionary psychologists have explained facts about sensation and perception. (For example, what would an evolutionary psychologist say is the purpose of pain?)

- _____
_____
_____
_____

- _____
_____
_____
_____

- _____
_____
_____
_____

- _____
_____
_____
_____

3. In Chapter 2, you learned about the importance of replication. Why is the ability to replicate studies on ESP so important? Why does the failure to replicate studies make psychologists skeptical about ESP? _____
_____
_____
_____
_____
_____

4. Despite the differences among the sense organs, there are many similarities in how sensory information is processed in the brain. Give some examples.

   - _____
   _____
   _____
   _____

   - _____
   _____
   _____
   _____

   - _____
   _____
   _____
   _____

After You Read . . . Thinking Ahead

1. At what time in life do you think the different senses develop? Do some develop before others? Which ones? When? _____

   _____

   _____

   _____

   _____

   _____

   _____

2. How does your memory (both its contents and its processes) affect what you sense and perceive?

   _____

   _____

   _____

   _____

   _____

   _____

3. How does what you sense and perceive affect your memory (both its contents and its processes)?

   _____

   _____

   _____

   _____

   _____

   _____

   _____

4. How might a person's stereotypes and/or prejudices influence his or her sensation and/or perception? _____

   _____

   _____

   _____

   _____

   _____

   _____

5. How might your sensations and perceptions influence your social interactions? _____

   _____

   _____

   _____

   _____

   _____

After You Read . . . Practice Tests

PRACTICE TEST #1

Multiple-Choice Questions

For each question, circle the best answer from the choices given.

1. Sensation is to perception as: (pp. 100-101)
   a. interpretation is to awareness
   b. awareness is to interpretation
   c. organizing is to interpretation
   d. interpretation is to awareness

2. The willingness to report noticing a stimulus is called: (p. 102)
   a. sensitivity
   b. reactivity
   c. bias
   d. vigilance

3. All of the following are characteristics of light waves EXCEPT: (p. 103)
   a. amplitude
   b. frequency
   c. duration
   d. wavelength

4. To distinguish an "F" from an "E" (which requires the processing of visual details) one must focus the light emanating from these stimuli onto which of the following structures of the eye? (p. 104)
   a. retina
   b. optic nerve
   c. blood vessels
   d. fovea

5. There are three types of cones in the eye which correspond to three wavelengths. All of the following are wavelengths that each cone is maximally sensitive to EXCEPT: (p. 106)
   a. Red
   b. Green
   c. Violet
   d. Blue

6. Which of the following best characterizes the appropriate sequence of processes necessary for perception to occur? (pp. 109-117)
   a. sensation, identification, organization, recognition
   b. sensation, recognition, organization, identification
   c. recognition, identification, sensations, organization
   d. sensation, organization, recognition, identification

7. According to your Kosslyn (1987), we use how many different ways to code for spatial relations? (p. 116)
   a. two
   b. three
   c. four
   d. five

8. Carol was paying close attention to the light on the corner, waiting for it to turn green. This form of attention is called: (p. 118)
   a. vigilance
   b. pop-out
   c. hypersensitivity
   d. reactivity

9. All of the following features of female faces are perceived to be attractive EXCEPT: (p. 120)
   a. smooth skin
   b. symmetry
   c. makeup
   d. male hormones

PRACTICE TEST #2

Multiple-Choice Questions

For each question, circle the best answer from the choices given.

1. Being exposed to sound at _____ dB will break your eardrum on the spot. (p. 124)
   a. 60
   b. 85
   c. 140
   d. 160

2. The pinna is located in the _____ ear. (p. 125)
   a. outer
   b. middle
   c. inner
   d. interior

3. A total of _____ little bones are located in the middle ear. (p. 125)
   a. two
   b. three
   c. four
   d. five

4. The authors review a total of _____ theories when discussing the manner in which the basilar membrane converts pressure waves into perceived sound. (p. 126)
   a. two
   b. three
   c. four
   d. five

5. Johnny jumped off the high dive at the pool which resulted in breaking his ear drum. As a result, he is most likely to have which of the following: (p. 1126)
   a. nerve deafness
   b. tinnitus
   c. conduction deafness
   d. auditory agnosia

6. Phase 1 of auditory perception mainly involves which of the following? (pp. 127-128)
   a. transduction
   b. organization
   c. recognition
   d. identification

7. The process by which we distinguish the sounds we want to hear (figure) from background noise (ground) is called: (p. 127)
   a. categorical processing.
   b. opponent-processing analysis.
   c. frequency processing.
   d. auditory scene analysis.

8. Suppose that you are at a party, talking to a friend, when all of a sudden you hear someone several feet away say your name. This is an example of: (p. 129)
   a. gestalt laws of processing.
   b. absolute pitch.
   c. plasticity.
   d. the cocktail party phenomenon.

9. Dichotic listening studies indicate that: (p. 129)
   a. attention is required for hearing.
   b. people hear in a single ear at a time.
   c. people "visualize" sounds that they didn't hear.
   d. even when not paying attention, people register some information from an unattended ear.

PRACTICE TEST #3

Multiple-Choice Questions

For each question, circle the best answer from the choices given.

1. Which of the following senses is (are) also referred to as a chemical sense(s)? (p. 130)
   a. olfaction
   b. taste
   c. kinesthesis
   d. a and b

2. Who is likely to be best at distinguishing among different smells? (p. 131)
   a. An elderly person
   b. A woman not on birth control pills
   c. A ten-year-old boy
   d. A woman on birth control pills

3. Based on research reviewed in your text, approximately how many genes have been identified that produce odor receptors? (p. 131)
   a. 10
   b. 1,000
   c. 10,000
   d. 100,000

4. Pheromones are similar to hormones in that they: (p. 132)
   a. modulate the functions of various organs.
   b. are released inside the body.
   c. are released by the frontal lobe.
   d. are accessed by the receptors spread all over the body.

5. Taste buds die and regenerate on average every _____ days. (p. 133)
   a. 5
   b. 10
   c. 15
   d. 20

6. To sense temperature there are receptors that register: (p. 135)
   a. only hot
   b. only cold
   c. only warm
   d. only hot or only cold

7. The role of top-down processing of pain is shown in: (p. 135)
   a. use of analgesics
   b. the placebo effect
   c. double pain
   d. paradoxical cold

8. Which of the following is an example of a counter-irritant? (p. 135)
   a. Acupuncture
   b. The placebo effect
   c. Double pain
   d. Paradoxical cold

9. It is believed that birds migrate long distances each year in part due to a _____ sense. (p. 136)
   a. kinesthetic
   b. vestibular
   c. somasthetic
   d. magnetic

10. All of the following are considered to be forms of "psi" EXCEPT: (p. 136)
    a. telepathy
    b. clairvoyance
    c. precognition
    d. psychokinesis

COMPREHENSIVE PRACTICE TEST

True/False Questions

Circle TRUE or FALSE for each of the following statements.

1.   TRUE   FALSE   Sensation is defined as the act of organizing and interpreting sensory input. (p. 100)

2.   TRUE   FALSE   According to your authors, recent research suggests that some women have four types of cones. (p. 106)

3.   TRUE   FALSE   Color blindness afflicts men more than women. (p. 108)

4.   TRUE   FALSE   An occlusion cue is an example of a binocular cue. (p. 112)

5.   TRUE   FALSE   The basilar membrane is located in the inner ear. (p. 125)

6.   TRUE   FALSE   Smell and taste are referred to as chemical senses. (p. 130)

7.   TRUE   FALSE   ESP is considered a somasthetic sense. (p. 134)

Multiple-Choice Questions

For each question, circle the best answer from the choices given.

1. All of the following were discussed in your text as Gestalt Laws of Organization EXCEPT: (p. 110)
   a. proximity
   b. similarity
   c. closure
   d. discontinuity

2. The light registered from watching a closing door will form different images on your retina, yet your perception of the door is one of being rectangular rather than changing shape. This phenomenon is most accurately referred to as a _____ constancy. (p. 111)
   a. sensational
   b. size
   c. shape
   d. geometrical

3. There is a total of _____ phases of visual perception according to your authors. (p. 109)
   a. two
   b. three
   c. four
   d. five

4. A proofreader may be unlikely to catch an error in which the word "the" occurs twice in succession (e.g., The boy had the the dog catch the Frisbee.). The error is attributed to which of the following? (p. 119)
   a. subliminal perception
   b. change blindness
   c. repetition blindness
   d. attentional blink

5. Increasing the volume of your radio is, in part, increasing which of the following properties of sound waves? (p. 124)
   a. cycle
   b. frequency
   c. hertz
   d. amplitude

6. The basilar membrane is located within which of the following structures? (p. 125)
   a. outer ear
   b. eardrum
   c. semicircular canals
   d. cochlea

7. If you receive damage to "hair cells" then you run the risk of getting which type of deafness? (p. 125)
   a. conduction
   b. tinnitus
   c. nerve
   d. receptor

8. Imagine that you are testing to see what information people gather when listening to two different streams of speech in a set of headphones (one stream of information in the left ear and an entirely different set of stream of information in the right ear). You ask people to only attend to the conversation stemming from the left ear by having them repeat it aloud. Employing this procedure is synonymous with which term? (p. 129)
   a. shadowing
   b. tracking
   c. phrasing
   d. vocalizing

9. One of the neural tracks that leaves the olfactory bulb passes through the, which is particularly involved in memory? (p. 131)
   a. hypothalamus
   b. hindbrain
   c. thalamus
   d. forebrain

10. Which region of the mouth is most sensitive to bitter tastes? (p. 133)
    a. front part of the tongue
    b. lateral sides of the mouth
    c. roof of the mouth
    d. back of the mouth

11. Which of the following somasthetic senses allows you to register movement and position of your limbs? (p. 134)
    a. kinesthetic
    b. vestibular
    c. magnetic
    d. psychokinesis

12. One way in which we deal with pain is by creating substances in our brains called _____, which serve as painkillers. (p. 135)
    a. neurotransmitters
    b. counter-irritants
    c. endorphins
    d. hormones

13. The ability to foretell future events is called: (p. 136)
    a. telepathy
    b. precognition
    c. clairvoyance
    d. psychokinesis

Short-Answer/Essay Questions
Answer each of the following questions in the space provided.

1. Describe the three stages of processing sensory input from the outside world. _____
_____
_____
_____
_____
_____
_____
_____
_____
_____
_____

2. Briefly describe, in order from first to last, the major eye structures that light strikes before it is transduced. _____
_____
_____
_____
_____

_____
_____
_____
_____
_____
_____

3. Discuss four reasons why psychologists are skeptical that ESP and PK exist. _____

_____
_____
_____
_____
_____
_____
_____
_____
_____
_____
_____

When You Are Finished . . . Puzzle It Out

Across

1. Leftover from previous visual perception
3. Where the optic nerve exits the retina
4. Defect in curvature of cornea
5. Strength of a sound
9. Sensitive to different tastes
12. Focusing on particular information
14. Like hormones, but outside the body
15. When different stimuli are obvious
17. Sense registering limp position

Puzzle created with Puzzlemaker at DiscoverySchool.com.

Down

2. Just-discovered receptor in the eye
6. Set of characteristics corresponding to an object
7. Person's willingness to report stimuli
8. Central region of the retina
10. Pain-killing chemicals produced by the brain
11. Retinal cells that register only gray
13. Processing guided by knowledge
14. How high or low a sound seems
16. Opening in the eye that light goes through

Chapter 4
Learning:
How Experience Changes Us

Before You Read . . .

In this chapter, you will discover the different ways that people learn. One way that you learn is by associating two things together. If you have ever gotten sick from something you ate or drank and now get nauseous just at the smell of that food or beverage, you experienced **classical conditioning.**

Operant conditioning also involves learning by association. However, in operant conditioning, you are associating the behavior and its consequence. For example, if you have learned that using this Grade Aid improves your exam performance, you have experienced operant conditioning. In this chapter, you will discover how behaviors are created and extinguished in classical and operant conditioning.

You will also learn that people can learn just by watching others; this is called **observational learning.** This type of learning explains why parents must watch their language so carefully around their children (lest their children pick up any curse words). In addition, Chapter 6 introduces **cognitive learning,** which is involved in learning complex tasks. Not surprisingly, cognitive learning involves cognitive (or intellectual) processes, such as memory and reasoning, which are covered in more depth in the next two chapters.

Chapter Objectives

After reading this chapter, you should be able to:

- Define classical conditioning and trace its history.

- Identify some common examples of classical conditioning in daily life.

- Define operant conditioning and explain how it occurs.

- Identify some common examples of classical conditioning in daily life.

- For both classical and operant conditioning, explain the principles of extinction, spontaneous recovery, generalization, and discrimination.

- Explain the brain functions involved in both classical and operant conditioning.

- Define cognitive learning.

- Define insight learning.

- Explain how watching others can help people learn and why some models are better   than others.

- Differentiate among the different forms of learning.

As You Read . . . Term Identification

Make flashcards using the following terms as you go. Use the definitions in the margins of this chapter for help. If you write the definitions in your own words, though, you will remember them better!

Acquisition
Avoidance learning
Behavior modification
Biological preparedness
Classical conditioning
Cognitive learning
Conditioned emotional response (CER)
Conditioned response (CR)
Conditioned stimulus (CS)
Continuous reinforcement
Contrapreparedness
Delayed reinforcement
Discrimination
Discriminative stimulus
Extinction (in classical conditioning)
Extinction (in operant conditioning)
Fixed interval schedule
Fixed ratio schedule
Food aversion (taste aversion)
Generalization
Habituation
Immediate reinforcement
Insight learning
Interval schedule
Latent learning
Law of Effect

Learning
Negative punishment
Negative reinforcement
Observational learning
Operant conditioning
Partial reinforcement
Phobia
Positive punishment
Positive reinforcement
Primary reinforcer
Ratio schedule
Reinforcement
Reinforcer
Response contingency
Secondary reinforcer
Shaping
Spontaneous recovery (in classical conditioning)
Spontaneous recovery (in operant conditioning)
Stimulus discrimination
Stimulus generalization
Successive approximations
Unconditioned response (UR)
Unconditioned stimulus (US)
Variable interval schedule
Variable ratio schedule

As You Read . . . Questions and Exercises

How does your text define learning? _____
_____

Are the following items examples of learning? Circle "YES" or "NO" as appropriate.

1. YES   NO   The cessation of thumb-sucking by an infant.

2. YES   NO   The acquisition of language in children.

3. YES   NO   A computer program generates random opening moves for its first 100 chess games and tabulates the outcomes of those games. Starting with the 101st game, the computer uses those tabulations to influence its choice of opening moves.

4. YES   NO   A worm is placed in a T maze. The left arm of the maze is brightly lit and dry; the right arm is dim and moist. On the first ten trials, the worm turns right seven times. On the next ten trials, the worm turns right all ten times.

5. YES   NO   Ethel stays up late the night before the October GRE administration and cnsumes large quantities of licit and illicit pharmacological agents. Her ombined (verbal plus quantitative) score is 410. The night before the Dcember GRE administration, she goes to bed early after a wholesome dinner and a glass of milk. Her score increases to 1210. Is her cange in pretest regimen due to learning?

6. YES   NO   A previously psychotic patient is given Dr. K's patented phrenological surgery and no longer exhibits any psychotic behaviors.

7. YES   NO   A lanky zinnia plant is pinched back and begins to grow denser foliage and flowers.

8. YES   NO   MYCIN is a computer program that does a rather good job of diagnosing human infections by consulting a large database of rules it has been given. If we add another rule to the database, has MYCIN learned something?

9. YES   NO   After pondering over a difficult puzzle for hours, Jane finally figures it out. From that point on, she can solve all similar puzzles in the time it takes her to read them.

10. YES   NO   After thirty years of smoking two packs a day, Zeb throws away his cigarettes and never smokes again.

Originally published in Rocklin, T. (1987). Defining learning: Two classroom activities. Teaching of Psychology, 14, 228–229. Reprinted with permission of the publisher and author.

Classical Conditioning

Pavlov's Experiments

In Pavlov's initial experiment, in which he paired a tone with the presentation of food, the _____ was the **unconditioned stimulus,** and the _____ was the **unconditioned response;** the _____ was the **conditioned stimulus,** and the _____ was the **conditioned response.**

Practice identifying the US, CS, UR, and CR.

1. Your professor slams her book down every day when she walks in, so that you now wince when you see her enter through the door.
   US: _____   UR: _____   CS: _____   CR: _____

2. Jack always smokes when he is in someone's car at school. When his mother picks him up for fall break, Jack immediately reaches for a cigarette when he gets in the car (even though he doesn't want his mother to know he smokes).
   US: _____   UR: _____   CS: _____   CR: _____

3. Mandi once got sick after eating Chinese food (because she was allergic to the MSG in it). Now even the smell of Chinese food makes her sick.
   US: _____   UR: _____   CS: _____   CR: _____

4. Marketing researchers have found that men are more likely to buy a car after viewing advertisements of attractive women sitting on the car.
   US: _____   UR: _____   CS: _____   CR: _____

5. John successfully quit drinking alcohol by participating in an Antabuse treatment program.
   US: _____   UR: _____   CS: _____   CR: _____

6. Ader and Cohen's rats died after drinking flavored water, even after they were *not* injected with an immune-suppressing drug.
   US: _____   UR: _____   CS: _____   CR: _____

7. Marcia was once in a bank robbery in which a robber pulled a gun from his inside coat pocket and held it to her face. Now, she jumps every time she sees a man place his hand in his inside coat pocket.
   US: _____   UR: _____   CS: _____   CR: _____

8. For her twenty-first birthday, Teri drank too much tequila and got sick. Now, whenever she sees a tequila bottle, she feels nauseous.
   US: _____   UR: _____   CS: _____   CR: _____

9. Every Sunday, Robin visits his mother, who makes him a delicious, six-course meal. Whenever he pulls into his mother's driveway, Robin's mouth begins to water.

    US: _____ UR: _____ CS: _____ CR: _____

10. Each time she meets with her boss, Michelle gets berated for having done something wrong. Now, whenever she even sees her boss, Michelle flinches.

    US: _____ UR: _____ CS: _____ CR: _____

GO SURFING . . .

...at Fullerton College's interactive demonstration of **classical conditioning:** http://www.uwm.edu/~johnchay/cc.htm. Try conditioning the dog to salivate when it sees a light. Click on each of the boxes to present that stimulus. The lines on the salivation bar represent the frequency of salivating.

In this situation, what is

- The US? _____
- The CS? _____
- The UR? _____
- The CR? _____

What did you do to try to **condition** the dog to salivate to a light? _____
_____
_____
_____

How many **trials** (or pairings) did it take for the dog to salivate before the food was presented? _____
_____
_____

If you stopped presenting the food, and only presented the light, what happened? _____
_____
_____

What happens if you again present the food and the light together? _____
_____
_____

Try doing this experiment a few different times. Is there anything that you can do to make the salivation occur for more trials, even without the food? _____

_____

_____

What is **conditioning?** _____

_____

Here are several different types of **conditioning.** Explain each and note whether it is effective.

Type of Conditioning	Explanation	Is It Effective?
Delayed conditioning		
Backward pairing		
Simultaneous conditioning		

Classical Conditioning: How It Works

What is **avoidance learning?** _____

_____

_____

How was **avoidance learning** discovered? _____

_____

_____

What is a **conditioned emotional response?** _____

_____

_____

What was the significance of the **Little Albert** study? _____

_____

_____

Do you have any **phobias?** If so, to what? _____

Do you know how these **phobias** developed? _____

_____

_____

Some stimuli are easier to **condition** than others.

List some stimuli that organisms seem to be biologically prepared to be conditioned to.	List some stimuli that organisms seem to be contraprepared to be conditioned to.

Why might it be easier to **condition** some stimuli than others? _____
_____
_____

When was **extinction** shown in the interactive demonstration you did earlier?

- What did you do to cause the **extinction**? _____
  _____

- What did the dog do when the behavior had been **extinguished**? _____
  _____

When was **spontaneous recovery** shown in the interactive demonstration you did earlier?

- What did you do to cause **spontaneous recovery**? _____
  _____

- What did the dog's behavior look like at this point? _____
  _____

How might you demonstrate **stimulus generalization** in a study like the one in the interactive demonstration you did earlier?

- What types of stimuli might the dog **generalize** to? _____
  _____

- What would the dog's behavior look like at this point? _____
  _____

Why might dogs (or people) **generalize** stimuli? _____
_____
_____

How might you demonstrate **stimulus discrimination** in a study like the one in the interactive demonstration you did earlier?

- What type of stimuli might the dog **discriminate** between? _____
  _____

- What would the dog's behavior look like at this point? _____

  _____

- How might you help the dog **discriminate** between stimuli? _____

  _____

In your own words, summarize three pieces of evidence showing that **cognitive processes** are involved in learning (contrary to what strict behaviorists would say):

- _____

  _____

  _____

  _____

- _____

  _____

  _____

  _____

  _____

- _____

  _____

  _____

  _____

Several distinct brain areas and processes are involved in **classical conditioning.** What are they?

Brain Part(s)	Function(s)

In your own words, explain why a **classically conditioned response** will never *really* be extinguished. _____

_____

_____

If this is true, then what is **extinction**? _____

_____

In your own words, explain how the brain is involved in **extinction**. _____

_____

Classical Conditioning Applied

In your own words, explain how **classical conditioning** can explain drug overdoses. _____
_____
_____

How is **classical conditioning** used as a therapeutic technique? _____
_____
_____

What is **evaluative conditioning**? _____
_____
_____

Find an example of **evaluative conditioning** in a magazine and staple it to this page.

In your example of **evaluative conditioning,** identify the following components of classical conditioning:

- US: _____
- CS: _____
- UR: _____
- CR: _____

Have you ever experienced a **taste aversion** to a particular food or drink? If so, explain what happened. (If not, think of a friend's taste aversion and explain that.) _____
_____
_____

Using your example, identify the following components of **classical conditioning:**

- US: _____
- CS: _____
- UR: _____
- CR: _____

In Ader and Cohen's study, identify the following components of **classical conditioning:**

- US: _____
- CS: _____
- UR: _____
- CR: _____

What was the significance of Ader and Cohen's study?
- _____
- _____

Explain an example of **classical conditioning** in your own life (other than those listed previously).

_____

_____

_____

In this example, identify the following components of **classical conditioning:**

- US: _____
- CS: _____
- UR: _____
- CR: _____

Operant Conditioning

The Roots of Operant Conditioning: Its Discovery and How It Works

Distinguish between **operant conditioning** and **classical conditioning.** _____

_____

_____

_____

Why does **"operant" conditioning** have its name? _____

_____

_____

What is the **Law of Effect?** _____

_____

_____

How did Thorndike develop the **Law of Effect?** _____

_____

_____

GO SURFING . . .

. . . at **Fullerton College**'s interactive demonstration of operant conditioning: http://www.uwm.edu/~johnchay/oc.htm. Familiarize yourself with all of the different parts of this computerized model of a **Skinner box.**

In this model, identify the following components of **operant conditioning:**

- The stimulus: _____
- The response: _____
- The consequence: _____

What happens when you click the button to **reinforce** the pigeon? _____
_____
_____
_____

What do the displayed numbers mean? _____
_____
_____
_____

GO SURFING . . .

One of the most successful treatments for autism is based on operant conditioning. Search (on www.google.com or another good search engine) for "applied behavioral analysis" and "autism." You can also search for the name "O. Ivar Lovaas," a pioneer in this field. How his childhood influenced him in developing this technique is particularly interesting.

Describe how **applied behavioral analysis** (ABA) is used with autistic children. _____
_____
_____
_____
_____

Principles of Operant Conditioning

The difference between **classical** and **operant conditioning** is exemplified in how responses are described as originating.

- In classical conditioning, responses are _____, exemplifying that they are usually reflexive and involuntary.

- In operant conditioning, responses are _____, exemplifying that they are usually voluntary.

What would happen if the pigeon (in the earlier interactive model) didn't like food pellets?_____
_____
_____

What is the difference between **reinforcement** and **punishment?** _____
_____
_____

In the terms **positive reinforcement, positive punishment, negative reinforcement,** and **negative reinforcement,** the words "positive" and "negative" do not refer to whether something is *good* or *bad.* What do the words mean in this context?

- Positive = _____

- Negative = _____

In the chart below, give an example that illustrates each type of feedback.

Effect ＼ Action	Giving a Stimulus	Removing or Withholding a Stimulus
To Increase Behavior		
To Decrease Behavior		

What type of feedback is involved in these situations: positive reinforcer (PR), positive punisher (PP), negative reinforcer (NR), or negative punisher (NP)?

1. _____ Your professor says that your class's performance on the last exam was so good that she is eliminating the cumulative final exam.

2. _____ Your boss yells at you because you arrived late to work.

3. _____ You clean your dorm room before your mother visits so that she won't nag you.

4. _____ Your grades are so bad that the coach takes away your basketball scholarship.

5. _____ Your professor praises your excellent term paper.

6. _____ You know from past experience that smoking reduces your anxiety, so you light up right before your final exam.

7. _____ Your professor gives you an F because you cheated.

8. _____ You get a bonus from work for going above and beyond the call of duty!

9. _____ Your coach makes you run an additional fifteen minutes for every pass you miss during practice.

10. _____ Your girlfriend refuses to kiss you because you smoke. (She says you taste like an ashtray!)

11. _____ Your professor has an attendance policy in which you lose four points for each unexcused absence.

12. _____ Your child gives you a hug every time you read her a bedtime story.

Describe three problems with using spankings as a means to control a child's behavior.

- _____
- _____
- _____

If you had children, would you spank them (as a form of **discipline**)? Why or why not? _____
_____
_____
_____

If you do plan to (or do) use spankings as a form of **discipline,** list three ways you could make them more effective.

- _____
- _____
- _____

Describe at least two alternatives to spankings that you could use to control a child's behavior.

- _____
  _____

- _____
  _____

In the list below, circle the **secondary reinforcers.**

| Food | Money | Attention | Praise | Sex |
| Promotion | Good grades | Water | Pain relief | Pay raises |

Using the principles of **immediate** and **delayed reinforcement,** explain why physical exercise is so difficult for some people to do. _____
_____
_____

Beyond Basic Reinforcement

Give an original example of **generalization** as it relates to operant conditioning. _____
_____
_____

Give an original example of **discrimination** as it relates to operant conditioning. _____
_____
_____

Underline the discriminative stimulus in each of the following situations:

- Jessica is sure to dress up and put her make-up on when she knows she will be seeing her boyfriend.

- Megan's dog, Cosmo, starts wagging his tail and jumping around whenever Megan comes home.

- You do all the assigned reading when you know that there will be a quiz.

- Jeff is careful to use polite language when his son is present.

How does **extinction** work in operant conditioning? _____
_____
_____
_____

How does **spontaneous recovery** occur in operant conditioning? _____
_____
_____
_____

GO SURFING . . .

...at the computerized model of the **Skinner box** that you visited earlier
(http://www.uwm.edu/~johnchay/oc.htm).

Shape the pigeon's behavior to get him to peck at the lever. How did you do this? _____
_____
_____

What type of **reinforcement schedule** did you use initially? _____
_____

Why might this be a good schedule to use initially? _____
_____
_____

Use a **fixed ratio schedule** for several minutes. Reinforce the pigeon for every sixth peck. What happens to the pigeon's other behaviors as you do this? _____
_____
_____

Graph the results of using this **schedule:**

Frequency
of
Pecking

Time

Now **extinguish** the behavior. How did you do this? _____
_____
_____

Restart the exercise and use a **variable interval schedule** of reinforcement. How did you do this?
_____
_____

Graph the results of using this **schedule:**

Frequency
of
Pecking

Time

Do the same thing using a **fixed interval schedule** of reinforcement. Graph your results below.

Frequency
of
Pecking

Time

Finally, use a **variable ratio schedule** of reinforcement. Graph your results below.

Frequency
of
Pecking

Time

After the behavior is well established using this schedule, try to **extinguish** the pecking behavior. What happens, especially in comparison to extinguishing the pecking following **a fixed ratio schedule**? _____

_____

Restart the program. Use **continuous reinforcement** to encourage the pigeon to flap its wings. What happens, especially in comparison to reinforcing pecking? _____

_____

_____

What does this result tell you about the relative frequency of pecking versus flapping in pigeons?

_____

_____

_____

Do you think you could **shape** a more complicated behavior in the pigeon (such as a peck followed by a flap)? If so, how would you do it? _____
_____
_____

Consider pigeons that were not immediately reinforced for their behaviors. (You can try it in the computer model, if you like!) These pigeons had to figure out what caused the food pellet to (eventually) appear. Was it the pecking? Was it because they walked in a circle? Explain how **delayed reinforcement** can help us to understand superstitious behaviors not only among pigeons but also among humans. _____
_____
_____
_____
_____
_____
_____

Which schedule of **reinforcement**

- Is most resistant to extinction? _____
- Causes exhaustion? _____
- Results in slow but consistent responding? _____
- Causes an individual to slow down right after reinforcement? _____

Describe how you could use these same **shaping** techniques to teach your roommate to clean up his room. Which **successive approximations** would you reward? Which schedule of reinforcement would you use? Explain your choices. _____
_____
_____
_____
_____
_____
_____
_____

GO SURFING . . .

. . .at **The Adaptive Mind Center** (http://epsych.msstate.edu/adaptive/index.html) to try another interactive model of **operant conditioning**.

Which type of reinforcement schedule is being used in these examples: FR, FI, VR, or VI?

1. _____   Picking up your paycheck at the end of each week

2. _____   Factory worker being paid for every three dresses she makes

3. _____   Slot machines at a gambling casino

4. _____   Calling a friend and getting no answer and then continuing to call until you reach her

5. _____   Buying lottery tickets

6. _____   A strawberry picker being paid per pints picked

7. _____   Looking at your watch during a lecture until the end of the lecture

8. _____   Mail-checking behavior, assuming that the mailman comes at different times each day

9. _____   Asking people out on dates

10. _____   Checking your e-mail

11. _____   Giving yourself a break from studying after every thirty minutes

12. _____   Getting your favorite cookies (which must bake for exactly seven minutes) from the oven

The Operant Brain

Dopamine helps you _____ and _____ your behavior so that you can reach your goals. Like humans, animals _____ their behaviors. Dopamine signals the _____ between what we expect will be the outcome of our behavior and what actually happens. A burst of activity in _____ neurons signals that an outcome was better than expected. A _____ in the activity of these neurons, which are located in the _____, signals that an outcome was worse than expected.

List the similarities between **classical** and **operant conditioning:**

- _____
- _____
- _____
- _____
- _____
- _____
- _____

Given these similarities, how do we know that **classical** and **operant conditioning** are different? (Or do we know that they are different?) _____
_____
_____
_____
_____

Looking at Levels:
Facial Expressions as Reinforcement and Punishment

List the factors at the **levels of the brain, person, and group** that influence how you perceive other people's facial expressions. Use arrows to indicate how events at the different levels may interact.

The Brain	The Person	The Group

Cognitive and Social Learning

Cognitive Learning

In what ways are **latent learning** and **observational learning** similar? _____

_____

_____

_____

_____

_____

_____

Give examples from your own experiences of **latent learning.** Is most of what we learn not evident at first? What does the educational setting typically require of students? _____

_____

_____

_____

_____

_____

_____

_____

Insight Learning: Seeing the Connection

GO SURFING . . .

. . .at one of the many Web sites that describe Wolfgang Köhler's work with tool-making chimpanzees. One place to start is http://www.pigeon.psy.tufts.edu/psych26/kohler.htm.

Do you have any other interpretations for Köhler's findings, besides that the chimps had **insights?**

_____

_____

_____

_____

Do you think that *all* animals can have **insights,** or is this ability limited to certain species?_____
_____
_____
_____

What type of psychologist was Köhler? _____

How does his theory of psychology relate to Köhler's work with chimpanzees? _____
_____
_____
_____

Have you ever had an **"aha experience,"** when things finally fell into place for you? If so, explain.
_____
_____
_____

Observational Learning/Learning from Models

Think about your role models. For each group listed below, think of at least one behavior that your models engage in. Then complete the following chart, indicating whether you imitate the behavior and listing factors that both promote and discourage imitation.

Role Models	Behavior	Do You Imitate This Behavior?	Factors Promoting Imitation	Factors Discouraging Imitation
Your parents				
Your siblings				
Other, older relatives				
Peers				

Your teachers/coaches				
Celebrities				

What type of learning is involved in each of the following examples?

1. _____ Nathan was a genius who didn't speak until he was three. When asked why he had not spoken earlier, Nathan said, "I didn't have anything important to say until then."

2. _____ You have been attending class all semester, but one day you suddenly understand statistics!

3. _____ You have noticed that your boss is always in a bad mood on Fridays, so you avoid him on those days.

4. _____ You have watched your roommate all semester and noticed that her study techniques have gotten her good grades. You begin using those techniques yourself.

5. _____ The food at your school's cafeteria is awful, and you feel sick every time you walk in the building.

6. _____ Bobby's dad has road rage and frequently curses at other drivers. One time, when he saw an upcoming roadblock, Bobby shouted the same expletives.

7. _____ You are returning to your hometown after a long break, but you find you can still navigate the roads as if you had never left.

8. _____ Your professor spits when he gets excited. Unfortunately, you sit in the front row. Now, whenever your professor's voice starts to rise, you keep your head down.

9. _____ You went to church every Sunday with your parents. They thought you didn't pay any attention, until one night you were watching *Jeopardy* with them and correctly answered all the questions in the religion category.

10. _____ You have been struggling with the organization of your thesis. One day, while you are taking a shower, the answer suddenly comes to you.

11. _____ Your boyfriend is so pleased that you have stopped smoking that he gives you a massage each day you don't light up. You love the massages, so you refrain from smoking.

12. _____ Despite your requests to the contrary, your roommate persists in burning aromatherapy candles that aggravate your allergies. Now, you begin coughing and sneezing as soon as you walk in the room, whether or not the candles are lit.

How could you use classical, operant, and/or social learning principles in each of the following situations? (Surf the Web for material if you can't think of any ideas yourself!)

1. After graduation, you take a job as a computer salesperson. Your income depends almost entirely on your sales. (Your base pay is very low.) How could you use learning principles to assist you in generating sales? _____

   _____
   _____
   _____
   _____
   _____
   _____

2. You are the parent of a four-year-old boy who STILL isn't potty-trained. How could you use learning principles to encourage him to potty-train? _____

   _____
   _____
   _____
   _____
   _____
   _____
   _____

3. Think of your favorite teacher of all time. How did he or she use learning principles in teaching?

   _____
   _____
   _____
   _____
   _____

4. After graduation, you get a job as a manager in a restaurant. How could you use your knowledge of learning principles in your management of others? _____
_____
_____
_____
_____
_____
_____

After You Read . . . Thinking Back

1. The Little Albert study is considered a classic study in the field of psychology and has led to many important findings. Today, however, it would not be allowed by Institutional Review Boards. Do you think the field of psychology is hindered by these ethical restraints? Should ethical standards be revised? Discuss. _____
_____
_____

2. Can you think of situations in which either classical or operant conditioning of an individual or group is unethical? How might individuals in positions of authority persuade reluctant followers to do what they want them to do, using learning principles? _____
_____
_____

3. Which of the learning theories discussed in Chapter 6 fall into the category of "behaviorism"?
_____

4. How can you remember this, given the content of the theories and the term "behaviorism"?
_____
_____

5. What were the lasting impacts of behaviorism (from Chapter 1)? _____
_____
_____

6. Tolman's studies of cognitive maps in rats were one factor that led to the end of the reign of behaviorism (as the predominant school of thought in psychology). Why? _____
_____
_____

7. What followed the fall of behaviorism? How would Tolman's studies contribute to this change?
_____
_____

8. The first phase of operant conditioning involves the hippocampus. What are the other functions of the hippocampus? How are all of these functions similar? _____

    _____

    _____

9. In classical conditioning, extinction involves the frontal lobe's active suppression of the amygdala's response. What are the other functions of the frontal lobes? How are all of these functions similar? _____

    _____

    _____

After You Read . . . *Thinking Ahead*

1. Insight is one method of problem solving. Can you rely on this method? How often does this method work for you? What are some other methods of problem solving? _____
   _____
   _____
   _____

2. Is there anything that you can do to increase the likelihood of having an "aha experience"? Explain. _____
   _____
   _____

3. The delay of gratification is one component of "emotional intelligence," which is discussed in Chapter 8. Can you think of other skills that might make someone "emotionally intelligent"?
   _____
   _____
   _____

4. Given what you know about biological preparedness and contrapreparedness, what do you think the most common phobias are? _____
   _____
   _____
   _____

5. What are the least common phobias? _____
   _____
   _____
   _____

6. Are there any personal characteristics that might make a person more or less likely to develop a phobia? What might those be? _____
   _____
   _____
   _____
   _____

7. If someone were to have *positive* symptoms of a disorder, what would you think that meant (given what *positive* reinforcement and *positive* punishment are)? _____
   _____
   _____

8. What do you think *negative* symptoms are? _____
   _____
   _____

After You Read . . . Practice Tests

PRACTICE TEST #1

Multiple-Choice Questions

For each question, circle the best answer from the choices given.

1. Which of the following represents the simplest form of learning? (p. 145)
   a. conditioning
   b. cognitive learning
   c. associative learning
   d. nonassociative learning

2. As you sit down to work at the computer you hear the buzzing of the hard drive, which is a bit annoying. However, after short period of time you no longer notice the irritable sound. This best illustrates which of the following terms? (p. 145)
   a. sensitization
   b. nonassociation
   c. habituation
   d. associative learning

3. The term "elicit" is most associated with which of the following? (p. 146)
   a. classical conditioning
   b. operant conditioning
   c. cognitive learning
   d. observational learning

4. Which of the following researchers is credited as being the discoverer of classical conditioning? (p. 146)
   a. Thorndike
   b. Watson
   c. Skinner
   d. Pavlov

5. All of the following are true about Ivan Pavlov EXCEPT: (p. 146)
   a. he was a Russian psychologist.
   b. he won a Nobel prize.
   c. he studied the digestive system of dogs.
   d. he was the first to study variables associated with classical conditioning.

6. If you were to use pepper to elicit sneezing in your conditioning study, pepper would be considered a(n) _____? (p. 146)
   a. CS
   b. CR
   c. US
   d. UR

7. The finding that we form associations between certain combinations of CSs and USs more quickly than other combinations is evidence for which of the following terms? (p. 148)
   a. phobia
   b. classical conditioning
   c. counterpreparedness
   d. biological preparedness

8. Which of the following brain structures has been implicated in fear conditioning? (p. 152)
   a. amygdala
   b. cerebellum
   c. hippocampus
   d. all of the above

PRACTICE TEST #2

Multiple-Choice Questions

For each question, circle the best answer from the choices given.

1. Operant conditioning is also known as _____ conditioning. (p. 159)
    a. classical
    b. Pavlovian
    c. instrumental
    d. vicarious

2. Behaviors that lead to favorable consequences are likely to be repeated according to the: (p. 159)
    a. Law of Experience
    b. Law of Effect
    c. Theory of Conditional Responses
    d. Theory of Reward

3. The association that is learned in operant conditioning technically consists of: (p. 160)
    a. two stimuli
    b. two behaviors
    c. a stimulus and behavior
    d. a stimulus, behavior, and consequence

4. In terms of responding, elicit is to emit as: (p. 160)
    a. voluntary is to involuntary
    b. involuntary is to voluntary
    c. receive is to give
    d. give is to receive

5. Each time your dog raises its paw you give it a treat. In terms of operant conditioning terminology, the treat technically serves as a _____. (p. 160)
    a. contingent
    b. snack
    c. reinforcer
    d. conditioned stimulus

6. Reinforcement is to punishment as: (pp. 160-164)
    a. good is to bad
    b. increase is to decrease
    c. conditioning is to learning
    d. learning is to memory

7. The color that is illuminated on a traffic light (red, yellow, or green) serves as a _____ stimulus. (p. 167)
   a. discriminative
   b. conditional
   c. unconditional
   d. generalized

8. _____ is a key neurotransmitter involved in learning associations between stimuli, responses, and consequences of making response. (p. 171)
   a. norepinephrine
   b. serotonin
   c. dopamine
   d. scopolamine

9. Those who took a common antianxiety medication were less likely to recognize: (pp. 172-173)
   a. happy emotional expressions
   b. sad emotional expressions
   c. angry emotional expressions
   d. facial expressions of emotion in general

PRACTICE TEST #3

Multiple-Choice Questions

For each question, circle the best answer from the choices given.

1. All of the following are forms of cognitive learning EXCEPT: (p. 175)
   a. salivating when you think of a lemon
   b. learning how to drive a car
   c. memorizing the names of your classmates
   d. evaluating the differences among the choices in this question

2. Latent learning refers to: (p. 176)
   a. learning information later in life.
   b. learning information by observing someone else.
   c. acquiring information through memorization.
   d. learning but not immediately displaying the learned behavior.

3. Which of the following brain structures is believed to be responsible for latent learning? (p. 176)
   a. amygdala
   b. hypothalamus
   c. hippocampus
   d. thalamus

4. The study of learning focuses on the _____ of information; in contrast, the study of memory focuses on the of information. (p. 176)
   a. retention; acquisition
   b. acquisition; retention
   c. generalization; discrimination
   d. discrimination; generalization

5. Suddenly knowing an answer to a question that you could not correctly answer at an earlier time is representative of _____. (p. 176)
   a. cognitive learning
   b. cognitive mapping
   c. insight learning
   d. observational learning

6. Albert Bandura is the psychologist who developed: (p. 177)
   a. social learning theory.
   b. classical conditioning.
   c. cognitive mapping.
   d. the latent hypothesis.

7. Social learning theory employs all of the following EXCEPT: (pp. 177-179)
    a. observational learning.
    b. modeling.
    c. the social context.
    d. reinforcement.

8. The process by which one learns new behaviors through observing others is known as
    _____. (p. 177)
    a. conditioning
    b. modeling
    c. shadowing
    d. none of the above

9. The Bobo doll was used in classic studies conducted by _____. (pp. 177-178)
    a. Tolman
    b. Piaget
    c. Köhler
    d. Bandura

COMPREHENSIVE PRACTICE TEST

True/False Questions
Circle TRUE or FALSE for each of the following statements.

1. TRUE   FALSE   Habituation is a form of nonassociative learning. (p. 145)

2. TRUE   FALSE   Simultaneous conditioning is a type of forward conditioning. (p. 147)

3. TRUE   FALSE   Once an organism has been classically conditioned, the relationship between the CS and the US can be completely vanquished via extinction. (pp. 150-151)

4. TRUE   FALSE   Responses voluntarily produced in operant conditioning are referred to as being "emitted." (p. 160)

5. TRUE   FALSE   Reinforcement is identical to reinforcer. (p. 160)

6. TRUE   FALSE   Fixed variable is a schedule of reinforcement. (pp. 168-170)

7. TRUE   FALSE   Research suggests that other people's facial expressions can act as reinforcement or punishment. (pp. 172-173)

8. TRUE   FALSE   Cognitive learning involves learning that may not involve any visible behaviors. (p. 175)

Multiple-Choice Questions
For each question, circle the best answer from the choices given.

1. Habituation is specifically referred to as a type of: (p. 145)
    a. nonassociative learning
    b. associative learning
    c. conditioning
    d. operant conditioning

2. If, in order to get people to sneeze as part of your conditioning study, you were to pair the sound of a gong with the inhalation of some pepper, the sound of the gong would be considered a(n) _____? (pp. 146-147)
    a. CR
    b. CS
    c. UR
    d. US

3. Which of the following behaviors would be a prime candidate as a UR? (p. 146-147)
   a. running
   b. walking
   c. hearing
   d. sneezing

4. The finding that it is difficult if not impossible to classically condition certain stimuli as CSs is evidence for which of the following terms? (p. 148)
   a. biological preparedness
   b. dishabituation
   c. contrapreparedness
   d. disinhibited preparedness

5. In taste aversion, the sight of the particular food serves as the _____. (p. 155)
   a. CR
   b. UR
   c. CS
   d. US

6. Who of the following learning theorists formulated the "Law of Effect"? (p. 159)
   a. Pavlov
   b. Thorndike
   c. Watson
   d. Skinner

7. Taking an aspirin to get rid of a headache illustrates: (p. 161)
   a. positive reinforcement
   b. negative reinforcement
   c. positive punishment
   d. negative punishment

8. _____ is also known as the "gambling reinforcement schedule." (p. 170)
   a. Fixed interval
   b. Variable interval
   c. Fixed ratio
   d. Variable ratio

9. If someone is depressed, he or she would be most unlikely to recognize which of the following facial expressions? (p. 173)
   a. sad
   b. mildly fearful
   c. mildly happy
   d. angry

10. Due to their ability to discriminate facial expressions: (p. 173)
    a. children versus adults may find smiles more reinforcing.
    b. young adults versus older adults may be more likely to find angry faces more punishing.
    c. men may be more likely to find smiles more reinforcing than women.
    d. women may find angry faces more punishing than men.

11. Tolman and Honzik's rats developed   to be able to use later when they were motivated to find their way around the maze. (pp. 175-176)
    a. insight
    b. cognitive maps
    c. neural networks
    d. conditioned responses

12. Jeremy just couldn't understand how to "do" geometry proofs. One day, after months of trying, Jeremy was walking down the street when suddenly it all became clear—he had found the key for doing proofs! Jeremy's experience is an example of: (p. 176)
    a. latent learning.
    b. observational learning.
    c. insight learning.
    d. classical conditioning.

13. Learning that is not dependent on reinforcement, occurs in a social context, and involves voluntary behaviors is called: (p. 177)
    a. latent learning
    b. observational learning
    c. classical conditioning
    d. insight learning

14. All of the following are characteristics of a model to whom a person is more likely to attend EXCEPT: (p. 179)
    a. kind
    b. expert in the field
    c. high status
    d. socially powerful

Short-Answer/Essay Questions
Answer the following questions in the space provided.

1. Define learning and briefly summarize the distinction between nonassociative and associative forms of learning. _____
_____
_____
_____
_____
_____
_____
_____
_____

2. Define and provide an example for each of the following schedules of reinforcement: Fixed Ratio, Variable Ratio, Fixed Interval, and Variable Interval._____

_____

_____

_____

_____

_____

_____

_____

3. Describe the characteristics of models that can make observational learning more effective. What is the underlying tenet for why such characteristics facilitate learning?_____

_____

_____

_____

_____

_____

_____

_____

4. Discuss how television can either negatively or positively impact children's behavior from an observational learning viewpoint, noting the role of modeling. Provide an example of a children's show that could affect children's behavior in a positive manner._____

_____

_____

_____

_____

_____

_____

When You Are Finished . . . Puzzle It Out

Across

2. Reinforcing successive approximations
5. Type of reinforcement that involves giving a desired reinforcer, such as food
7. What happens when the CS is repeatedly presented without the US
11. Primary rule of operant conditioning, developed by Thorndike
14. Brain part involved in storing the stimulus-response associations underlying fear
16. 20th century's foremost proponent of behaviorism
17. Type of learning involved in pairing actions with consequences
19. By studying rats in mazes, he developed the idea of cognitive maps
20. First person to systematically investigate classical conditioning

Puzzle created with Puzzlemaker at DiscoverySchool.com.

Down

1. Type of learning that occurs when repeated exposure to a stimulus decreases a person's responsiveness to it
3. Type of learning in which an organism tries to avoid the CS (which is paired with an unpleasant US)
4. He developed social learning theory
6. The food in Pavlov's studies or the noise in the Little Albert study
8. Learning that occurs without behavioral signs
9. Noncontinuous reinforcement
10. An irrational fear of a specific object
12. Type of learning involving associations between stimuli
13. Type of reinforcement schedule based on numbers of responses
15. Watson's famous subject
18. Type of learning involving "aha experiences"

Chapter 5
Memory: Living with Yesterday

Before You Read . . .

Do you think of yourself as having a good memory or a bad memory? In fact, as you will learn in this chapter, memory is not one unit or process. Rather, memory consists of multiple memory stores and processes. For example, there are three memory stores: sensory memory, short-term memory, and long-term memory (of which there are several different types). To move information first into the memory system and then from one store to the next, a person must use different strategies, including encoding and mnemonic devices.

Memory is not just about remembering, but about forgetting. People forget information for many different reasons. In addition to losing information, we can create false memories and suffer from amnesia. And what about repressed memories? Are they real? The chapter attempts to shed some light on this most controversial topic in psychology.

Chapter 7 ends with information you can use in all your classes: how to improve your memory.

Chapter Objectives

After reading this chapter, you should be able to:

- Differentiate between and describe the three memory stores: sensory memory, short-term memory, and long-term memory.

- Describe the different stores within LTM, including modality-specific stores, semantic and episodic memory, and explicit and implicit memory.

- Explain the concept of working memory and its components.

- Discuss the genetic foundations of memory.

- Explain how memories are made, stored, and retrieved.

- Discuss how memory can be disrupted, including false memories, forgetting, amnesia, and repression.

- Provide examples of how memory can be improved, both at storage and retrieval.

As You Read . . . Term Identification

Make flashcards using the following terms as you go. Use the definitions in the margins of this chapter for help. If you write the definitions in your own words, though, you will remember them better!

Amnesia
Anterograde amnesia
Automatic processing
Breadth of processing
Central executive
Chunk
Code
Consolidation
Controlled processing
Cues
Decay
Depth of processing
Elaborative encoding
Encoding
Encoding failure
Episodic memories
Explicit (or declarative) memories
False memories
Flashbulb memory
Forgetting curve
Habit
Implicit (or nondeclarative) memories
Incidental learning
Intentional learning
Interference

Long-term memory (LTM)
Memory store
Mnemonic devices
Modality-specific memory stores
Primacy effect
Priming
Proactive interference
Reality monitoring
Recall
Recency effect
Recognition
Rehearsal
Repetition priming
Repressed memories
Retrieval
Retroactive interference
Retrograde amnesia
Semantic memories
Sensory memory (SM)
Short-term memory (STM)
State-dependent retrieval
Storage
Transfer appropriate processing
Working memory (WM)

As You Read . . . Questions and Exercises

Encoding Information Into Memory: Time and Space Are of the Essence

Types of Memory Stores

How is **working memory** different from **short-term memory**? _____
_____
_____
_____

Provide three examples from your own life of when you use your **working memory**.

- _____
- _____
- _____

In the following table, compare and contrast the differences between **sensory, short-term,** and **long-term memory.**

	Sensory Memory (SM)	Short-Term Memory (STM)	Long-Term Memory (LTM)
What does it hold?			
How much does it hold?			
How long does it hold information?			
Does it have sub-components? If so, what are they?			

For the following events, indicate whether **sensory, short-term,** or **long-term memory** is being activated.

Event	Type of Memory
Trying to remember the names of the states and their capitals	
Believing you hear your name during a loud and busy conference	
Trying to remember a phone number long enough to dial it	
"Committing" the phone number to memory	
Fleeting visual images as you watch a movie	
Looking at an object for a few seconds before sketching it	

Draw a picture of the **memory curve,** and indicate where the **primacy effect** and **recency effect** are evident.

What do the **primacy effect** and **recency effect** tell us about the number of memory stores we have? Why? _____

_____

_____

_____

Making Memories

What are **codes?** _____

_____

_____

_____

What kind of **codes** are there? List and describe them:

1) _____
_____
_____

2) _____
_____
_____

Think of a time when you knew information very well but later forgot it. For example, you may have memorized the Gettysburg Address for a school performance, but now can't remember any more than "Fourscore and seven years ago . . . ." Describe this material and the situation. _____
_____
_____
_____
_____
_____
_____
_____

Explain why you once knew this material and later forgot it, using the concept of **consolidation**.
_____
_____
_____
_____

Describe some material that you have probably stored as **dynamic memory**. _____
_____
_____
_____
_____

Describe some material that you have probably stored as **structural memory**. _____
_____
_____
_____
_____

How long does it take for information to be **consolidated**? _____
_____
_____
_____
_____

How are **consolidation** and **reconsolidation** different? _____

_____

_____

_____

_____

Under what circumstances is **reconsolidation** necessary? _____

_____

_____

_____

Why is it a good idea to do the Test Yourself, Think It Through!, and Review and Remember! exercises in the textbook? _____

_____

_____

_____

Using the following concepts, explain how you would teach someone to study for an exam in this class: **consolidation, breadth of processing, depth of processing, transfer appropriate processing, elaborative encoding.** _____

_____

_____

_____

_____

_____

_____

_____

_____

_____

If you were a college professor, how difficult would you make the tasks in the general psychology course? Why? _____

_____

_____

_____

Why is it better to study in small chunks of time, spread out over time, than to cram for an exam?

_____

_____

_____

Why is it not a good idea to say to your professor, "I *tried* really hard to learn the material for this test."? _____

_____

_____

_____

Describe a time when you _tried_ to learn something (called **intentional learning**). _____

_____

_____

_____

Describe a time when you learned something without intention (called **incidental learning**).

_____

_____

_____

How is it possible to learn material without trying? _____

_____

_____

_____

Read through the following list of words once. Try to remember as many of them as you can.

planet	bottle
briefcase	piano
smile	friend
paper	journey
table	explosion
account	magazine
cancer	giraffe

Now cover these words and write as many of them as you can on a separate sheet of paper.

Take a look at the words you remembered. Chances are that you remembered the emotionally laden words (e.g., smile, cancer, friend, explosion). Was this true for you? Why is it true for most people? Explain using research on the effects of emotion on memory. _____

_____

_____

_____

_____

_____

At the level of the brain, how does emotion affect memory? _____

_____

_____

_____

_____

_____

Describe, in as much detail as you can, how you remember learning about the terrorist attacks on the World Trade Center and Pentagon on September 11, 2001. _____

_____
_____
_____
_____
_____
_____
_____
_____
_____

Were any other people with you at the time you heard about these attacks? If so, who? _____

_____

CALL . . .

...the people who were present when you first learned of the September 11 terrorist attacks and record their memories related to hearing about the plane crashes into the World Trade Center and Pentagon. _____

_____
_____
_____
_____
_____
_____
_____
_____
_____
_____
_____
_____

How does your recall compare to their recall? What does the research say about the accuracy (or inaccuracy) of **flashbulb memories**? _____

_____
_____
_____
_____
_____
_____

Storing Information: Not Just One LTM

Modality-Specific Memories: The Multimedia Brain

In the following table, describe material that you hold in each of the following **modality-specific memory stores**.

Modality-Specific Memory Store	Material
Visual memory store	
Auditory memory store	
Olfactory memory store	
Memory store for touch	
Memory store for movement	
Memory store for language	

Semantic versus Episodic Memory

Identify the following experiences as **semantic** or **episodic memories**.

Experience	Type of Memory (Semantic or Episodic?)
Your sixteenth birthday party	
What you had for breakfast this morning	
The largest country in the world	
The difference between dogs and cats	
The smell of your grandmother's baking	
The first president of the United States	
The meaning of the word "psychology"	
The image of the World Trade Center towers collapsing	
The square root of 36	
The death of Princess Diana	

Explicit versus Implicit Memories

Identify the following memories as either **explicit** or **implicit**.

Experience	Type of Memory (Explicit or Implicit?)
Riding a bike	
Spelling the word "psychology"	
The names of the fifty states	
Tying your shoe	
Your first kiss	
The Pledge of Allegiance	
Walking	
How to skip	
The birthdates of your immediate family members	
What you ate for dinner last night	

There are five types of **implicit memories.** Give a personal example of each.

Type of Implicit Memory	Personal Example
Classically conditioned response	
Nonassociative learning (e.g., habituation)	
Habit	
Skill	
Priming	

Genetic Foundations of Memory

What are **knockout mice?** _____

_____

_____

_____

What do **knockout mice** tell us about the biological basis for memory? _____

_____

_____

_____

What do blinking rabbits tell us about the biological basis for memory? _____
_____
_____
_____

What does the Human Genome Project tell us about the biological basis for memory? _____
_____
_____
_____

Stressed Memories

Given the negative effects of stress on the **hippocampus,** explain why it is crucial to keep your anxiety level down when studying for and taking an exam. _____
_____
_____
_____
_____

In what other ways does stress affect memory? _____
_____
_____
_____
_____

Is the memory damage caused by stress permanent? Explain. _____
_____
_____
_____
_____

Looking at Levels: Autobiographical Memory

Explain the factors at each of the three levels that contribute to the formation of **autobiographical memories**. Use arrows to indicate how events at the three levels may interact.

The Brain	The Person	The Group

Retrieving Information from Memory: More Than Reactivating the Past

The Act of Remembering: Reconstructing Buried Cities

How is remembering like **reconstructing** buried cities? Why do Kosslyn and Rosenberg use this analogy? _____

_____

_____

_____

_____ `

_____

Recognition versus Recall

Distinguish between **recognition** and **recall**. Do you perform better on essay tests or multiple-choice tests? What does this tell you about your own memory abilities? _____

_____

_____

_____

_____

_____

_____

_____

How can you use what you now know about **cues and state-dependent retrieval** to help you study for an exam? _____

_____

_____

_____

_____

_____

_____

_____

Why won't most courts accept testimony based on recall that occurs during hypnosis? _____

_____

_____

_____

_____

_____

_____

When Memory Goes Wrong—and What to Do About It

False Memories

When you did the "sweet" experiment in Figures 7.14 and 7.15 in the textbook, did you incorrectly recall any words? If so, which ones? _____
_____

Why does this happen? _____
_____
_____
_____
_____

How could a criminal lawyer question his or her witnesses so as to avoid interfering with the witnesses' memories of a crime? _____
_____
_____
_____
_____

How do real memories and false memories differ, in terms of brain functioning? _____
_____
_____
_____
_____

Give an example from your own life of a time when you had difficulty with reality monitoring:
_____
_____
_____
_____
_____

Forgetting

Identify the likely sources of forgetting for each of the following experiences, choosing from **encoding failure, decay, retroactive interference,** and **proactive interference**.

Experience	Type of Forgetting
Susan met numerous people at a party, but when she bumps into them the next week, she can't remember their names.	
Having just moved last month and memorized her new address, Kristy can't remember her previous address.	
Sam can't remember whether he passed a drugstore on the way home from his new job.	
James called his new girlfriend by his old girlfriend's name.	
Sixty-year-old Frank can't remember what his second-grade teacher looked like.	

Complete the following table to distinguish between **organic amnesia** and **functional amnesia**.

Type of Amnesia / Characteristic	Organic Amnesia	Functional Amnesia
Triggering event		
Relative frequency		
Brain changes		
Type of memory disrupted		

Distinguish between **anterograde** and **retrograde amnesia.** _____
_____
_____
_____
_____

Do you have any memories of your childhood before the age of three? Given that memory before this age is pretty poor, what do you think accounts for your memories? _____
_____
_____
_____
_____

How does Alzheimer's disease affect memory? _____
_____
_____
_____
_____
_____

Repressed Memories

What evidence suggests that traumatic memories can be repressed? _____
_____
_____
_____
_____
_____

Explain how events with highly charged emotional content (e.g., abuse) can be forgotten, when such emotional tone usually enhances memory. _____
_____
_____
_____
_____
_____

Improving Memory: Tricks and Tools

Create a hierarchical organization for memory-related terms to help you remember the material from this chapter.

List ways that you can apply the material from this chapter to your studying, so as to help you best learn the material.

- _____

- _____

- _____

- _____
- _____
- _____

Use **interactive images** to remember these ten items on a grocery list: apples, milk, tissues, hotdogs, cereal, bananas, juice, pasta, green beans, rice. Study the list for about one minute, and then cover it up and write as many items as you can remember in the space below.

How many could you remember? _____

Use the **method of loci** to remember the following list: asparagus, paper towels, dog food, hamburger, bread, syrup, olives, cookies, peaches, peanut butter. Study the list for about one minute, and then cover it up and write as many items as you can remember in the space below.

How many could you remember? _____

Use the **pegword system** to remember this list: waffles, peas, tissues, ice cream, spaghetti, potatoes, popcorn, soda, lemons, shampoo. Study the list for about one minute, and then cover it up and write as many items as you can remember in the space below.

How many could you remember? _____

Which of the above methods worked best? Did you experience **interference** in trying to learn the lists? If so, what type of interference did you experience? _____
_____
_____

Can you remember the five methods suggested to enhance **retrieval**? Use what you have learned in this section to memorize the five methods. List your mnemonic devices below:

- _____
  _____
  _____
  _____

- _____
  _____
  _____
  _____

-

-

-

After You Read . . . Thinking Back

1. In Chapter 1, you considered the impact of the cognitive revolution. Certainly, memory research has benefited from the cognitive revolution. However, some of the key studies in memory also contributed to the cognitive revolution. Name two important people and/or studies in memory, and explain how they influenced the cognitive revolution. _____

_____

_____

_____

_____

_____

_____

2. In Chapter 2, you learned about different kinds of psychological studies, including correlational, quasi-experimental, and experimental studies. Which methods lend themselves particularly well to memory studies? Why? _____

_____

_____

_____

_____

_____

_____

3. In Chapter 4, you learned about top-down and bottom-up processing. How does top-down processing affect memory? _____

_____

_____

_____

_____

_____

_____

4. How does bottom-up processing affect memory? _____

_____

_____

_____

_____

_____

5. What is the difference between learning, as described in Chapter 6, and memory? Is there any such difference? Discuss. _____

_____

_____

_____

_____

After You Read . . . Thinking Ahead

1. Which memory strengths, if any, do you think might facilitate problem-solving abilities? Why?
    _____
    _____
    _____
    _____
    _____

2. Is memory a component of intelligence? If so, which aspect(s) of memory are involved in intelligence? _____
    _____
    _____
    _____
    _____
    _____

3. Do you think that your memories affect your emotions? If so, how? _____
    _____
    _____
    _____
    _____
    _____

4. Can you think of any reasons why people might not have first memories before the age of approximately three or four? Why? _____
    _____
    _____
    _____
    _____
    _____

5. How might memory skills affect a person's stress level, or vice versa? Discuss. _____
    _____
    _____
    _____
    _____
    _____

6. How do memories affect how we perceive other people? Discuss. _____
    _____
    _____
    _____
    _____
    _____

After You Read . . . Practice Tests

PRACTICE TEST #1

Multiple-Choice Questions

For each question, circle the best answer from the choices given.

1. The process of organizing and transforming incoming information so that it can be entered into memory is called _____. (p. 186)
   a. decoding
   b. rehearsal
   c. storage
   d. retrieval
   e. encoding

2. According to psychologists, sensory memory _____. (p. 188)
   a. holds a large amount of perceptual input for a very brief time
   b. holds analyzed information for brief periods of time
   c. is also called working memory
   d. is the system used to maintain information for extended periods of time
   e. can hold unanalyzed information indefinitely

3. Which of the following would NOT be an example of a semantic memory? (p. 198)
   a. knowing that Pluto is the outmost planet
   b. knowing the chemical formula for salt
   c. remembering the definition of "semantic memory"
   d. knowing where you parked your car
   e. knowing that Paris is in France

4. Modality-specific memories stores retain input from _____. (p. 197)
   a. all our sensory systems in a common sensory register
   b. only our visual and auditory systems
   c. a single sense or processing system
   d. all parts of the brain
   e. two to three senses combined into one sensory modality

5. How do cues help you to remember? (p. 207)
   a. They provide inferences
   b. They assign numbers to memories
   c. They help with the chunking of information
   d. They are differential memory stores
   e. They direct you to key stored fragments

6. Recent research indicates that STM can hold about how many chunks? (p. 189)
   a. four
   b. five to nine
   c. it is unknown
   d. about twenty
   e. close to ten

7. As Cinnamon was getting ready to give her speech she kept repeating the main points silently to herself. What part of working memory is she utilizing? (p. 190)
   a. the visuospatial sketchpad
   b. her echoic memory
   c. the articulatory loop
   d. the central executive
   e. her sensory memory

8. The fact that you recognize "X" as a letter when reading a word suggests that _____. (p. 190)
   a. only ltm is meaningful
   b. most information is stm is meaningful
   c. no information in stm is meaningful
   d. the central executive is working
   e. echoic memory is meaningful

9. Consolidation of memory usually happens _____. (p. 193)
   a. over the course of one day
   b. during sleep
   c. overnight
   d. after much time has passed
   e. almost immediately

10. Conditioned responses and habits are examples of what type of memory? (pp. 198-199)
    a. iconic memory
    b. implicit memory
    c. modality-specific memory
    d. semantic memory
    e. working memory

PRACTICE TEST #2

Multiple-Choice Questions

For each question, circle the best answer from the choices given.

1. When the brain is encoding new memories, the _____ is/are activated. (p. 190)
   a. frontal lobes
   b. occipital lobes
   c. temporal lobes
   d. parietal lobes
   e. hypothalamus

2. Memory research indicates that the memory system which has the largest capacity is _____. (p. 190)
   a. long-term memory
   b. short-term memory
   c. sensory memory
   d. somatic memory
   e. working memory

3. The capacity of LTM is _____. (p. 190)
   a. very limited
   b. somewhat larger than STM
   c. equal to the number of neurons
   d. so large that some researchers question whether it has a limit
   e. the same as working memory

4. According to psychologists, episodic memories include: (p. 198)
   a. memories of factual information
   b. knowledge about the world in general
   c. memories of particular events that w have personally experienced
   d. knowledge about how to perform complex tasks
   e. knowledge about facts learned in school

5. Semantic memories and episodic memories are _____. (p. 198)
   a. virtually the same thing
   b. processed in different parts of the frontal lobes
   c. stored as wholes rather than parts
   d. equally likely to be personal incidents
   e. aspects of working memory

6. Primacy effects occur for material that is (p. 191)
   a. at the beginning of the list
   b. at the end of the list
   c. in the middle of the list
   d. encoded last
   e. encoded unconsciously

7. Suppose you have very vivid memories of you sixteenth birthday party, when all your friends got together and threw you a surprise party. Even though a number of years have passed, you can still recall every detail of the party, right down to what everyone was wearing. Psychologists refer to vivid memories of this type as: (p. 195)
   a. procedural memory
   b. a flashbulb memory
   c. semantic memory
   d. déjà vu
   e. unconscious memories

8. You have a big psychology test next week that requires you to learn a long list of important terms. Based on what memory research has shown regarding distributed versus massed practice, what should you do? (p. 218)
   a. spend one intense study session early in the week, and the relax
   b. space your study sessions out over the full week
   c. spend one intense study session the night before the test
   d. only read the terms through once before the test, to reduce interference
   e. memorize all the terms in the first night and then do the same thing right before the test

PRACTICE TEST #3

Multiple-Choice Questions

For each question, circle the best answer from the choices given.

1. What causes interference in memory? (pp. 213-214)
   a. retrieval cues that are similar
   b. we do not want to remember some things
   c. the brain has a limited capacity for storage
   d. memory is for recognition only
   e. false memories

2. Martha remembers the day she was born very vividly, down to the things that people were saying. This is most likely _____. (p. 216)
   a. a true memory
   b. a false memory
   c. a common event
   d. due to her episodic memory
   e. due to her semantic memory

3. When previously established memories interfere with the creation of new memories, _____ has occurred. (p. 213)
   a. retroactive interference
   b. proactive interference
   c. retroactive amnesia
   d. proactive amnesia
   e. repression

4. What effect does hypnosis have on memory? (p. 208)
   a. it increases accuracy of memory
   b. it causes false memories to be recalled
   c. it has no effect on memory
   d. it can increase confidence in a memory, but not necessarily accuracy
   e. it greatly increases memory ability

5. How do mnemonic devices help memory? (p. 218)
   a. they increase the capacity of LTM
   b. they enable effective organization and integration
   c. they provide more elaborate and better retrieval cues
   d. they decrease interference
   e. they have no effect on memory

6. If you want a better memory, what does your textbook recommend you do? (pp. 217-219)
   a. take vitamins and supplements
   b. use strategies to help you remember
   c. eat more brain foods like fish
   d. nothing will improve your memory
   e. put more effort into recalling information

7. What do good memory strategies all have in common? (pp. 217-219)
   a. they are interactive and require active learning
   b. they all use visual images
   c. they all use auditory information
   d. they increase brain functioning
   e. they suppress interference

8. What aspect of memory do organizational strategies attempt to enhance? (p. 217)
   a. encoding
   b. retrieval
   c. storage
   d. interference
   e. visual cues

COMPREHENSIVE PRACTICE TEST

True/False Questions

Circle TRUE or FALSE for each of the following statements.

1.   TRUE   FALSE   Sensory memory can last for several days. (pp. 187-188)

2.   TRUE   FALSE   STM can hold an unlimited amount of information for only a short time. (p. 189)

3.   TRUE   FALSE   A code is a physical representation. (p. 191)

4.   TRUE   FALSE   Reality monitoring involves remembering that movies are real. (p. 211)

5.   TRUE   FALSE   What you remember from your first day at school may not be exactly what happened. (p. 210)

6.   TRUE   FALSE   There is an unlimited number of memory stores. (p. 187)

7.   TRUE   FALSE   If you are exposed to emotional stimuli, it will always lead to poor memory. (pp. 194-195)

8.   TRUE   FALSE   Genetics are the main determinant of whether someone has a good memory or not. (p. 297)

Multiple-Choice Questions

For each question, circle the best answer from the choices given.

1. Jennifer listens attentively in her psychology class and translates the information into new memories. This illustrates _____. (p. 186)
   a. storage
   b. retrieval
   c. encoding
   d. partitioning
   e. forgetting

2. The capacity of short-term memory can be enhanced by (p. 189)
   a. willful effort
   b. chunking information together
   c. certain vitamins
   d. rehearsal
   e. there is no way to increase STM capacity

3. Automatic processing requires _____. (p. 200)
    a. a lack of practice
    b. effort
    c. attention
    d. little or no attention
    e. a large working memory

4. Condolisa is trying to remember the names of the cranial nerves for her anatomy exam. She read the names through several times, and then tested herself on how well she could recall them. According to the serial position curve, you should predict that Condolisa will show the worst memory for the names of the nerves: (p. 191)
    a. at the beginning of the list
    b. at the end of the list
    c. in the middle of the list
    d. at both the beginning and the end of the list
    e. that have the longest names

5. The visuospatial sketchpad, the articulatory loop, and the central executive are all parts of _____. (p. 189)
    a. primacy memory
    b. long-term memory
    c. rehearsal memory
    d. working memory
    e. consolidation memory

6. In working memory, the role of the central executive is _____. (p. 190)
    a. to put information into STM
    b. to plan and problem-solve
    c. to keep interference from happening
    d. to dampened meaningless information
    e. unknown at this time

7. According to psychologists, flashbulb memories are: (p. 195)
    a. relatively pure, unanalyzed representations of incoming information
    b. memories of factual information and knowledge about the world in general
    c. unrehearsed memories of how to execute complex tasks and behaviors
    d. unusually vivid and accurate memories of dramatic events
    e. memories for photographs and film

8. Your first memory of playing tennis is stored in: (p. 198)
    a. semantic memory
    b. procedural memory
    c. episodic memory
    d. sensory memory
    e. working memory

9. Every time you see a potato chip commercial, you feel compelled to eat some chips. This classically conditioned response is an example of what type of memory? (p. 199)
   a. working memory
   b. short-term memory
   c. episodic memory
   d. semantic memory
   e. procedural memory

10. The act of remembering involves _____. (p. 206)
    a. looking up files in the brain
    b. retrieving fragments and reconstructing the memory
    c. pulling entire memories from the brain
    d. recall instead of recognition
    e. completely unconscious processes

11. Repressed memories are _____. (p. 216)
    a. definitely real memories
    b. most likely false memories
    c. an example of conscious forgetting
    d. a controversial and unsolved issue
    e. implanted memories

12. People who suffer memory loss from brain damage most likely have what part of the brain damaged? (p. 215)
    a. the hypothalamus
    b. the occipital lobe
    c. the hippocampus and its connections
    d. the entire cortex
    e. the cerebellum

13. Memory can be improved by _____. (pp. 217-219)
    a. organizing the way it is encoded
    b. processing the information thoroughly
    c. connecting new to old information
    d. distributing its learning over time
    e. all of the above

14. Creating interactive images and associating them with a previously memorized, ordered list of objects is a mnemonic device known as: (p. 219)
    a. the locus word system
    b. the method of loci
    c. chunking
    d. context-specific processing
    e. the pegword system

Short-Answer/Essay Questions

Answer the following questions in the space provided.

1. What are some ways that the theory of working memory is an advance over the original theory of STM? _____

_____

_____

_____

_____

_____

_____

_____

_____

2. What physiological evidence exists for different types of memory stores?_____

_____

_____

_____

_____

_____

_____

_____

_____

3. Why is reconsolidation necessary for some types of memories but not for others? _____

_____

_____

_____

_____

_____

_____

_____

_____

4.. How do good memory cues work?_____

_____

_____

_____

_____

_____

_____

_____

5. What are some reasons that you forget information?_____

_____

_____

_____

_____

_____

_____

When You Are Finished . . . Puzzle It Out

Across

3. Studied S., who had an almost superhuman memory
4. Stimuli that trigger remembering
6. Process of repeating information over and over
10. A unit of information
11. Encoding an input and matching it to a stored code
13. A well-learned, automatic response
14. Also called "immediate memory"
16. Means "a memory aid"

Puzzle created with Puzzlemaker at DiscoverySchool.com.

Down

1. Loss of memory over an entire time span
2. Type of memory for dramatic event
5. Developed the forgetting curve
7. The process of retaining information in memory
8. Converting stored information in LTM into structural changes in the brain
9. Process of accessing information
12. A type of mental representation
15. Fading away of memories with time because the relevant connections between neurons are lost
16. Mnemonic device discovered by Simonides
17. Memories of events associated with a context

Chapter 6
Language, Thinking, and Intelligence:
What Humans Do Best

Before You Read . . .

What sets humans apart from other mammals? Many people would point to our intelligence and our ability to speak and to reason. In this chapter, you will learn how psychologists think about these important aspects of life. What makes a language? Could we reason without language? Given our ability to reason, why do humans so often fail to think logically or rationally about a problem? What makes a person smart? These are just some of the topics you'll be reading about in the coming chapters.

Chapter Objectives

After reading this chapter, you should be able to:

- Identify the essential characteristics of all languages.

- Explain how first and second languages are learned and used.

- Explain whether language molds our thoughts.

- Describe how we think with mental images.

- Explain the idea of concepts and the different levels of concepts.

- Describe the methods used to solve problems.

- Understand whether people reason logically.

- Explain why we commit reasoning errors.

- Compare and contrast different theories of intelligence.

- Identify and explain how intelligence is measured.

- Describe what IQ tests are, how they are scored, and what they say about a person's future.

- Discuss what makes people intelligent.

- Discuss heritability and the problems with heritability studies.

- Describe research on group differences in intelligence.

- Explain and summarize research on mental retardation and giftedness.

- Describe creativity and explain why some people are more creative than others.

- Analyze efforts to enhance intelligence and creativity.

As You Read . . . Term Identification

Make flashcards using the following terms as you go. Use the definitions in the margins of this chapter for help. If you write the definitions in your own words, though, you will remember them better!

Affirming the consequent
Algorithm
Availability heuristic
Base-rate rule
Basic level
Category
Concept
Confirmation bias
Creativity
Crystallized intelligence
Deductive reasoning
Down syndrome
Emotional intelligence
Factor analysis
Fetal alcohol syndrome
Fluid intelligence
Functional fixedness
g
Gifted
Grammar
Heuristic
Inductive reasoning
Intelligence
Intelligence quotient (IQ)
Language comprehension
Language production
Linguistic relativity hypothesis

Logic
Mental images
Mental set
Mentally retarded
Microenvironment
Morpheme
Norming
Phoneme
Phonology
Pragmatics
Primary mental abilities
Problem
Prodigies
Propositional representation
Prototype
Representation problem
Representativeness heuristic
s
Semantics
Standardized sample
Strategy
Syntax
Test bias
Theory of multiple intelligences
Typicality
Wechsler Adult Intelligence Scale (WAIS)

As You Read . . . Questions and Exercises

Language: More Than Meaningful Sounds

The Essentials: What Makes Language Language?

Language is best understood as having four aspects: **phonology, syntax, semantics,** and **pragmatics.** Indicate below which function is illustrated by each example.

Example	Function (Phonology, Syntax, Semantics, or Pragmatics?)
Grammar produces this aspect of language	
Represented by morphemes	
Helps us to understand jokes and metaphors	
The difference between "cat" and bat"	
Can't program a computer to do this (at least, so far!)	
A sentence needs a noun and verb phrase	
The difference between "read" and "reading"	
The basic building blocks of speech	

In the following sentence, identify a **phoneme**, the **syntax**, a **morpheme**, the **semantic meaning** of the words, and the **pragmatic meaning** of the entire phrase:

People in glass houses should not throw stones.

Phoneme: _____

Syntax: _____

Morpheme: _____

Semantic meaning: _____

Pragmatic meaning: _____

How many **morphemes** are in the word *transcontinental?* What are they? What do they mean?

_____

_____

_____

_____

_____

Write a sentence that has meaning, but is **syntactically incorrect**: _____

_____

Write a sentence that is **syntactically correct,** but has no meaning: _____

_____

Suppose that you were a lawyer, questioning a child witness. How could you use your knowledge of children's skills in pragmatics to elicit the best testimony? _____

_____

_____

_____

How is each of the **hemispheres** involved in **pragmatics?**

Left	Right

In your own words, explain how **speech production** and **comprehension** draw on the same brain mechanisms in each of the following four areas.

- **Phonology:** _____

_____

- **Syntax:** _____

_____

- **Semantics:** _____

_____

- **Pragmatics:** _____

_____

Bilingualism: A Window of Opportunity?

Have you taken a course in some foreign language in high school or college? Which aspects of the **language** were the hardest to learn? The **vocabulary**? The **grammar**? **Reading** or **writing**? Given what you have learned in this chapter, explain why you may have (or may not have) had difficulty learning a **second language**. _____

_____

_____

_____

_____

_____

_____

_____

_____

Thinking: Understanding the World and Guiding Behavior

Words: Inner Speech and Spoken Thoughts

What are the three problems with asserting that **thinking** is just talking to yourself?

- _____
- _____
- _____

What evidence suggests that **language** shapes **thought?**

- _____
  _____
  _____
  _____

- _____
  _____
  _____

How can you use the research on how language enhances memory in your studying? _____
_____
_____
_____
_____

Mental Imagery: Perception without Sensation

Does the Statue of Liberty hold the torch in her left or right hand? _____

GO SURFING . . .

...at http://www.nps.gov/stli/mainmenu.htm to see if you were correct. Were you? _____

In your own words, describe and explain the three properties of **mental space**:

- _____
  _____
  _____
  _____

- _____
  _____
  _____
  _____

- _____
  _____
  _____
  _____

What are the limits of mental images?

- _____
- _____
- _____
- _____

Concepts: Neither Images nor Words

How are **concepts** different from words or images? For each of the following ideas, indicate whether you think of a word, an image, or neither (a concept).

Idea	Word/Image/Concept
Book	
Angry	
Freedom	
Hungry	
Automobile	
Excitement	

Why was Aristotle's definition of the features of a **concept** (necessary and sufficient) inaccurate? ___

_____

_____

_____

For the following **concepts,** see if you can come up with **necessary and sufficient features.**

Concept	Necessary Feature	Sufficient Feature
Bird		
Friend		
Depression		
Hunger		

Name a **prototype** and a **non-prototype** to illustrate each of the following **concepts.**

Concept	Prototype	Non-prototype
Bird		
Mammal		
Furniture		
Fruit		

How do **prototypes** affect our thought and behaviors?

- _____

  _____

  _____

- _____

  _____

  _____

For the following **basic-level** words, describe a related **concept** that is more **general** and more **specific.**

More General	Basic-Level Word	More Specific
	Apple	
	Car	
	House	
	Angry	
	Computer	

How to Solve Problems: More than Inspiration

Name and briefly describe a **problem** that you are currently facing. _____
_____
_____
_____

Is there a different way of **representing** this problem that may make it easier to solve? Try it! Report your results here. _____
_____
_____
_____

In general, what difficulties can arise during the **representation** of a problem that can make it difficult to solve the problem? _____
_____
_____
_____

Name one instance in which you use an **algorithm,** and describe when you use it. _____
_____
_____
_____

Name one instance in which you use a **heuristic,** and describe when you use it. _____
_____
_____
_____

Can you remember a time that you used **analogical reasoning** to solve a problem? If so, describe it. _____
_____
_____
_____

Overcoming Obstacles to Problem Solving

Name and briefly describe five ways that you can overcome obstacles to **problem solving:**

- _____
  _____
- _____
  _____
- _____
  _____
- _____
  _____
- _____
  _____

GO SURFING . . .

...at one of the following sites and try some of the **logic** puzzles there:
- http://www.thakur.demon.nl/
- http://crpuzzles.com/logic/
- http://www.mysterymaster.com/puzzles.html

What **obstacles** did you face in doing the logic puzzles online? How did you overcome them? (Or did you?) _____
_____
_____
_____

Logic, Reasoning, and Decision Making

Are People Logical?

Identify the type of reasoning—**deductive** or **inductive**—in the following situations.

Situation	Type of Reasoning
In her new town, Susan met three people, all of whom were rude to her. She therefore assumed that all people in the new town would be rude.	
All aliens have an antenna. An antenna allows aliens to communicate with the mothership. All aliens can communicate with the mothership.	
Frank bought a car that turned out to be a lemon. He told his friends not to buy a car from that dealer, as all of the cars on the lot were sure to be lemons.	
When the pressure drops, it rains. When it rains, the plants grow. When the pressure drops, the plants grow.	

Identify the type of error—**affirming the consequent** or **confirmation bias**—in the following situations.

Situation	Error
All babies are bald. Jim is bald. Jim must be a baby.	
Lara is convinced that she is psychic because yesterday she picked up the phone to call a friend just as her friend called her.	
Ignoring her dissatisfaction, poor coworker relationships, and demanding boss, Paula convinced herself that she loved her job because she was well paid.	
If it rains today, people will carry umbrellas. People are carrying umbrellas, so it must be raining.	

Heuristics and Biases: Cognitive Illusions?

People do not always use the **rules of logic,** but instead sometimes rely on sets of heuristics. These heuristics can result in wrong conclusions being drawn.

Define each of the following **heuristics** and explain how it may result in errors.

Heuristic	Definition	How May It Result in Errors?
Representativeness		
Availability		

Emotions and Decision Making: Having a Hunch

What is the evidence that **emotions** can facilitate **decision making?** _____
_____
_____
_____
_____
_____
_____

Intelligence: Is there More than One Way to Be Smart?

Who is the smartest person you know? Describe him or her. _____
_____
_____
_____
_____

What makes that person so **intelligent**? _____
_____
_____
_____
_____

Based on the preceding answer, what is your definition of **intelligence**? _____
_____
_____
_____
_____

How does your definition of **intelligence** compare with psychologists' definition? _____
_____
_____
_____
_____

A Brief History of Intelligence Testing

Who started **intelligence** tests and why? _____
_____
_____
_____
_____

What kinds of tasks were included on this first **intelligence** test? _____
_____
_____
_____
_____

How were **IQ** tests originally scored? What was the problem with that method? _____
_____
_____
_____
_____

What is the modern test based on the original test developed by Simon and Binet? _____
_____
_____
_____
_____

Why did Wechsler develop a new **intelligence** test?

- _____
- _____
- _____
- _____

Which **intelligence** test did Wechsler develop for adults? _____
_____

Which **intelligence** test did Wechsler develop for children? _____
_____

What are the most widely used **intelligence** tests in the United States? _____
_____

What are the two major parts of Wechsler's tests?
- _____
- _____

Scoring IQ Tests: Measuring the Mind

How did William Stern propose that **IQ** scores should be computed? _____
_____
_____
_____
_____

What was the problem with that method? _____
_____
_____
_____
_____

How are **intelligence** tests scored now? Why? _____
_____
_____
_____
_____

What is the mean **IQ** score? _____

Describe the two steps involved in **norming** a test.

- _____
  _____
  _____
  _____

- _____
  _____
  _____
  _____

Draw a normal curve below. On it, indicate the mean and mark off the standard deviation of the WISC-III.

Describe a measurement in your everyday life that is not *reliable*. For instance, do you have a thermometer that yields different temperatures at two close intervals? Do you have a scale that shows a ten-pound difference in weight for the same object over a short period of time? _____

_____
_____
_____
_____

Describe a measurement in your everyday life that is not *valid*. For example, is a thermometer a valid instrument to measure illness? _____

_____
_____
_____
_____

IQ and Achievement: IQ in the Real World

What do **IQ** scores predict?

- _____
- _____
- _____
- _____
- _____
- _____
- _____
- _____
- _____

Recall the smartest person you know, who you described earlier. Which of these variables are true of that person? _____

_____
_____
_____
_____

How much variability in job performance can be predicted by **IQ?** _____

What other variables predict job success?

- _____
- _____
- _____
- _____
- _____
- _____

Is the smartest person you know successful on the job? _____
_____
_____
_____
_____

Which of the other characteristics that predict job success does this person have? _____
_____
_____
_____
_____

Analyzing Intelligence: One Ability or Many?

GO SURFING . . .

...at the following site and take the **IQ** tests there:
- http://www.iqtest.com/ (traditional psychometric test)

What was your score on this test? _____

In the normal curve you drew (on the previous page), mark an X indicating where you fall, using the score from the traditional psychometric test you just took.

What is *g*? _____
_____
_____
_____
_____

What evidence is there for *g*? _____
_____
_____
_____
_____

What technique did Charles Spearman develop to analyze sets of test scores? _____
_____
_____
_____
_____

What did Louis Thurstone believe that **intelligence** consists of? _____
_____
_____
_____

In your own words, what are **fluid** and **crystallized intelligence**?

- **Fluid intelligence:** _____
  _____
  _____

- **Crystallized intelligence:** _____
  _____
  _____

Why do you think **fluid intelligence** tends to diminish as a person ages, but **crystallized intelligence** does not? _____
_____
_____
_____
_____

Do you think that people can improve their **crystallized** or **fluid intelligence**? If so, how?
_____
_____
_____
_____
_____

Name three types of careers in which you think **crystallized intelligence** would be vital. Briefly explain why it would be so important in each.

- _____
  _____
  _____

- _____
  _____
  _____

- _____
  _____
  _____

Name three types of careers in which you think **fluid intelligence** would be vital. Briefly explain why it would be so important in each.

- _____
  _____
  _____
- _____
  _____
  _____
- _____
  _____
  _____

Do you think most of your school tests measure **fluid** or **crystallized intelligence** better? _____
_____
_____

In 1993, John Carroll proposed a hierarchical structure of **intelligence** that fits many earlier theories into a single framework. Fill in the boxes below to indicate what appears at each level of the hierarchy.

Two areas of debate surround Carroll's three-stratum theory of the structure of **intelligence.** Describe them.

- _____
  _____
  _____
  _____
- _____
  _____
  _____
  _____

Emotional Intelligence: Knowing Feelings

GO SURFING . . .

...at the following site and take the IQ tests there:
- http://www.utne.com/interact/test_iq.html (emotional intelligence test)

There are two major facets of **emotional intelligence (EI).** Describe each of these facets in the chart below.

Intelligence, as Usually Defined	Subjective Experiences and Inclinations

Can you think of someone who may or may not be highly **intelligent** (using a traditional definition), but who is very **emotionally intelligent?** Describe him or her. How successful has this person been? Why? _____

_____

_____

_____

Circle the correct choice to indicate who typically has higher emotional intelligence.

Men   Women

Minorities   Whites

Older people   Younger people

Multiple Intelligences: More Than One Way to Shine?

GO SURFING . . .

...at the following site and take the **IQ** tests there:
- http://www.mitest.com/o7inte~1.htm (multiple intelligences test)

Describe your *profile of intelligences* based on that test. _____
_____
_____
_____
_____

What are the three observations on which Gardner based his **theory of multiple intelligences?**
- _____
_____
_____
- _____
_____
_____
- _____
_____
_____

Imagine that you are a social studies teacher and are trying to teach students about the Revolutionary War. How could you teach this material so that students with each of the following intellectual strengths could best grasp it?

- **Linguistic:** _____
_____

- **Spatial:** _____
_____

- **Musical:** _____
_____

- **Logical-mathematical:** _____
_____
_____

- **Bodily-kinesthetic:** _____
  _____

- **Intrapersonal:** _____
  _____

- **Interpersonal:** _____
  _____

- **Naturalist:** _____
  _____

- **Existentialist:** _____
  _____
  _____

Do you agree that Gardner's theory is one of **intelligence,** or do you agree with his critics, who claim that some of these are talents, not intelligences? Explain. _____
_____
_____
_____
_____

Write a question (on intelligence) that would test each of the following types of **intelligence** (from Sternberg's theory).

- **Analytic:** _____
  _____
  _____

- **Practical:** _____
  _____
  _____

- **Creative:** _____
  _____
  _____

What part of Sternberg's theory is tested by **IQ** tests? _____

After having taken **intelligence** tests, how do you feel about using IQ tests for school placement?
_____
_____
_____
_____

What Makes Us Smart? Nature and Nurture

Smart Genes, Smart Environment: A Single System

How are *adoption studies* conducted? _____
_____
_____
_____
_____

What are the two major findings of *adoption studies?*

- _____
_____
_____

- _____
_____
_____

Some studies compare the **IQ**s of people with different numbers of genes in common. What is the major finding from such research? _____
_____
_____
_____
_____

The usual estimate of the heritability of **intelligence** is .50. What does this mean? _____
_____
_____
_____
_____

What is the evidence for an environmental contribution to **intelligence?** _____
_____
_____
_____
_____
_____
_____

Describe some of the difficulties in interpreting heritability estimates.

- _____
  _____
  _____

- _____
  _____
  _____

- _____
  _____
  _____

- _____
  _____
  _____

- _____
  _____
  _____

Group Differences in Intelligence

Put the following groups in order of how they typically perform on **IQ** tests, from highest to lowest:

Asian Americans	Hispanic Americans
Black Americans	White Americans

Highest: _____

_____

_____

Lowest: _____

Why don't heritability estimates tell us anything about group differences in **intelligence?** _____
_____
_____
_____
_____
_____
_____

Five theories for explaining racial differences in **IQ** have been proposed. For each of the following theories, describe the evidence that supports or refutes it.

Theory	Supporting Evidence	Refuting Evidence
Test bias		
Text anxiety		
Bad environments		
Inferior schooling		
Microenvironment		

How do men's and women's intellectual strengths differ? _____

_____

_____

_____

_____

What is the evidence that these differences are biologically determined? _____

_____

_____

_____

_____

What is the evidence that these differences are environmentally determined? _____

_____

_____

_____

_____

Some research findings indicate that biology affects gender differences in **intelligence**; other findings indicate that the environment affects these differences. How can both sets of research findings be correct? Explain. _____

_____

_____

_____

_____

Looking at Levels: Stereotype Threat

At each level, list some of the factors that may affect how Blacks perform on the GREs. Draw arrows to indicate the interactions between events at the different levels.

The Brain	The Person	The Group

Diversity in Intelligence

Mental Retardation: People with Special Needs

What are the three criteria for **mental retardation?**

- _____
- _____
- _____

Return to the **normal curve** you drew earlier in this chapter. In a different-colored ink, mark the borderline for mental retardation. Mark the average IQ for people with mental retardation.

Have you ever known anyone with **mental retardation?** If so, describe his or her level of functioning. _____

_____

_____

_____

Consider some causes of retardation. In the chart below, describe the four listed disorders, explain what causes these disorders, and list the risk factors for developing these disorders.

Disorder / Characteristic	Down Syndrome	Fragile X Syndrome	Autism	Fetal Alcohol Syndrome
Description of the disorder				
Cause of the disorder				
Risk factors for developing the disorder				

The Gifted

What does it mean to be **gifted?** _____

_____

_____

_____

_____

What evidence is there for a possible biological basis for **giftedness?** _____

_____

_____

_____

_____

Have you ever known a **prodigy?** If so, describe that person. If not, describe what such a person might be like, intellectually. _____

_____

_____

_____

_____

In what ways, other than their IQs, do **gifted** individuals differ from average children?
- _____
- _____
- _____

What are the possible "prices" of **giftedness?** _____

_____

_____

_____

_____

Why do you think that these "prices" might exist? _____

_____

_____

_____

_____

Creative Smarts

What is the two-stage process of **creativity?** Name and briefly describe each of the stages.

- _____
- _____

Use the shapes below. Combine them (using rotation, size adjustment, and other measures) and make as many objects as you can. Then try to interpret what you created.

How difficult was this exercise? Which part was difficult? _____
_____
_____
_____
_____

Give yourself exactly two minutes to think of as many uses for a brick as you can. List them here:

Divide the total number by two. The answer is your **creativity score:** _____.
(The average score is four; eight is a very high score.)

Do you think these tests are good measures of **creativity?** Why or why not? _____
_____
_____
_____
_____

Here is a checklist of some of the special abilities that **creative** people appear to have. Check all of those abilities that you think describe you.

_____	1.	The ability to generate many solutions
_____	2.	The ability to choose among solutions well
_____	3.	The ability to keep options open
_____	4.	The ability to keep from making snap decisions about the likely outcome of an effort
_____	5.	The ability to see problems from multiple vantage points
_____	6.	The ability to be flexible
_____	7.	The ability to reorganize information
_____	8.	The ability to think in terms of analogies
_____	9.	High intelligence
_____	10.	Wide interests
_____	11.	Not liking traditional dogmas
_____	12.	High self-esteem
_____	13.	Fondness for hard work
_____	14.	High motivation and persistence
_____	15.	Being driven to create

Do you think of yourself as **creative?** Why or why not? _____

_____

_____

_____

_____

Which environmental factors do you think contributed to your **creativity?** _____

_____

_____

_____

_____

After You Read . . . Thinking Back

1. How do you think myelination of different brain parts (discussed in Chapter 3) affects individuals' language and thinking? _____

   _____

   _____

   _____

   _____

2. How do you think the paradigm shift from behaviorism to cognitive psychology (as discussed in Chapter 1) influenced the study of thinking? _____

   _____

   _____

   _____

   _____

3. Do you think that there are particular difficulties with the research methodology used to study thinking, as opposed to some other topics in psychology? _____

   _____

   _____

   _____

   _____

4. The importance of imagery was demonstrated in Tolman's study of cognitive maps. What did Tolman find? _____

   _____

   _____

   _____

   _____

5. What type of studies are adoption studies (e.g., experiments, correlational studies, quasi-experiments)? What are the advantages and disadvantages of this type of study? How is that reflected in adoption studies on intelligence? _____

   _____

   _____

   _____

   _____

6. Why can't we draw causal conclusions from correlational studies? Explain. _____

   _____

   _____

   _____

   _____

7. Do you think that people with high IQs might differ from people with low IQs in terms of learning? If so, for what type of learning (classical, operant, social, cognitive)? How? What evidence supports your opinion? _____

_____

_____

_____

_____

8. Your text discussed the relationship between intelligence and working memory. Can you think of any other aspects of memory (either storage or processing components) that might be related to intelligence? Defend your answer. _____

_____

_____

_____

_____

After You Read . . . Thinking Ahead

1. Can you think of group interactions that might help (or hurt) problem solving? Explain.

   _____
   _____
   _____
   _____
   _____
   _____
   _____

2. Can thinking provide a motivation for some people? Do you know anyone like this? Discuss. ___

   _____
   _____
   _____
   _____
   _____
   _____
   _____

3. How do people with high intelligence differ from others with regard to motivation? Why might this be? _____

   _____
   _____
   _____
   _____
   _____
   _____
   _____

4. How could parents encourage this type of motivation? _____

   _____
   _____
   _____
   _____
   _____

5. What do you think the first signs of giftedness might be? Why? _____

   _____
   _____
   _____
   _____
   _____

6. Are there particular points in the lifespan during which being gifted might be particularly difficult? Why? _____

_____

_____

_____

_____

_____

_____

7. How do groups react to people who are retarded or gifted? Why do you think this is? How does this affect the person? _____

_____

_____

_____

_____

_____

_____

After You Read . . . Practice Tests

PRACTICE TEST #1

Multiple-Choice Questions

For each question, circle the best answer from the choices given.

1. The basic building blocks of speech sounds that combine into meaningful speech are called: (p. 29)
   a. morphemes
   b. phonemes
   c. syntax
   d. pragmatics

2. The sentence, "The watchful the barked mean at man dog," would be difficult for an English speaker to understand because the sentence violates the rules of : (p. 230)
   a. phonology
   b. morphology
   c. syntax
   d. pragmatics

3. The phase "I go," has _____ morphemes. (p. 229)
   a. one
   b. two
   c. three
   d. four

4. Semantics refers to: (p. 230)
   a. rules for combining sounds to make words
   b. rules for combining words to make sentences
   c. the practical knowledge used to comprehend and produce spoken language
   d. the meaning of a word or sentence

5. Binet and Simon's specific aim for developing an intelligence test was _____. (p. 253)
   a. to identify gifted children
   b. to identify children who needed extra classroom help
   c. to show that the French were the smartest people
   d. to illustrate the genetic component of intelligence

6. On Wechsler's IQ test, if you were repeating digits you had heard, you would be taking which subtest? (p. 254)
   a. performance
   b. digit span
   c. arithmetic
   d. matrix reasoning

7. In reference to intelligence testing, what is a population? (p. 255)
   a. a random selection of people drawn from a larger group
   b. the process of setting the mean and standard deviation
   c. the specific subgroup that is tested
   d. a group of people who share more specific attributes

8. One way to asses the validity of IQ tests is to _____. (p. 256)
   a. see if scores are related to performance on other measures of intelligence
   b. make sure they are all correlated
   c. choose a very small sample and compare it to the population
   d. look at genetic components underlying the scores

9. Like Spearman, Cattell and Horn postulated two type of intelligence, but their types were different and called _____. (pp. 258-259)
   a. fluid and crystallized
   b. primary and secondary
   c. F-factor and C-factor
   d. analytical and practical

10. Carroll organized intelligence into _____. (pp. 259-260)
    a. three specific kinds of intelligence
    b. five types of intelligence
    c. three strata of intelligence
    d. hundreds of different types of intelligence

11. Gardner based his theory of intelligence on _____. (p. 262)
    a. studies of animals
    b. correlations of different IQ tests
    c. observations of children as they aged
    d. the behavior of brain damaged patients

12. Sternberg's theory of intelligence added two concepts to the idea that intelligence is based on analytic knowledge like you learn in school. Those two new types are _____ intelligence. (p. 263)
    a. practical and creative
    b. practical and convergent
    c. creative and divergent
    d. verbal and performance

PRACTICE TEST #2

Multiple-Choice Questions

For each question, circle the best answer from the choices given.

1. The most common form of imagery is: (p. 237)
   a. visual
   b. auditory
   c. dreams
   d. nightmares

2. Visual images rely on: (p. 239)
   a. most of the same brain areas as perception
   b. none of the same brain areas as perception
   c. mostly the frontal lobe
   d. the temporal lobes and frontal lobes

3. Relying completely on visual imagery can be a problem sometimes because: (p. 240)
   a. images are abstract
   b. the vividness of the image
   c. it is so easy for everyone to do
   d. images can be ambiguous

4. An unambiguous internal representation that defines a group of objects is called: (p. 240)
   a. a visual image
   b. a concept
   c. a category
   d. a prototype

5. A class of objects in which people generally agree on the members as specific cases of a more general type is called: (p. 242)
   a. an algorithm
   b. a hierarchy
   c. a category
   d. a prototype

6. Which bird would most likely be the prototypical bird? (p. 242)
   a. an ostrich
   b. a parrot
   c. a dodo
   d. a robin

7. When asked what kind of pet they have, most people respond with: (p. 242)
   a. the most specific response
   b. the basic level response
   c. the prototype
   d. the schema

8. The reason that people chose the same three names for pictures of apples, trees, and dogs, is that these concepts are: (p. 243)

   a. at the basic level of the category
   b. the prototype of the category
   c. formally related
   d. an informal relationship

10. The representational problem involves determining: (p. 243)
    a. how to understand the problem
    b. how to best formulate the nature of the problem
    c. how to use a strategy
    d. how to assess your solution

11. When you get stuck solving a problem, it could be because you are stuck on one interpretation or use of an object. This is called: (p. 244)
    a. functional fixedness
    b. the representational problem
    c. heuristic processing
    d. IDEAL solving

12. If you want to solve a problem and get the same answer each time, you will need to use a: (p. 244)
    a. heuristic
    b. algorithm
    c. an analogy
    d. a schema

13. Unlike using an algorithm, analogical thinking requires: (p. 244-245)
    a. knowing the steps or procedures
    b. knowing the exact algorithm to use
    c. unconscious problem solving
    d. having solutions to previous problems in memory

14. You are a student, and all students are people; therefore, you are a person. This conclusion involves: (p. 247)
    a. inductive reasoning
    b. deductive reasoning
    c. faulty reasoning
    d. mental model reasoning

15. You ate a piece of fish and it tasted rotten; therefore all fish taste rotten. This conclusion involves: (p. 247)
    a. inductive reasoning
    b. deductive reasoning
    c. base-rule reasoning
    d. mental model reasoning

16. When you select a person from the population at random, the chance of that person being a lawyer is directly proportional to the percentage of lawyers in the population. This is called: (p. 249)
    a. the framing question
    b. the availability heuristic
    c. the representativeness heuristic
    d. the Base-rule rule

17. What effect does emotion have on decision making? (p. 250)
    a. emotion always impairs decision making
    b. emotion always improves decision making
    c. emotion has been found to sometimes help decision making and to sometimes hurt decision making
    d. the effects of emotion of decision making can not be determined

PRACTICE TEST #3

Multiple-Choice Questions
For each question, circle the best answer from the choices given.

1. What is the heritability of IQ? (p. 266)
   a. about .33
   b. about .50
   c. about .66
   d. about .10

2. A person's genes can help shape aspects of their environment. One way genetics influence the environment is through the _____. (p. 268)
   a. way a child is educated
   b. microenvironment
   c. prenatal influences of the Y chromosome
   d. reinforcement of certain behaviors

3. Similar to genetic and environmental causes for differences in intelligence, if you plant identical seeds in two types of soil, the differences between the plants in the two areas will most likely be due to _____. (pp. 269-271)
   a. differences in the soil
   b. differences in the genetics of the seeds
   c. differences within the groups
   d. random differences

4. According to your textbook, the most likely reason(s) for race differences in IQ is (are) _____. (pp. 271-272)
   a. true differences in intelligence
   b. cultural learning styles
   c. poor parenting
   d. a combination of several environmental factors

5. In terms of nature and nurture, sex differences in verbal and spatial reasoning are _____. (p. 273)
   a. a byproduct of our culture
   b. found in at least thirty different cultures
   c. mostly environmental
   d. a byproduct of education in the United States

6. Mental retardation can be defined as having an IQ score that is more than _____ standard deviations below the mean? (p. 276)
   a. one
   b. two
   c. three
   d. four

7. Down syndrome and fragile X syndrome are both _____. (p. 277)
    a. related to drug use
    b. problems with educational opportunities
    c. genetically related
    d. related to toxins in the air

8. Gifted girls, relative to non-gifted girls, may have higher levels of which hormone? (p. 277)
    a. testosterone
    b. cortisol
    c. all steroids
    d. both estrogen and testosterone

9. How do gifted children compare to other children socially? (p. 278)
    a. They have twice the rate of emotional and social problems
    b. There are no differences in social or emotional functioning
    c. Gifted children are much more popular than non-gifted children
    d. Gifted children can not adjust to adult life

10. Prodigies are _____. (p. 278)
    a. gifted in all areas
    b. usually only gifted in a specific area
    c. not truly gifted
    d. most likely extremely dull in all areas other than their specialty

11. Creativity has been generally found to be _____. (p. 279)
    a. highly inheritable
    b. a form of mental illness
    c. a function of hard work
    d. strongly influenced by shared aspects of the home

12. How is convergent thinking related to creativity? (p. 279)
    a. It is not related
    b. It is involved with setting up the problem to be creatively solved
    c. It allows for the generation of multiple solutions
    d. It allows for insight into the problem

13. Divergent thinking would be most useful for which of the following? (p. 279)
    a. Setting up a problem
    b. Reducing the number of solutions to a problem
    c. Generating several solutions to a problem
    d. Choosing only one solution

COMPREHENSIVE PRACTICE TEST

True/False Questions
Circle TRUE or FALSE for each of the following statements.

1. TRUE   FALSE   Syntax refers to the internal structure of the sentence. (p. 230)

2. TRUE   FALSE   Understanding metaphors requires an understanding of pragmatics. (p. 232)

3. TRUE   FALSE   Prototypes of categories are sometimes the oddest member. (p. 242)

4. TRUE   FALSE   Emotion clouds reasoning in most circumstances. (pp. 250-251)

5. TRUE   FALSE   Intelligence can be quantified like any concrete entity. (p. 252)

6. TRUE   FALSE   The mean of IQ in the population is always 100. (p. 255)

7. TRUE   FALSE   IQ is not correlated with achievement in the real world. (pp. 256-257)

8. TRUE   FALSE   If intelligence is all g, then you would expect all of the scores from different intelligence tests to be correlated to the same degree. (p. 258)

9. TRUE   FALSE   According to your textbook, most modern researchers agree that intelligence has a hierarchical structure. (p. 259-260)

10. TRUE   FALSE   There has been very little modern interest in the idea of emotional intelligence. (p. 260)

11. TRUE   FALSE   Creativity is less influenced by genetic factors than analytical intelligence. (p. 279)

Multiple-Choice Questions
For each question, circle the best answer from the choices given.

1. The words "seem" and "seam" differ in: (p. 230)
    a. phonemes and semantics
    b. phonemes only
    c. semantics
    d. the number of morphemes

2. Mental sentences that expresses the unambiguous meaning of an utterance is called: (p. 231)
   a. the propositional representation
   b. the prepositional representation
   c. the pragmatics
   d. the semantic awareness

3. Research participants have a harder time visualizing details in smaller sizes than they do in larger sizes. This is due to: (pp. 238-239)
   a. the grain of mental space
   b. the blurriness of mental space
   c. the ambiguity of mental images
   d. the spatial extent of the object

4. Which of the following would be at the basic level of the category? (pp. 242-243)
   a. furniture
   b. chair
   c. objects
   d. Swedish massage chair

5. Your textbook defines a problem as: (p. 243)
   a. self created obstacles
   b. a complex interconnected phenomenon
   c. an obstacle that must be overcome to reach a goal
   d. a conscious decision

6. One way to solve a problem is to take a short-cut and look at only a few ways to solve it. This is called: (p. 244)
   a. an algorithm
   b. a heuristic
   c. a mental set
   d. functional fixedness

7. According to your textbook the first intelligence test was created by _____. (p. 253)
   a. Lewis Terman
   b. Binet and Simon
   c. Wecshler
   d. Thurston

8. William Stern's formula for IQ was (MA/CA) X 100. MA is _____. (p. 255)
   a. your mean age
   b. your chronological age minus 10
   c. your mental age
   d. your math ability

9. For the WAIS-III, the _____ is 100, and the _____ is 15. (p. 255)
    a. mean; standard deviation
    b. standard deviation; mean
    c. distribution; variance
    d. norm; difference

10. In Spearman's theory of intelligence, g and s are _____. (pp. 257-258)
    a. highly correlated
    b. distinct from one another
    c. measures of general ability
    d. two types of crystallized intelligence

11. Factor analyses of the correlations among different measures of performance show that _____ is/are one of the important factor in many tasks related to intelligence. (p. 257)
    a. speed of processing
    b. genetics
    c. head size
    d. reaction ranges

12. Gardner's theory is very appealing, but a major problem is that _____. (pp. 261-262)
    a. it is based solely on brain damage
    b. it only applies to Western society
    c. there is currently no way to measure all the separate intelligences, making the theory impossible to test rigorously
    d. some children have only one intelligence

13. Sternberg's sub-theory of creative intelligence is closely related to what other type of intelligence? (p. 263)
    a. Thurston's primary ability
    b. Gardner's naturalistic intelligence
    c. Cattell and Horn's fluid intelligence
    d. Carroll's three-strata

14. Most researchers would agree that intelligence is _____. (p. 266)
    a. about 90% genetic and 10 environmental
    b. about 50% genetic and 10% environmental
    c. about 50% genetic and close to 50% environmental
    d. almost completely environmental

15. Consider the statement that the most important aspect of creativity is the unconstrained and unstructured freedom to make creative choices. Does the research in your book agree with this statement? (pp. 279-280)
    a. yes, creativity is hurt by any constraint
    b. no, structure can sometimes help creativity
    c. no, creativity always requires high levels of structure
    d. yes, creativity IS the lack of structure

Short-Answer/Essay Questions

Answer the following questions in the space provided.

1. What evidence exists that mental imagery is similar to perception? _____

_____

_____

_____

_____

_____

_____

_____

_____

2. Imagine that you lost your lecture notes. Use an algorithm and a heuristic to find them. _____

_____

_____

_____

_____

_____

_____

_____

_____

3. Outline the means to overcoming obstacles to problem solving listed in your textbook. _____

_____

_____

_____

_____

_____

_____

_____

4. Outline the history of intelligence testing. _____

_____

_____

_____

_____

_____

_____

_____

5. Which aspects of Carroll's model are generally accepted and which are not? _____

_____

_____

_____

_____

_____

_____

_____

_____

6. What are the main components and criticisms of Sternberg's theory? _____

_____

_____

_____

_____

_____

_____

_____

When You Are Finished . . . Puzzle It Out

Across

3. Type of studies used to study genetic roles
4. Child with immense talent in one area
5. Type of memory related to fluid intelligence
6. Cattell's problem-solving type of intelligence
8. One explanation for racial differences in IQ
13. Guarantees a solution to a problem
16. Number of morphemes in "reread"
17. Earliest, simplest sentence
19. Grammatical structure of sentence

Puzzle created with Puzzlemaker at DiscoverySchool.com.

Down

1. Theory saying language comes from learning
2. Statistical analysis used in developing IQ tests
7. Said there was one g and multiple s's
8. Hormone implicated in spatial ability
9. Meaning of a word or sentence
10. Said there are 8-9 intelligences
11. Ability to produce original thinking
12. Setting the mean and SD of a test
14. People who have IQs of 135+
15. Rule of thumb
18. Basic building block of speech

Chapter 7
Emotion and Motivation: Feeling and Striving

Before You Read . . .

How are you feeling right now: Happy? Excited? Bored? Angry? Why do you feel that way? In this chapter, you will gain an overview of emotion, ranging from basic emotions to more complex ones. You will also learn about several theories of the causes of emotion and examine the evidence that supports or refutes them. Of special interest will be the role of cognition in emotion.

The chapter then moves to motivation—that is, the needs and wants of humans and animals. The concepts of drives and incentives, being pushed away from and pulled toward certain events, are explained, as are the different needs of people. The needs for achievement and cognition are examined in greater detail. Lastly, the motivations of eating and sex are set out in separate sections, with the reasons why we eat and have sex being discussed.

Chapter Objectives

After reading this chapter, you will be able to:

- Name the different emotions.

- Understand what causes emotion.

- Explain how culture affects our emotional lives.

- Name the sources of motivation.

- Explain the differences between "needs" and "wants" and describe how culture affects them.

- Explain the nature of sexual response.

- Understand what determines whether we are attracted to the same sex or the opposite sex.

As You Read . . . Term Identification

Make flashcards using the following terms as you go. Use the definitions in the margins of this chapter for help. If you write the definitions in your own words, though, you will remember them better!

Androgens
Basic emotion
Bisexual
Collectivist culture
Deprived reward
Display rule
Drive
Emotion
Estrogens
Facial feedback hypothesis
Heterosexual
Homeostasis
Homosexual
Implicit motive
Incentive

Individualist culture
Instinct
Insulin
Learned helplessness
Metabolism
Misattribution of arousal
Motivation
Need
Need for achievement (nAch)
Nondeprived reward
Polygraph
Set point
Sexual response cycle
Want

As You Read . . . Questions and Exercises

Emotion: I Feel, Therefore I Am

Types of Emotions: What Can You Feel?

Before reading this section, list below the various <u>distinct</u> **emotions** you believe individuals have.

_____

_____

_____

_____

What did Ekman and Friesen (1971) find when they showed the Caucasian facial expressions of emotion to members of a New Guinea tribe? _____

_____

_____

_____

_____

_____

_____

_____

What are the six **basic emotions** as outlined by Ekman (1984)?

- _____
- _____
- _____
- _____
- _____
- _____

Does your list differ from Ekman's? How so? _____
_____
_____
_____

Describe three challenges to Ekman's finding that there are six basic, innate **emotions**.

- _____
  _____
  _____
  _____

- _____
  _____
  _____
  _____

- _____
  _____
  _____
  _____

Define approach and withdrawal **emotions.** Which parts of the brain do these emotions activate?

Approach: _____
_____

Withdrawal: _____
_____
_____

Complete the following chart to indicate which hemisphere is more active in each of the following populations.

Population	More Active Hemisphere
People who have approach emotions	
People who have withdrawal emotions	
People who have a rosier outlook on life	
People who have clinical depression	

What Causes Emotions?

Complete the following paragraph, which contrasts the various theories of emotion. The earliest theory of emotion, put forth by _____ and _____, argued that emotions arise *after* your body reacts—that different emotions arise from different sets of bodily reactions. In 1927, Cannon and Bard argued that _____ and _____ occur in tandem, arising at the same time. The _____ theory, by contrast, holds that we interpret situations differently, which gives rise to different emotions. But Joseph LeDoux (1996) argued that interpretation takes place only for emotions such as _____, not for other emotions such as _____, because these emotions arise from different parts of the brain. Other modern researchers claim that people's brain and body reactions produce _____, or "simplest raw feelings," which are then categorized. Categories may be based on _____ and _____.

Since the leading theories of **emotion** have been posited, evidence has been found that casts doubt on their veracity. For each of the theories below, indicate what evidence serves to refute it:

Theory	Evidence to Refute
James–Lange	
Cannon–Bard	
Cognitive interpretation	

What is the **facial feedback hypothesis?** How can you use it in your daily life? _____

_____

_____

_____

What are the four important findings about fear that researchers have discovered?

- _____
  _____
  _____

- _____
  _____
  _____

- _____
  _____
  _____

- _____
  _____
  _____

How do these four findings about fear support the following theories?

Theory	Support
James–Lange	
Cannon–Bard	
Cognitive	

Which theory of **emotion** best explains fear? Why? _____
_____
_____
_____

List the factors involved in happiness among Americans.

- _____
- _____
- _____
- _____
- _____
- _____
- _____
- _____

List the benefits of having positive states of mind.

- _____
- _____
- _____
- _____
- _____
- _____
- _____

Expressing Emotions: Letting It All Hang Out?

For the following situations, define which **display rules** are present.

Situation	Display Rules
A bar	
A funeral	
A classroom	
Thanksgiving dinner at home	
A football game	

Can people control their **emotions?** Why is this important? _____

_____

_____

_____

_____

GO SURFING . . .

...at the following sites and take one of the road rage tests there:

- http://webhome.idirect.com/~kehamilt/rage.htm
- http://www.aaafoundation.org/quizzes/index.cfm?button=aggressive
- http://www.roadrageiq.org/home.asp

What do these tests say about you? Do you "let it all hang out" on the road? _____

_____

Which areas of the brain appear to be involved in emotional regulation? _____

_____

If so, what are some ways that you could try to control your road rage in the future? _____

_____

_____

_____

Perceiving Emotions: A Form of Mind Reading

List the variables that affect how good people are at reading **emotions.**

- _____
- _____
- _____
- _____
- _____

Looking at Levels: Lie Detection

Suppose you were falsely accused of committing a crime. If the police offered you the opportunity to take a **polygraph** to demonstrate your innocence, would you take it? Why or why not? _____
_____
_____
_____

Which technique would you want the police to use? Why? _____
_____
_____
_____

Why is it so difficult to detect lies? _____
_____
_____
_____

What cues do you (and others) use to detect whether someone is lying? _____
_____
_____
_____

What does the **polygraph** really detect? _____

Why may a **polygraph** fail to detect a lie? _____
_____
_____
_____

Motivation and Reward: More Than Feeling Good

Getting Motivated: Sources and Theories of Motivation

Describe the focus of the following theories of **motivation.**

Theory	Focus
Instinct theory	
Evolutionary theory	
Drive theory	
Arousal theory	

What is the **drive** that motivates you to:

- Drink alcohol? _____
- Go to a party? _____
- Eat chocolate? _____
- Study for a test? _____

Graph and explain the Yerkes–Dodson law.

_____
_____
_____
_____

GO SURFING . . .

. . .to discover how much arousal you need in your life. Take the following test, at the following site:

- **Sensation Seeking Scale**
  http://www.bbc.co.uk/science/humanbody/mind/sensation/

What do the results of this test say about your need for arousal? How do you see this need in your everyday life? How can you modify your life to meet the level of your needs for arousal?

_____
_____
_____
_____
_____
_____

What expectations for reinforcement do you have, and how do these expectations affect your behavior? _____
_____
_____
_____
_____
_____

How is the brain involved in expectations for reinforcement and in determining what is an **incentive**? _____
_____
_____
_____

Which of the following are **drive-related motivations**, and which are **incentive-related motivations?**

Sex	drive-related	**OR**	incentive-related
Food	drive-related	**OR**	incentive-related
Praise	drive-related	**OR**	incentive-related
Money	drive-related	**OR**	incentive-related
Water	drive-related	**OR**	incentive-related

How can **learned helplessness** explain why some people stay in abusive relationships?

_____
_____
_____
_____

What are the possible long-term consequences of **learned helplessness?** _____
_____
_____

Needs and Wants: The Stick and the Carrot

Describe a time when you have been motivated by a **deprived reward.** _____
_____
_____
_____

How is the brain involved in **deprived rewards?** _____
_____
_____
_____

Describe a time when you have been motivated by a **nondeprived reward.** _____
_____
_____
_____

How is the brain involved in **nondeprived rewards**? _____

_____

_____

_____

_____

GO SURFING . . .

…to discover what various scales say about your motivations:

- **Entrepreneur Test**
  http://www.liraz.com/webquiz.htm
- **Need for Cognition Scale**
  http://www.prenhall.com/divisions/hss/app/social/chap7_2.html

Based on the results of these tests, what do you think **motivates** you? What doesn't? _____

_____

_____

The following list includes **needs** as proposed by researchers. Given your results on the preceding surveys, rank-order these **needs** in terms of importance to you (i.e., "1" would indicate the need that is most important to you).

The need to be competent   _____

The need to be autonomous   _____

The need to have social approval   _____

The need to be dominant   _____

The need for affiliation   _____

The need to be powerful   _____

The need for closure   _____

The need to understand   _____

The need to maintain self-esteem   _____

The need to find the world
 benevolent   _____

The need for achievement   _____

Do you agree with the priorities established by this list? Why or why not? _____

_____

_____

_____

_____

How can you use knowledge of your **motivations** in everyday life? _____
_____
_____
_____
_____

List the seven needs as outlined by Maslow, from lowest to highest:

- _____
- _____
- _____
- _____
- _____
- _____
- _____

What evidence do we have that casts doubt on Maslow's theory? _____
_____
_____
_____
_____
_____

People in **individualist cultures** have stronger needs for _____, but they also
_____.

Hunger and Sex: Two Important Motivations

Eating Behavior: The Hungry Mind in the Hungry Body

There are two distinct brain systems involved in eating.

- **One system leads you to feel a need to eat.**
  This feeling arises when your brain senses that one of two types of food molecules is too low:
    - _____ or
    - _____.

- **The other system leads you to feel full.**
  This feeling arises because of signals sent by the _____ in the
  _____ to the brain.

What role does lateral hypothalamus play in eating behaviors? _____
_____
_____
_____
_____

What role does the ventromedial hypothalamus play in eating behaviors? _____
_____
_____
_____
_____

What role does learning play in eating behaviors? _____
_____
_____
_____
_____

What effect do the following factors have on the size and/or timing of your appetite?

Factor	Effect
Opioids	
Changes in flavor, texture, color, or shape of food	
Presence of other people	
Insulin	
Culture	
Memory	
The clock/time of day	

Overeating: When Enough Is Not Enough

Using the terms **set point** and **metabolism,** explain why dieting can actually lead to eventual increases in weight rather than to decreases. _____
_____
_____
_____
_____

What is your **set point?** _____

How firmly set is a **set point**? _____
_____
_____
_____
_____

GO SURFING . . .

...to discover to find your current and ideal body mass index. Visit one of the following sites:

- **National Heart, Lung and Blood Institute**
  http://nhlbisupport.com/bmi/bmicalc.htm
- **Total Health Dynamics**
  http://www.totalhealthdynamics.com/bodymass.htm

The maximum recommended BMI is 24.9. What is your BMI? _____

Use the charts on the Web site to calculate how many pounds you would have to gain or lose to reach a BMI of 24.9. How many? _____

What is the best way that you could gain or lose this weight? _____
_____
_____
_____
_____
_____
_____

For each reason given below, provide the various explanations for obesity.

Reason	Explanation
Psychodynamic theory	
Genetics	

Reason	Explanation
Environmental factors	

Dieting

Have you ever dieted? If so, which diets have you tried? _____
_____
_____
_____
_____

What is the most commonly recommended diet for obese people? _____
_____
_____
_____
_____

What were the long-term effects of this diet? _____
_____
_____
_____
_____

As your textbook points out, the science of dieting is clear. To lose weight, you must do two things. What are they?

- _____
- _____

Sexual Behavior: A Many-Splendored Thing

Would you volunteer to be in a study of sexual behavior? Why or why not? _____
_____
_____
_____
_____

How are volunteers in sexual behavior studies different from non-volunteers? _____
_____
_____
_____

What does this mean for the validity of the studies? _____

_____

_____

_____

_____

Fill in the arrows, indicating a comprehensive description of the **sexual response cycle.** Provide a brief description of each of the stages.

```
┌─────────────────────────┐
│                         │
│                         │
│                         │
└─────────────────────────┘
            ↓
┌─────────────────────────┐
│                         │
│                         │
│                         │
└─────────────────────────┘
            ↓
┌─────────────────────────┐
│                         │
│                         │
│                         │
└─────────────────────────┘
            ↓
┌─────────────────────────┐
│                         │
│                         │
│                         │
└─────────────────────────┘
```

Fill in the blanks in the following paragraph.

Hormones are _____ that trigger _____ on neurons and other types of cells. Hormones are controlled largely by the _____, which in turn is controlled by the _____. Hormones are secreted into the bloodstream by the _____.

Testosterone is one male hormone. The "male hormones," _____, have the following effects:

- _____
- _____

The "female hormones," or _____, cause many characteristics, including:

- _____
- _____

What type of hormone(s) do you have in your body? _____
_____

What is the role of hormones in behavior? _____
_____

Describe androgen insensitivity syndrome. _____
_____
_____
_____
_____
_____

Women's sex hormones change over the course of their menstrual cycles. This has the following effects:

- _____
  _____
- _____
  _____
  _____
- _____
  _____

How do the testosterone levels of married and single men compare? _____
_____
_____
_____
_____
_____
_____

How does oxytocin affect people's sex lives? _____
_____
_____
_____
_____
_____
_____

Sexual Stimuli

Describe the different motives that people have for having sex, including the two dimensions described by Cooper and colleagues. _____
_____
_____
_____

The evolutionary theory suggests that men should be more interested in short-term sex and less particular about mates; females, who are typically very invested in nurturing and raising children, should have opposite preferences. What evidence supports this theory? _____

_____

_____

_____

Another evolutionary theory suggests that men are particularly alert to their female partners' sexual infidelity because men can never be absolutely certain that a baby is theirs. What evidence supports this theory? _____

_____

_____

_____

How do researchers avoid problems of social desirability in studies of participants' judgments about preferred characteristics in mates? _____

_____

Sexual Orientation: More Than a Choice

What evidence supports the idea that sexual orientation has a biological basis?

- _____
  _____
  _____

- _____
  _____

- _____
  _____

- _____
  _____

- _____
  _____

After You Read . . . Thinking Back

1. In Chapter 2, you learned about how people sense and perceive. How do you think people's emotions affect what they sense and perceive? _____
    _____
    _____
    _____
    _____

2. How is classical conditioning involved in emotions? _____
    _____
    _____
    _____
    _____

3. How does emotion affect memory? _____
    _____
    _____
    _____
    _____

4. Does memory also affect emotion? If so, how? _____
    _____
    _____
    _____
    _____

5. Is there a relationship between intelligence scores and motivation? If so, what types of
    motivation? _____
    _____
    _____
    _____
    _____

6. How is learning involved in motivation? _____
    _____
    _____
    _____
    _____

7. Which other aspects of emotions, besides control of them, are involved in emotional
    intelligence? _____
    _____
    _____
    _____
    _____

After You Read . . . Thinking Ahead

1. How do you think children might develop emotional control? _____

   _____

   _____

   _____

   _____

2. How do you think children develop knowledge of display rules? _____

   _____

   _____

   _____

   _____

3. Do you think emotions affect health? If so, in a positive or a negative way? _____

   _____

   _____

   _____

   _____

4. How do you know when emotions are normal versus when they have become a disorder (e.g., depression)? _____

   _____

   _____

   _____

   _____

5. How might knowing whether cognition precedes emotion assist a therapist in treating a psychological disorder? _____

   _____

   _____

   _____

6. How do our social groups influence our happiness? _____

   _____

   _____

   _____

   _____

7. What can parents do to motivate children without pressuring them? _____

   _____

   _____

   _____

   _____

After You Read . . . Practice Tests

PRACTICE TEST #1

Multiple-Choice Questions

For each question, circle the best answer from the choices given.

1. A psychological state that includes subjective experience, bodily arousal, overt behavior and specific mental processes is called _____. (p. 289)
   a. a motive
   b. a drive
   c. an emotion
   d. an instinct

2. _____ theory argues that an emotion arises when you interpret a situation, not when you notice your bodily arousal. (p. 293)
   a. Cannon-Bard
   b. Cognitive
   c. James-Lange
   d. Control

3. Your text suggests that effective coping strategies are promoted by _____. (pp. 298-299)
   a. internal motives
   b. external values
   c. positive emotions
   d. negative emotions

4. According to your text, the internal imbalance that causes us to strive to achieve a particular goal that will reduce that imbalance is called: (p. 308)
   a. a drive
   b. an instinct
   c. a motive
   d. an emotion

5. Which of the following is NOT a basic psychological need, according to your text? (p. 312)
   a. achievement
   b. affiliation with others
   c. dominance/control
   d. food and water

6. The _____ contains detectors that register the food value of what we eat and transmit this information to the brain. (p. 315)
   a. large intestine
   b. small intestine
   c. stomach
   d. esophagus

7. Carol periodically gains or loses a little weight from dieting, but she seems to revert right back to the same weight as soon as she stops dieting. When she stops dieting, Carol's body is probably reverting to her _____. (p. 318)
   a. metabolism
   b. set point
   c. ideal weight
   d. goal weight

8. Which statement is true regarding the findings of Masters and Johnson? (p. 321)
   a. Men and women are different in their bodily reactions to sex.
   b. Women do not tend to stay aroused as long as men do.
   c. Both men and women can easily have multiple orgasms, if their partners are experienced.
   d. Women reported that penis size is not related to sexual performance unless the man is worried about it.

PRACTICE TEST #2

Multiple-Choice Questions

For each question, circle the best answer from the choices given.

1. Which theory suggests that emotions arise simply because of our internal recognition of different body states? (pp. 292-293)
   a. Cannon-Bard
   b. James-Lange
   c. Cognitive
   d. LeDoux

2. Which statement is true regarding happiness? (p. 299)
   a. Individuals' personalities affect their happiness.
   b. Nonassertive people tend to be happier than assertive people.
   c. Introverts tend to be happier than extroverts.
   d. People with more activation in the right frontal lobe tend to be happier than people with more activation in the left frontal lobe.

3. A(n) _____ an inherited tendency to produce organized and unalterable responses to particular stimuli. (p. 307)
   a. instinct
   b. drive
   c. stasis
   d. motive

4. Sarah has a compact car but really wishes she had an SUV. Sarah's desire for an SUV would fit the description of a(n) _____. (p. 310)
   a. need
   b. want
   c. implicit desire
   d. deprived reward

5. Elizabeth is twelve years old. Like her friends, her breasts are developing. Biologically, this is attributed to the hormone _____. (p. 468)
   a. androgen
   b. testosterone
   c. estrogen
   d. progesterone

6. _____ is the hormone that is thought to assist in mother-child bonding. (p. 470)
   a. Progesterone
   b. Estrogen
   c. Oxytocin
   d. Androgen

7. One theorist argues that men typically invest less in child rearing and are more interested in short-term sex—thus being less particular about mates. This theory is known as _____. (p. 471)
    a. sexual preference
    b. parental investment
    c. mate selection
    d. short-term selection

PRACTICE TEST #3

Multiple-Choice Questions

For each question, circle the best answer from the choices given.

1. The four components of emotion are: _____, characteristic overt behavior, activation of specific mental processes and bodily arousal. (p. 289)
   a. a positive or negative subjective experience
   b. learned behavior
   c. classical conditioning
   d. operant conditioning

2. The emerging synthesis discussed in your chapter suggests that emotion is the result of a.) interpretations and memories that pertain to the situation and b.) _____. (pp. 293-294)
   a. operant conditioning
   b. independent thought
   c. cognitive appraisals
   d. brain and body reactions

3. Which of the following statements regarding fear is true? (p. 297)
   a. After you learn to fear an object, you must think about it to fear it in the future.
   b. Fear is a response only of bodily arousal – such as the activation of the amygdala.
   c. Evidence suggests that once you learn to associate fear with an object, you will always do so.
   d. Once you become afraid, you are less susceptible to a fear-potentiated startle.

4. According to your text, being happy is one focus of what is called _____. (p. 299)
   a. social psychology
   b. positive psychology
   c. cognitive psychology
   d. emotional psychology

5. The very existence of display rules supports the idea that: (p. 300)
   a. individuals have little control over their emotions.
   b. culture is not particularly relevant to emotions.
   c. we have at least some voluntary control over our emotions.
   d. controlling our emotions is irrelevant to culture.

6. Sarah is working hard to improve her time in the back stroke so that she can qualify for a college athletic scholarship. In this case, the scholarship is considered to be a(n) _____. (p. 309)
   a. conditioned stimulus
   b. incentive
   c. basic need
   d. neutral stimulus

COMPREHENSIVE PRACTICE TEST

True/False Questions

Circle TRUE or FALSE for each of the following statements.

1.   TRUE   FALSE   Charles Darwin believed that our basic emotions are learned. (p. 290)

2.   TRUE   FALSE   According to facial feedback hypothesis, if you force yourself to smile, you might actually feel a little happier. (p. 295)

3.   TRUE   FALSE   Body language is rarely affected by culture. (p. 300)

4.   TRUE   FALSE   Stiff body posture combined withy direct eye contact is often a sign of deception. (p. 304)

5.   TRUE   FALSE   A condition that arises from the lack of a requirement is called a need. (p. 310)

6.   TRUE   FALSE   Someone who is more than 20% over their ideal weight is considered to be obese. (p. 318)

7.   TRUE   FALSE   The stages of the sexual response cycle have sharp divisions that distinguish them from each other. (p. 321)

8.   TRUE   FALSE   According to one study, in homosexual men, a particular part of the hypothalamus was found to be half the size of the same part in heterosexual men. (pp. 324-325)

Multiple-Choice Questions

For each question, circle the best answer from the choices given.

1. Which of the following is considered to be a basic emotion? (p. 290)
    a. indifference
    b. depression
    c. anxiety
    d. disgust

2. Overt behavior and bodily arousal are two of the four components of _____. (p. 289)
    a. motivation
    b. incentive
    c. emotion
    d. learning

3. Your text identifies _____ basic emotions that appear to be innate and shared by all humans. (p. 290)
   a. four
   b. five
   c. six
   d. seven

4. Love is a _____ emotion, while disgust is a _____ emotion. (p. 292)
   a. complex; simple
   b. simple; complex
   c. approach; withdrawal
   d. impressive; depressive

5. Tanisha saw her old boyfriend in the parking lot. Her heart began to race and her mouth went dry. Based on her bodily responses, she wasn't really sure if she was excited or frightened to see him. This situation is called _____. (p. 296)
   a. cognitive reinterpretation
   b. misattribution of arousal
   c. attribution theory
   d. physiological feedback hypothesis

6. With regard to fear, which statement is true? (pp. 297-298)
   a. The biological changes associated with fear are not distinct events.
   b. Emotions such as fear can be identified with the activation of a single area of the brain.
   c. The amygdala plays a direct role in producing the "emotional feel" associated with fear.
   d. Fear is typically the strongest emotion.

7. Which lie-detector technique uses neutral questions along with questions related directly to the crime in question? (p. 303)
   a. guilty knowledge test
   b. relevant/irrelevant technique
   c. guilty actions test
   d. control question technique

8. According to Yerkes-Dodson Law, we prefer _____ level of arousal. (p. 308)
   a. an intermittent
   b. an intermediate
   c. a conditioned
   d. a complex

9. Greg has a teacher who is constantly criticizing his work. No matter how hard he tries or what he does, he seems to stay on his teacher's "bad side." Finally Greg just gives up trying to please that teacher. He says it was hopeless anyway, so why bother. Greg's attitude represents _____. (p. 310)
   a. heightened arousal
   b. learned helplessness
   c. Yerkes-Dodson Law
   d. LeDoux's theory

10. Which type of sugar is one of the basic food molecules registered by the brain? (p. 315)
    a. sucrose
    b. fructose
    c. sorbitol
    d. glucose

11. Your text suggests that at least _____ percent of Americans are either overweight or obese. (p. 318)
    a. 31
    b. 34
    c. 65
    d. 69

12. With regard to diets, which statement is FALSE? (p. 465)
    a. Overweight people lost modest amounts of weight when following any of four popular diets.
    b. Low carbohydrate diets lead obese people to lose more weight than standard diets.
    c. In research studies, at least one third of the people who began did not stick to the diets.
    d. The most commonly recommended diet for obese people requires cutting their normal food intake in half.

13. Motivation for sex is thought to fall along two dimensions: self/social and _____. (p. 323)
    a. introvert/extrovert
    b. stimulus/response
    c. avoidance/approach
    d. hetero/homosexual

Short-Answer/Essay Questions

Answer the following questions in the space provided.

1. Compare and contrast James-Lange theory with the cognitive theory of emotion. _____
   _____
   _____
   _____
   _____
   _____
   _____
   _____

2. Based on research of the brain's systems, what are the four important conclusions drawn about fear? _____
   _____
   _____
   _____
   _____
   _____
   _____

3. Your text lists three reasons that emotional regulation is important. Give a brief, substantive explanation of one of them. _____

_____

_____

_____

_____

_____

_____

_____

4. What is learned helplessness? _____

_____

_____

_____

_____

_____

_____

5. Summarize the four general conclusions drawn by Masters and Johnson regarding human sexuality. _____

_____

_____

_____

_____

_____

_____

When You Are Finished . . . Puzzle It Out

Puzzle created with Puzzlemaker at DiscoverySchool.com.

Across

1. Maintaining a steady state
7. A draw toward a goal
9. Internal imbalance pushing toward a goal
12. Proposed hierarchy of motivation
17. Female hormones
18. Emotions that are generally positive
20. Motive that is unconscious

Down

2. Being 20% above ideal weight
3. Highest of Maslow's levels
4. Rules about showing emotions
5. Male hormones
6. Arises from lack of requirement
8. Proposed most accepted emotion theory
10. First researcher to discover basic emotions
11. Hormone that stimulates fat storage
13. Person attracted to both sexes
14. Turns goals into incentives
15. Commonly known as a lie detector
16. Body weight easiest to maintain
19. Number of basic emotions, as proposed by answer 1

Chapter 8
Personality: Vive la Différence!

Before You Read . . .

Are you the same person with your parents as you are with your best friend? How are you the same or different? In this chapter, you will learn about personality, including how and why it changes. You will also learn more about how different types of personalities can be described and how personality is measured.

In addition, you will apply the three levels of analysis to personality. As you will see, personality has its roots in genetics, but is also affected by a variety of personal characteristics. You will learn how psychodynamic theorists, humanistic psychologists, cognitive psychologists, and behaviorists believe that personality is formed. Finally, you will review some of the environmental factors that may affect personality, including birth order, peer influences, and culture.

Chapter Objectives

After reading this chapter, you should be able to:

- Explain and critique Freud's view of personality, including the three parts of personality, the stages of development, and defense mechanisms.

- Summarize the humanistic theory of personality.

- Define personality.

- Describe the roles of traits and situations and how they interact in forming personality.

- Describe the number of dimensions in the various models of personality.

- Explain the different ways that personality can be measured, and the pros and cons of each of these methods.

- Define temperament, and describe different types of temperaments.

- Describe the role that genetics plays in personality.

- Compare biologically based theories of personality.

- Describe learning theorists' view of personality.

- Discuss the sociocognitive view of personality.

- Discuss the role of family, peers, birth order, gender, and culture on personality.

As You Read . . . Term Identification

Make flashcards using the following terms as you go. Use the definitions in the margins of this chapter for help. If you write the definitions in your own words, though, you will remember them better!

Activity
Big Five
Castration anxiety
Defense mechanism
Ego
Emotionality
Expectancies
Id
Impulsivity
Locus of control
Minnesota Multiphasic Personality
   Inventory-2 (MMPI-2)
Neurosis
Personality

Personality inventory
Personality trait
Projective test
Psychological determinism
Psychosexual stages
Repression
Rorschach test
Self-actualization
Self-efficacy
Sociability
Social desirability
Superego
Temperament
Thematic Apperception Test (TAT)
Unconditional positive regard

As You Read . . . Questions and Exercises

Personality is a set of _____, _____, and _____ tendencies that people display _____ and _____ and that distinguish individuals from each other.

Personality traits are consistent characteristics exhibited in different situations. Name some of your personality characteristics that you think are consistent:

- _____
- _____
- _____
- _____
- _____

Personality: Historical Perspectives

Freud's Theory: The Dynamic Personality

According to Freud, in what part of your **consciousness** would the following information be found?

Information	Part of Consciousness
Your favorite color	
Feelings of aggression toward your teacher	
What you did on your last birthday	
Sexual feelings for your parent	
The name of your roommate	
Your mother's maiden name	

According to Freud, which part of your **personality** would be responsible for the following behaviors?

Behavior	Part of Personality
Delaying gratification	
Making you feel guilty	
Balancing reality and needs	
Eating a gallon of ice cream	
Telling you something is morally wrong	
Screaming when you're angry	

Describe the **developmental tasks** and **consequences of fixation** (if any) for each of the following stages of development:

Stage	Developmental Task
Oral	
Anal	
Phallic	
Latency	
Genital	

Describe the **Oedipus** and **Electra complexes** as explained by psychodynamic theory. _____

_____
_____
_____
_____
_____
_____
_____
_____
_____
_____
_____

Give an example from your own life of each of the **common defense mechanisms** listed below:

Defense Mechanism	Example
Denial	
Intellectualization	
Projection	
Rationalization	
Reaction formation	
Repression	
Sublimation	
Undoing	

For each of the following theorists, describe his or her unique contribution to the understanding of **personality development:**

Theorist	Contribution
Carl Jung	
Alfred Adler	
Karen Horney	

Name three criticisms of the **psychodynamic theory** of personality development.

- _____

- _____

- _____

Name three aspects of **psychodynamic theory** that have been supported.

- _____

- _____

- _____

Humanistic Psychology: Thinking Positively

Unlike psychodynamic theorists, humanistic theorists focus on the positive aspects of the individual. They say people have a drive toward **self-actualization,** which is _____

_____

Do you know anyone who you believe is **self-actualized**? Describe him or her. What characteristics does this person have that makes you think he or she is self-actualized? (If you don't know anyone who is self-actualized, just write the characteristics of self-actualized people.) _____

_____

What are the criticisms of the **humanistic theory** of personality? _____

_____

What Exactly *Is* Personality?

Personality: Traits and Situations

Some theorists say that personality is largely determined by situations. Think of a characteristic that you display in some situations, but not in others. Explain. What determines whether or not you display this characteristic? _____

_____

_____

_____

_____

_____

What is the advantage to defining a personality trait narrowly? _____

_____

_____

What is the disadvantage to defining a personality trait narrowly? _____

_____

_____

Interactionism says that there is an interaction between the person and the situation. What are the three major ways that personality affects situations?

- _____
  _____
- _____
  _____
- _____
  _____

Factors of Personality: The Big Five? Three? More?

GO SURFING . . .

...to learn more about your personality. Take a Web version of the **NEO-PI-R,** which is used to measure the **Big Five** or the *Five Factor Model.* You can find it online at either of the following Web sites:

- http://www.personal.psu.edu/~j5j/IPIP
- http://www.outofservice.com/bigfive

How did you score on each of the following five **superfactors?**

- **Extraversion:** _____
- **Neuroticism:** _____
- **Agreeableness:** _____
- **Conscientiousness:** _____
- **Openness:** _____

List some of the **traits** that contribute to each of these **superfactors.**

- **Extraversion:** _____
  _____
- **Neuroticism:** _____
  _____
- **Agreeableness:** _____
  _____
- **Conscientiousness:** _____
  _____
- **Openness:** _____
  _____

Name two problems with the **superfactors** approach to personality.

- _____
  _____
- _____
  _____

Below are lists of the five **superfactors** of the **Five Factor Model** and **Eysenck**'s three superfactors. Draw lines between the factors that are similar to each other.

Five-Factor Model	**Eysenck's Three Personality Dimensions**
Extraversion	Extraversion
Neuroticism	Neuroticism
Agreeableness	Psychoticism
Conscientiousness	
Openness	

What would be a more accurate name for Eysenck's personality dimension of *psychoticism?* Why would this name be more accurate? _____
_____
_____

Measuring Personality: Is Grumpy Really Grumpy?

List the pros and cons of using the following types of personality assessments.

	Pros	Cons
Interviews		
Observation		
Inventories		
Projective test		

Read the following list of traits to a friend and ask how he or she thinks you would score on each **superfactor.** Write his or her predictions below.

- **Extraversion:** _____
- **Neuroticism:** _____
- **Agreeableness:** _____
- **Conscientiousness:** _____
- **Openness:** _____

How did your friend's observations compare with your results? Why do you think he or she was so accurate (or inaccurate)? Discuss. _____
_____
_____
_____

List three criticisms of the use of the **Rorschach test.**

- _____
_____
- _____
_____
- _____
_____

List two criticisms of the use of the **Thematic Apperception Test (TAT).**

- _____
  _____
- _____
  _____

How do some psychologists defend the use of the **TAT** and the **Rorschach test?** _____
_____
_____

Biology's Influences on Personality

Temperament: Waxing Hot or Cold

How is **temperament** different from **personality?** _____
_____
_____

CALL . . .

...a parent or someone who knew you when you were young. Ask him or her to describe what you were like at age three. Write his or her comments below. Be sure to ask specifically about the following dimensions.

- Your **sociability** (preference of being with others): _____
  _____

- Your **emotionality** (inclination to be aroused in emotional situations): _____
  _____

- Your **vigor** (intensity of activity): _____
  _____

- Your **tempo** (speed of activity): _____
  _____

- Your **impulsivity** (tendency to respond to stimuli immediately): _____
  _____

- Your **reactivity** (response to novel or challenging events): _____
  _____

- Your **self-regulation** (ability to control attention and inhibit responses): _____
_____
_____

- Other observations: _____
_____
_____

How are these dimensions of temperament similar to the **Big Five factors** of personality?
_____
_____
_____
_____
_____
_____

Longitudinal studies have found correlations between children's temperaments at age three and their personalities at age 18. Is this true of you? Why or why not? _____
_____
_____
_____
_____

What is the evidence that temperament is inherited? _____
_____
_____
_____

Do you know anyone who is shy? Name and describe this person. _____
_____
_____
_____

CALL . . .

...this person and ask this shy individual to describe what he or she was like as a child.

Report your findings here: _____
_____
_____
_____

Do this person's childhood experiences represent the research on shy children? _____
_____
_____
_____
_____

How might the environment have affected this person's shyness? _____
_____
_____
_____
_____

If you had a child who was shy, what would you do to help him or her overcome this shyness? _____
_____
_____
_____
_____

GO SURFING . . .

...to find out whether you are high or low in *sensation seeking*. Tests can be found online at the following Web sites:

- http://www.bbc.co.uk/science/humanbody/mind/sensation/
- http://www.dushkin.com/connectext/psy/ch09/survey9.mhtml

Are you high or low in **sensation seeking**? _____

Would these tests suggest that you like or don't like to take physical risks? _____
_____
_____

Do you or don't you like to take physical risks? _____
_____
_____

Compare and contrast the two biological systems proposed by Jeffrey Gray in the table below.

Characteristic	Behavioral Activation System (BAS)	Behavioral Inhibition System (BIS)
Basis of system		
Nickname for the system		
Associated Big Five superfactor and/or Eysenck dimension		
Feelings and behaviors triggered by the system		
Associated difficulties		

Eysenck has also proposed a biological basis for his three personality dimensions. In the table below, list the evidence that supports the idea that each element is a unique personality dimension.

Dimension	Supporting Evidence
Extraversion	
Neuroticism	
Psychoticism	

What are the four basic personality dimensions on which Cloninger and his colleagues propose that people differ?

- _____
- _____
- _____
- _____

Answer the following questions about Cloninger's **novelty seeking** dimension.

- What is another name for this dimension? _____
- What Big Five factors does this dimension correspond to? _____
  _____
- What brain pathway is this dimension related to? _____

Below is a list of the five **superfactors** of the **Five Factor Model**. In the second column, provide the corresponding dimensions of Zuckerman's *alternative five*.

Five Factor Model	Zuckerman's Alternative Five
Extraversion	_____
Neuroticism	_____
Agreeableness	_____
Conscientiousness	_____
Openness	_____

Genes and Personality: Born to Be Mild?

What does **MISTRA** stand for? What is it? Explain. _____
_____
_____
_____
_____

MISTRA has found substantial **heritability** for two of the Big Five factors:

- _____
- _____

In general, MISTRA and other studies have found that families do not play a large role in personality. However, several aspects of twin studies may compromise this finding. Describe two of them:

- _____
  _____
- _____
  _____

List some behaviors that researchers suggest may have genetic origins.

- _____
- _____
- _____
- _____
- _____
- _____

How do researchers believe that genes influence behaviors? _____
_____
_____
_____
_____
_____
_____

What is the difference between shared and nonshared environmental influences? Give an example of each from your own life. _____
_____
_____
_____
_____

Name two ways that genes may influence personality.

- _____
  _____
- _____
  _____

Learning and the Cognitive Elements of Personality

Learning to Have Personality: Genes Are Not Destiny

Describe how one of your personality traits may have its roots in classical conditioning.

_____
_____
_____
_____
_____
_____

Describe how one of your personality traits may have its roots in operant conditioning.

_____
_____
_____
_____
_____
_____

Describe how one of your personality traits may have its roots in observations.

_____
_____
_____
_____
_____
_____

Are the behaviorists' views of personality currently supported by research? Why or why not?

_____
_____
_____
_____
_____
_____

According to the sociocognitive perspective, how can personality be explained?

_____
_____
_____
_____
_____
_____

Give an example of the sociocognitive view of personality from your own life.

_____
_____
_____
_____
_____
_____

The Sociocognitive View of Personality: You Are What You Expect

Describe a situation in which you have **expectancies**. _____

_____
_____
_____
_____

How do these **expectancies** shape your thoughts, feelings, and behaviors—and hence your personality? _____

_____
_____
_____
_____
_____

GO SURFING . . .

...and take a **locus of control** test at one of the following sites:

- http://discoveryhealth.queendom.com/questions/lc_short_1.html
- http://www.dushkin.com/connectext/psy/ch11/survey11.mhtml
- http://www.psych.uncc.edu/pagoolka/LocusofControl-intro.html
- http://www.ballarat.edu.au/ard/bssh/psych/rot.htm

According to this test, do you have an **internal** or **external locus of control**?

_____

Describe someone who you believe has a strong **internal locus of control**. _____

_____
_____
_____
_____

Describe someone who you believe has a strong **external locus of control**. _____

_____
_____
_____

Do you think you have high **self-efficacy?** Support your answer. _____

_____
_____
_____

Are you **self-reflective?** Support your answer. _____

_____
_____
_____

Provide an example of how you self-regulate your behavior. _____
_____
_____
_____

Consider how you felt about your performance on your last exam. Using the following terms, describe how you interpreted your success (or failure!) and how your experience will affect how you study for your next exam.

Term	My Interpretation
Reinforcements	
Expectancies	
Locus of control	

Sociocultural Influences on Personality

Birth Order: Are You Number One?

Think of a family you know with at least three children (e.g., your own, one of your parent's, a friend's). In the table below, describe the firstborn, middle-born, and later-born children. Then, describe Sulloway's findings on the personalities of children with these different birth orders.

Birth Order	Your Example	Sulloway's Findings
Firstborn		
Middle-born(s)		
Later-born		

Sex Differences in Personality: Nature and Nurture

For each of the following **personality traits,** indicate with a mark in the appropriate column whether men or women have consistently displayed the trait *more*, or if there have been mixed or inconsistent findings (or if men and women don't differ on the trait).

Trait	More in Women	More in Men	Mixed, etc.
Social connectedness			
Individuality and autonomy			
Empathy			
Nurturing			
Assessing emotion			
Spotting deception			
Neuroticism			
Anger			
Aggression			
Assertiveness			

Describe how each of the following theories explains the sex differences in personality:

Theory	Explanation
Social role	
Expectancy effects	
Context	
Biological	

Culture and Personality

List four ways that personality has changed over time.

- _____
- _____
- _____
- _____

Describe some difficulties that arise in cross-cultural studies of personality. _____
_____
_____
_____

List the traits that distinguish **individualist** from **collectivist** cultures.

Individualist Cultures Are More . . .	Collectivist Cultures Are More . . .

List the traits that distinguish the personalities of people in **individualist** cultures from the personalities of people in **collectivist** cultures.

People from Individualist Cultures Are More . . .	People from Collectivist Cultures Are More . . .

Where are you from? _____

Is that area **individualistic** or **collectivistic?** _____

Looking at Levels: Attachment

In the chart below, describe how attachment styles arise and how they exert their influence, using the levels-of-analysis perspective.

	The Brain	The Person	The World
How attachment styles arise			
How attachment styles exert their influence			

After You Read . . . Thinking Back

1. Can you think of any ways to overcome the difficulties associated with response biases that are present in self-report methodologies, such as personality inventories? _____
    _____
    _____
    _____

2. How could the validity and reliability of personality inventories be established? Why is this important? _____
    _____
    _____
    _____

3. In Chapter 4, you learned about top-down and bottom-up processing. Which theory of personality best represents top-down processing? Explain. _____
    _____
    _____
    _____

4. Which theory best represents bottom-up processing? Explain. _____
    _____
    _____
    _____

5. In previous chapters, you examined evolutionary theories. What is the evolutionary theory of gender differences in personality? What are some of the criticisms of evolutionary theories?
    _____
    _____
    _____
    _____

6. Do you think there is any relationship between intelligence (discussed in Chapter 9) and personality? Why or why not? _____
    _____
    _____
    _____

After You Read . . . Thinking Ahead

1. Which types of early life experiences might shape temperament? How so? _____
   _____
   _____
   _____
   _____

2. What do you think might happen if a child of one temperament was born to parents with very
   different personalities? _____
   _____
   _____
   _____

3. Which types of temperamental dimensions would be more difficult for parents to cope with?
   Why? _____
   _____
   _____
   _____

4. Which personality variables would help a person cope with stress and/or improve his or her
   health? Explain. _____
   _____
   _____
   _____

5. There are several "personality disorders." What distinguishes a normal personality from a
   disordered one? Explain. _____
   _____
   _____
   _____

6. Do you think a personality disorder could be treated? Why or why not? If so, how?
   _____
   _____
   _____
   _____

After You Read . . . Practice Tests

PRACTICE TEST #1

Multiple-Choice Questions

For each question, circle the best answer from the choices given.

1. According to Freud, your normal awareness is called your _____. (p. 335)
   a. id
   b. ego
   c. conscious
   d. preconscious

2. Which theorist is most closely associated with the inferiority complex? (p. 338)
   a. Freud
   b. Jung
   c. Adler
   d. Horney

3. If you believe that you create your own circumstances, not just by your actions – but by who you are, then you follow the ideas associated with _____. (p. 342)
   a. interactionism
   b. situationism
   c. the id
   d. trait theory

4. Thirty personality traits from the Five-Factor Model are assessed by the _____. (p. 346)
   a. Cattell 16-pf
   b. MMPI-2
   c. NEO-PI-R
   d. TAT

5. According to the MISTRA study, which personality traits seem most likely to be affected by family environment? (p. 355)
   a. social closeness and positive emotionality
   b. extroversion and agreeableness
   c. social closeness and agreeableness
   d. extroversion and positive emotionality

6. Britt seems to have a sense that she can accomplish whatever she really sets her mind to. According to Bandura, Britt: (p. 361)
   a. has low self-esteem.
   b. has high self-efficacy.
   c. is narcissistic.
   d. has a superiority complex.

7. Compared to first and later-borns, middle children are: (p. 362)
    a. more responsible.
    b. more temperamental.
    c. more agreeable.
    d. more rebellious.

8. Which attachment style are American children LEAST likely to have? (pp. 367-369)
    a. secure
    b. anxious
    c. avoidant
    d. organized

9. Which statement about avoidantly attached children is true? (pp. 367-369)
    a. They require less time to remember sad occasions.
    b. They pay more attention to emotional events.
    c. They are likely to deny feelings of distress when their bodily responses suggest that they are distressed.
    d. They seem to encode more information when listening to someone speak about relationship issues.

PRACTICE TEST #2

Multiple-Choice Questions

For each question, circle the best answer from the choices given.

1. Grayson was asked for her social security number when he applied for a job. Freud would say that Grayson retrieved the information from his _____. (p. 335)
   a. superego
   b. conscious mind
   c. preconscious mind
   d. subconscious mind

2. Kayla ordered an ice cream sundae and a diet soda. She said that the ice cream treat was not as big of a deal since she was having a diet drink instead of a regular one. Which of Freud's defense mechanisms is Kayla falling back on? (p.337)
   a. denial
   b. rationalization
   c. intellectualization
   d. sublimation

3. How many personality traits did Cattell originally identify? (p. 344)
   a. three
   b. five
   c. twelve
   d. sixteen

4. Which of the following is a test generally used to measure psychopathology? (p. 346)
   a. Cattell 12-pf
   b. MMPI-2
   c. NEO-PI-R
   d. Five FM

5. Eysenck's theory suggests that extroverts have cortex responses that are: (p. 352)
   a. less easily aroused than introverts.
   b. more easily aroused than introverts.
   c. much larger than introverts.
   d. much smaller than introverts.

6. If your activity level is both low vigor and low tempo, then you are more likely to: (p. 357)
   a. spend time in group activities.
   b. spend time walking for exercise.
   c. watch TV alone.
   d. play poker with friends.

7. Which statement about culture and personality is true? (p. 367)
    a. Children in a given culture are socialized according to that culture's values.
    b. Social desirability bias prohibits us from answering personality tests in a deceptive manner.
    c. Temperaments are culturally – not genetically influenced.
    d. North American personalities have remained constant over time.

PRACTICE TEST #3

Multiple-Choice Questions

For each question, circle the best answer from the choices given.

1. The _____ is the seat of morality. (p. 335)
   a. conscious
   b. ego
   c. superego
   d. preconscious mind

2. A relatively consistent characteristic exhibited in different situations is called _____. (p. 341)
   a. personality
   b. a personality trait
   c. temperament
   d. a type of temperament

3. Eysenck's personality superfactors are: (p. 344)
   a. introversion, agreeableness and psychoticism.
   b. neuroticism, psychoticism and agreeableness.
   c. deviance, conformity and extroversion.
   d. extroversion, neuroticism and psychoticism.

4. The "inkblot test" refers to the _____. (p. 347)
   a. MMPI-2
   b. Cattell 16-pf
   c. Rorschach
   d. NEO-PI-R

5. Which statement about high-reactive infants is true? (p. 350)
   a. They tend to have slower heart rates.
   b. They are usually not as fussy than other babies.
   c. They have higher levels of cortisol.
   d. They prefer situation they lead to higher levels of arousal.

6. Sam loves to sky-dive and play games of chance. Mike does not particularly care for either activity. Cloninger would suggest that such differences in novelty seeking is: (p. 353)
   a. abnormal
   b. genetically determined
   c. caused by intellectual differences
   d. caused by family environmental influences

7. Which statement about heritability of personality is true? (p. 355)
   a. Not all traits are equally heritable.
   b. Genetic origins for specific trait behaviors are nonexistent.
   c. Neuroticism shows the highest level of heritability.
   d. Aggression shows the lowest level of heritability.

8. Compared to first and middle-born children, later-born children are: (p. 363)
   a. more rebellious.
   b. more assertive.
   c. more dominant.
   d. more adventurous.

COMPREHENSIVE PRACTICE TEST

True/False Questions

Circle TRUE or FALSE for each of the following statements.

1.   TRUE   FALSE   In Freud's view, more of your thoughts and feelings are in your unconscious than your conscious mind. (p. 335)

2.   TRUE   FALSE   Tess was angry with her boyfriend so she went to the gym and worked out for an extra hour. This is an example of the defense mechanism, displacement. (p. 337)

3.   TRUE   FALSE   Accepting another person without any conditions is what Carl Rogers called efficacy. (p. 340)

4.   TRUE   FALSE   The term *central traits* is most closely associated with Gordon Allport. (p. 342)

5.   TRUE   FALSE   Among the "Big Five," sociability is another term for extroversion. (p. 344)

6.   TRUE   FALSE   Highly reactive infants are likely to become inhibited and shy as older children. (p. 350)

7.   TRUE   FALSE   Most aspects of personality are affected by individual genes. (p. 355)

8.   TRUE   FALSE   Many American psychological terms do not translate well in other cultures, but it does not affect the outcome of some personality tests. (pp. 365-366)

Multiple-Choice Questions

For each question, circle the best answer from the choices given.

1. Freud believed that personality development progressed through and depended upon stages based on erogenous zones. These were called _____ stages. (p. 336)
   a. psychosocial
   b. psychosexual
   c. psychodynamic
   d. social-emotional

2. The highest emotional and intellectual potential recognized by Maslow is called _____. (p. 340)
   a. humanism
   b. spirituality
   c. self-actualization
   d. fulfillment

3. Which statement about personality traits is FALSE? (pp. 342-343)
   a. Over longer periods of time and over many similar situations, people become less consistent and traits are less evident.
   b. The more narrowly a trait is defined, the better it predicts behavior.
   c. Narrowly defined traits can be applied to limited situations.
   d. Personality affects situations and situations affect behavior.

4. Gary was shown detailed black and white drawings and asked to explain various elements of them. He was most likely taking the projective test called the _____. (p. 347)
   a. MMPI-2
   b. Rorschach
   c. TAT
   d. NEO-PI-R

5. Gray has proposed that many aspects of personality are best explained in terms of two biological systems known as the behavioral activation system and the: (p. 351)
   a. behavioral stimulation system.
   b. behavioral exhibition system.
   c. behavioral inhibition system.
   d. behavioral discrimination system.

6. Raine's study found that underarousal at age fifteen predicted _____ at age twenty-four in 75% of cases. (p. 353)
   a. criminality
   b. marriage
   c. homosexuality
   d. introversion

7. Which of Zuckerman's alternative five is associated with antisocial behavior? (p. 354)
   a. sociability
   b. neuroticism-anxiety
   c. impulsive sensation-seeking
   d. aggression-hostility

8. The results of the MISTRA study indicated that _____ has substantial heritability. (p. 355)
   a. agreeableness
   b. psychoticism
   c. extroversion
   d. social deviance

9. Ninth graders who believe that drinking will make them more popular are more likely to drink at an earlier age. This demonstrates the sociocognitive concept of _____. (p. 360)
   a. self-fulfilling prophesy
   b. self-efficacy
   c. expectancies
   d. peer pressure

10. Compared to middle and later-borns, first born children are: (p. 362)
    a. more sociable.
    b. more adventurous.
    c. more self-conscious.
    d. more responsible

11. Women tend to score higher on _____. (p. 364)
    a. autonomy
    b. social connectedness
    c. individuality
    d. assertiveness

12. According to your text, over time, college students are increasingly reporting: (p. 360)
    a. an external locus of control.
    b. an internal locus of control.
    c. decreased autonomy.
    d. disrupted self-esteem.

13. Two attachment styles are avoidant and _____. (p. 367)
    a. reactive
    b. anxious
    c. responsive
    d. relational

Short-Answer/Essay Questions

Answer the following questions in the space provided.

1. Compare and contrast the defense mechanisms of denial and rationalization. _____

_____
_____
_____
_____
_____
_____
_____
_____

2. What is the drawback of recognizing fewer specific personality traits? _____

_____
_____
_____
_____
_____
_____
_____
_____

3. Explain the characteristics associated with a "high-reactive" infant. _____

_____

_____

_____

_____

_____

_____

_____

4. What are the criticisms of using twins studies in personality research? _____

_____

_____

_____

_____

_____

_____

_____

5. Compare and contrast locus of control: internal versus external. _____

_____

_____

_____

_____

_____

_____

_____

6. How do collectivist and individualist cultures differ? _____

_____

_____

_____

_____

_____

_____

When You Are Finished . . . Puzzle It Out

Across

2. Hypothesized that self-efficacy helps people believe in themselves
3. The sense of being able to follow through and produce desired behaviors
8. Expectations that influence personality
12. Proposed that biological mechanisms underlie three personality dimensions
13. Developed client-centered therapy
14. _____ Factor Model
17. Children with this birth status are often more assertive and dominant
18. Number of superfactors, per Eysenck
19. Said conscious can be divided into three levels

Down

1. Rorschach test, for example
3. Freud's personality structure that houses the sense of right and wrong
4. Psychologists suggest calling this nonconformity or social deviance
5. Most common type of adult attachment style
6. Developed theory of self-actualization
7. Defense mechanism in which unconscious prevents threatening thoughts from entering consciousness
9. A set of behavioral, emotional, and cognitive tendencies that people display over time and across situations
10. Two components are vigor and tempo
11. Behavioral _____ System
15. Important study of personality, using twins
16. Hong Kong is an example of this type of culture

Puzzle created with Puzzlemaker at DiscoverySchool.com.

Chapter 9
Psychology over the Life Span:
Growing Up, Growing Older, Growing Wiser

Before You Read . . .

Did your mother enjoy being pregnant with you? When did you start walking and talking? Are you the same person now as you were as a child? Will you be the same person in your sixties? How will you change?

This chapter presents an overview of human development, from conception to old age. You will learn about prenatal development, from the gametes that start it to the infant who is born. You will discover both positive factors and negative events (teratogens) that can affect the developing fetus. Later, you will learn about the newborn—its perceptual abilities, reflexes, and even personality (temperament).

In childhood, children grow rapidly and undergo remarkable physical changes. You will learn about this physical transformation as well as the qualitative and quantitative changes children experience in language and cognition. You will explore Piaget's classical framework for understanding child development as well as the new areas of understanding developed by more modern researchers.

You will also learn about adolescence and adulthood, including changes that you can expect in your sense of self, morality, and gender identity and changes that will occur as you develop new, mature relationships that wax and wane over time.

Chapter Objectives

After reading this chapter, you should be able to:

- Describe how development progresses in the womb.

- Describe the capabilities of a newborn.

- Explain how the ability to control the body develops with age.

- Explain physical, cognitive, social, and emotional development during childhood and adolescence.

- Discuss whether adolescence is inevitably a time of emotional upheaval.

- Explain how aging affects a person's physical abilities, perception, memory, and intelligence.

- Describe the course of social and emotional development during adulthood.

As You Read . . . Term Identification

Make flashcards using the following terms as you go. Use the definitions in the margins of this chapter for help. If you write the definitions in your own words, though, you will remember them better!

Accommodation
Adolescence
Assimilation
Attachment
Child-directed speech (CDS)
Concrete operation
Conservation
Critical period
Cross-sectional study
Egocentrism
Embryo
Fetus
Formal operation
Gender roles
Grammar
Language acquisition device (LAD)

Longitudinal study
Maturation
Moral dilemma
Nativism
Object permanence
Overextension
Overregularization error
Psychosocial development
Puberty
Schema
Self-concept
Separation anxiety
Telegraphic speech
Teratogen
Underextension
Zygote

As You Read . . . Questions and Exercises

In the Beginning: From Conception to Birth

Prenatal Development: Nature and Nurture from the Start

GO SURFING . . .

. . .to see photographs of the developing **embryo.**
- http://www.visembryo.com
- http://www.w-cpc.org/fetal.html
- http://anatomy.med.unsw.edu.au/CBL/Embryo/embryo.htm

Name the important developments that happen at each of the following prenatal stages:

- 3 days: _____

- 2 weeks: _____

- 8 weeks: _____

- 20–25 weeks: _____

- 28 weeks: _____

- 25–34 weeks: _____

What do fetuses do in utero? _____
_____
_____

What evidence is there that fetuses can learn? _____
_____
_____
_____

Describe what effect the following factors can have on developing babies:

Teratogen	Effect
Rubella in the embryonic period	
HIV	
Alcohol	
Heroin or cocaine	
Excessive caffeine	
Smoking	
Poor maternal diet	

Teratogen	Effect
Environmental pollutants	
Maternal stress	

What can a pregnant woman do to enhance her unborn child's development? _____
_____
_____
_____
_____
_____

The Newborn: A Work in Progress

Describe a newborn's sensory capabilities.

- Sight: _____
    _____
    _____
    _____

- Hearing: _____
    _____
    _____
    _____

- Smell: _____
    _____
    _____

Complete the following table of **reflexes:**

Reflex	Description
Rooting	
	The startle reflex
Babinski	

What is *temperament?* _____

_____

_____

_____

_____

What is meant by an "approach" temperament? What is meant by a "withdrawal" temperament?

_____

_____

_____

_____

_____

What is the evidence that biological factors affect infant *temperament?*

- _____

_____

- _____

_____

- _____

_____

- _____

_____

- _____

_____

- _____

_____

How stable is *temperament?* _____
_____
_____
_____

How might the environment influence the stability of *temperament?* _____
_____
_____
_____

Infancy and Childhood: Taking Off

Physical and Motor Development: Getting Control

In what order is motor control gained? _____
_____
_____
_____

What evidence, if any, suggests that the environment plays a role in the development of motor control? _____
_____
_____
_____
_____
_____

Perceptual and Cognitive Development: Extended Horizons

Describe the visual abilities of infants. _____
_____
_____
_____
_____
_____
_____
_____

Describe the auditory abilities of infants. _____
_____
_____
_____
_____
_____
_____
_____

Explain the habituation technique. What does this technique tell us about infants? _____
_____
_____
_____
_____
_____
_____

Given infants' visual and auditory preferences, name some gifts that a newborn would particularly enjoy. Explain why these items would be particularly appropriate gifts.

- _____
  _____
  _____
- _____
  _____
  _____
- _____
  _____
  _____

Summarize the facts that support various language theories and the problems with these theories in the chart below.

	Supporting Facts	Problems
Behaviorist theory		
Nativist theory		
Interactionist theory		

If you had a child, how would you most likely talk to your baby? _____

What are the characteristics of this form of language?

- _____
- _____
- _____

In some ways, infants have better language skills than adults. Name and describe one such way.

_____
_____
_____

Name the **language skills** that develop at each of the following ages.

Language Acquisition

- **2–3 months:** _____
- **6 months:** _____
- **8 months:** _____
- **12 months:** _____
- **13 months:** _____
- **18 months:** _____
- **2 years:** _____
- **3 months:** _____
- **4 months:** _____
- **6 years:** _____
- **9 years:** _____

Provide a new example (not from the textbook) of an **overextension:** _____
_____
_____

Provide a new example (not from the textbook) of an **underextension:** _____
_____
_____

CALL . . .

...your parents and ask what your first sentence was. How does this match the research on **telegraphic speech?**

Discuss. _____
_____
_____

Provide a new example (not from the textbook) of **overregularization:** _____
_____
_____

Complete the table below, indicating the approximate age of each stage and the accomplishments by the end of each period. Use the hypothesis developed by Piaget, not the information put forth by more contemporary researchers.

Cognitive Stage	Approximate Age	Accomplishments	Limitations
Sensorimotor			
Preoperational			
Concrete operational			
Formal operational			

What are **schemas,** according to Piaget? _____

_____

_____

_____

_____

_____

_____

What two processes does the child use to change his or her **schemas?**

- _____

_____

- _____

_____

_____

Contemporary researchers, using different research methodology, have suggested that Piaget underestimated the age at which children achieve certain cognitive goals. In the table below, indicate the age at which contemporary researchers believe children attain each goal.

Goal	Age of Attainment and Evidence
Imitation	
Object permanence	
Conservation of amount/mass	

How does working memory change throughout childhood? _____
_____

How might changes in information processing explain the qualitative changes that Piaget observed?
_____
_____
_____
_____
_____
_____

How might brain changes affect these information-processing abilities? _____
_____
_____
_____
_____
_____
_____

Briefly summarize Lev Vygotsky's ideas about the following topics, in your own words.

- **The role of adults in cognitive development:** _____
_____
_____
_____

- **The role of language in cognitive development:** _____
_____
_____
_____

Social and Emotional Development: The Child in the World

Why does **separation anxiety** occur between the ages of six months and two years? _____

_____

_____

_____

Provide the name of the type of **attachment** described by the following reactions of babies to the Strange Situation.

Reaction	Type of Attachment
Babies will leave mother, but are upset when mother leaves and are not comforted by a stranger. Babies calm down when mother returns.	
Babies stay close to mother and become angry when she leaves. When mother returns, babies are still angry and won't calm down easily.	
Babies don't care if mother is present or absent, and are easily comforted by a stranger.	
Babies become depressed and unresponsive, with sudden spurts of emotion at the end of the *Strange Situation*.	

What type of **attachment** do you think you had as a child? Support your answer. _____

_____

_____

_____

_____

_____

_____

GO SURFING . . .

...to the following sites and take the attachment quizzes there. These quizzes measure attachment in romantic relationships. Researchers believe that a person's romantic attachment style may have its roots in the individual's early parental attachment style.

- http://www.web-research-design.net/cgi-bin/crq/crq.pl
- http://psychcentral.com/romancequiz.htm

Describe your results here. _____
_____
_____
_____
_____

Is this consistent with your **attachment** type as a child? _____
_____
_____
_____
_____

Would you send your child to daycare? Why or why not? _____
_____
_____
_____
_____

What is **self-concept?** _____
_____
_____
_____
_____

At what age do children first exhibit a **self-concept?** _____

What research shows this? _____
_____
_____
_____
_____

How would a child define himself or herself at the following ages:

- Three years old: _____
- Eight to eleven years old: _____

How does culture influence **self-concept?** _____
_____
_____
_____
_____

Name and describe three factors involved in the development of **gender identity.**

- _____
  _____
  _____

- _____
  _____
  _____

- _____
  _____
  _____

In the table below, describe **gender roles** for males and females in your culture.

Males	Females

Bobby just received too much money from the teller at the bank. At which of Kohlberg's levels of moral development is Bobby if he says to himself:

Bobby's Thought	Level of Moral Development
"I could use this money to buy a bike, as long as I don't get caught!"	
"If I kept this money, my dad would think I'm a bad person."	
"It would be in the best interests of everyone who has an account at this bank if I give the money back."	
"Taking this money is the same thing as stealing, and stealing is wrong."	

Explain Gilligan's criticisms of Kohlberg's theory of moral development. _____
_____
_____
_____

What has later work concluded about Gilligan's criticisms? _____
_____
_____
_____

Adolescence: Between Two Worlds

Physical Development: In Puberty's Wake

Describe the physical changes that happen to boys and girls during **puberty.**

Changes to Boys	Changes to Girls

What is the secular trend? What has caused it? _____

_____

_____

_____

_____

_____

Cognitive Development: Getting It All Together

According to Piaget, what are the two major changes in thinking during **adolescence?**

- _____

- _____

Think back to adolescence. What were you interested in doing and reading? Were these changes from earlier in your life? How do they reflect changes in thinking during **adolescence?**

_____

_____

_____

_____

Describe the possible reasons for these cognitive changes.

- _____
  _____
  _____

- _____
  _____
  _____

What is an _imaginary audience?_ Give a personal example of a time when you experienced this phenomenon. _____
_____
_____
_____
_____

What is a _personal fable?_ Give a personal example of a time when you experienced this. _____
_____
_____
_____
_____

Social and Emotional Development: New Rules, New Roles

What are the three problems that have been identified as "normal" during **adolescence?**

- _____
  _____

- _____
  _____

- _____
  _____

Did you experience any or all of these problems during **adolescence?** Discuss. _____
_____
_____
_____

How do biology and culture interact to affect adolescents? _____
_____
_____
_____
_____

Did you experience "storm and stress" during **adolescence?** Why or why not, do you think?

_____
_____
_____
_____
_____

Which types of life experiences will positively affect later intimate relationships?

- _____
- _____

Which types of negative peer relationships sometimes occur during **adolescence?** _____

_____
_____
_____

Did you experience positive or negative peer relationships during **adolescence?** Describe.

_____
_____
_____
_____

List the factors that appear to put a teenage girl at risk of becoming pregnant.

- _____
- _____
- _____
- _____

What are some of the likely consequences of teenage pregnancies?

- _____
- _____
- _____
- _____

Adulthood and Aging: The Continuously Changing Self

The Changing Body: What's Inevitable, What's Not

What are the two aspects of aging?

- _____
- _____

What are some of the inevitable age-related changes that are programmed into our genes?

_____
_____
_____
_____
_____
_____

Perception and Cognition in Adulthood: Taking the Good with the Bad

Describe the age-related changes, if any, in each of the following areas.

Area	Age-Related Changes
Vision	
Hearing	
Fluid intelligence	
Crystallized intelligence	
Memory	

Think of any elderly people you know. Do they appear to have experienced age-related changes in any of the preceding areas? If so, which ones? How do you know? _____

_____

_____

_____

_____

_____

Why is it important to note what type of research design was used when examining intelligence during adulthood? _____

_____

_____

_____

_____

_____

Social and Emotional Development During Adulthood

What are the three **psychosocial stages** of adulthood (according to Erik Erikson) and the goal at each stage?

Stage	Goal

Do people generally feel happier or sadder as they get older? Explain emotional changes associated with aging. _____

_____

_____

_____

_____

Do interpersonal relationships improve or weaken over time? Explain. _____

_____

_____

_____

_____

Looking at Levels: Keeping the Aging Brain Sharp

Should elderly people be encouraged to engage in mental workouts to keep their minds sharp? What about the elderly person who does not wish to do so? Which factors, at the levels of the brain, the person, and the group, may lead to diminished motivation for such tasks? Use arrows to indicate how these factors may interact.

The Brain	The Person	The Group

After You Read . . . Thinking Back

1. This chapter underscores a point made earlier: Memory is not a single entity, but rather consists of multiple systems that develop at different rates. What are these different systems? _____
   _____
   _____
   _____
   _____
   _____
   _____

2. This chapter revisits an issue initially raised in Chapter 3: the nature–nurture debate. What are some of the ways that theorists have thought about nature and nurture interacting? _____
   _____
   _____
   _____
   _____
   _____
   _____

3. Given that even young infants have been shown to learn, what does this finding say about the biological basis of learning? _____
   _____
   _____
   _____
   _____
   _____
   _____

4. Can you think of confounds that may influence what appear to be age-related changes in intelligence? Explain. _____
   _____
   _____
   _____
   _____
   _____
   _____

5. Think back to Chapter 2, where you learned about research in psychology. Why is it particularly difficult to make causal statements in developmental studies? For example, why can't you say, "Age causes memory decline?" _____
   _____
   _____
   _____
   _____
   _____
   _____

After You Read . . . Thinking Ahead

1. Which environmental factors may influence whether people behave morally? For example, which types of situations in World War II contributed to the immoral acts of the Nazis?

    _____
    _____
    _____
    _____
    _____
    _____

2. Why do you think that peer interactions are positive for some adolescents and negative for others? Could any environmental changes be made that would facilitate more positive interactions? _____

    _____
    _____
    _____
    _____
    _____
    _____

3. How might stress affect a person's development, at all three levels of analysis? _____

    _____
    _____
    _____
    _____
    _____

4. What can a parent do for a child to facilitate his or her later social interactions, both in groups and in intimate relationships? _____

    _____
    _____
    _____
    _____

5. Can you think of any environmental factors in childhood that might contribute to later psychological disorders? _____

    _____
    _____
    _____
    _____

After You Read . . . Practice Tests

PRACTICE TEST #1:
IN THE BEGINNING

Multiple-Choice Questions
For each question, circle the best answer from the choices given.

1. Another name for the specialized cells or sex cells is _____. (p. 377)
   a. gamete
   b. embryo
   c. zygote
   d. blastocyst

2. What signals the embryotic stage of human development? (p. 378)
   a. all of the major body structures are present.
   b. the chromosomes in each parent cell are exchanged.
   c. the placenta becomes fully functional.
   d. the major axis of the body is present.

3. Alexis strokes the cheek of her baby sister. Her sister, Naomi, turns her head and starts to suck. Alexis has elicited the _____ reflex. (p. 382)
   a. sucking
   b. stepping
   c. rooting
   d. moro

4. Differences in temperament are apparent as early as: (p. 383)
   a. birth.
   b. one month.
   c. one week.
   d. two months.

5. Which of the following depicts the order of prenatal development? (pp. 378-379)
   a. zygote → fetus → embryo → blastocyst
   b. blastocyst → zygote → fetus → embryo
   c. ovum → zygote → fetus → embryo
   d. zygote → blastocyst → embryo → fetus

6. Sunnel is a young pregnant mother who experiences high levels of stress due to her job. What is a possible result of her high level of stress? (p. 381)
   a. the baby will be born with a smaller head.
   b. the baby will be born with larger feet.
   c. the baby will be born with lower than normal stress levels.
   d. none of the above—mother's stress does not affect the baby.

7. Which of the following statements is FALSE regarding the development of a baby? (p. 383)
    a. babies are born sensitive to a range of women's voices.
    b. babies are a blank slate, waiting to learn from their environment.
    c. babies are equipped with a range of abilities.
    d. babies can process information from their senses as early as two days old.

8. Babies with greater activation in the right frontal lobe tend to be _____ later. (p. 383)
    a. more difficult
    b. happier
    c. depressed
    d. less inhibited

PRACTICE TEST #2:
INFANCY AND CHILDHOOD

Multiple-Choice Questions

For each question, circle the best answer from the choices given.

1. What movement has aided in SIDS cases declining 30%? (p. 385)
   a. tummy sleep
   b. walk on your own
   c. play with your kid
   d. back to sleep

2. Alan is a nine-month-old infant. What motor milestone should he MOST likely have accomplished? (p. 385)
   a. potty training.
   b. rolling over.
   c. turning the pages of a book.
   d. throwing a ball.

3. In the _____ experiment, six-month-old infants didn't want to crawl over the "deep end." This experiment provided evidence that infants can perceive depth before they are able to speak. (p. 386)
   a. habituation
   b. where the Sidewalk Ends
   c. visual Cliff
   d. none of the above

4. Skinner believed that language was: (p. 388)
   a. innate
   b. completely learned
   c. partially learned and partially innate
   d. biological

5. An interactionist sees language development as: (p. 388)
   a. innate
   b. completely learned
   c. partially learned and partially innate
   d. biological

6. A child might use the word dog to refer to all four-legged animals. This is an example of: (p. 390)
   a. overextension
   b. underextension
   c. syntactic confusion
   d. pragmatic language

7. Hamid is given an array of objects and asked whether a specific object is included in the array. In a very organized and systematic way, he scans the objects and makes his conclusion. Most likely, Hamid is _____ year(s) old. (p. 548)
   a. one
   b. four
   c. nine
   d. Can't tell from the information given

8. Which theorist is known for work on the stages of cognitive development? (p. 392)
   a. Piaget
   b. Vygotsky
   c. Bowlby
   d. Maccoby

9. Baby Loyla knows to suck on her new yellow pacifier. The yellow pacifier could be considered a new stimulus in that her old pacifier was green. Loyla is using the process of _____. (p. 392)
   a. conservation
   b. accommodation
   c. assimilation
   d. frustration

10. The period of cognitive development during which the child first develops mobility is known as _____. (p. 393)
    a. sensation
    b. preoperational
    c. formal operations
    d. sensorimotor

11. John's mother has just baked a fresh apple pie for his birthday. She asks him how many pieces he would like the pie into -- 8 or 12. John replies, "I am very hungry. Cut it into 12 pieces." John's answer reflects which major development of the preoperational period? (p. 394)
    a. conservation
    b. object permanence
    c. assimilation
    d. accommodation

12. Which style of attachment describes babies that appear depressed and have periods of lack of interest? (p. 398)
    a. secure
    b. avoidant
    c. resistant
    d. none of the above

PRACTICE TEST #3:
ADOLESCENCE and ADULTHOOD AND AGING

Multiple-Choice Questions

For each question, circle the best answer from the choices given.

1. Puberty begins around the age of _____ for girls and _____ for boys. (p. 404)
   a. 8-14; 9-15
   b. 12-14; 13-15
   c. 10-12; 12-15
   d. 6-8; 9-15

2. A cognitive distortion that can be found in some adolescents is _____. (p. 407)
   a. imaginary audience
   b. allegory
   c. theory of mind
   d. fear of isolation

3. Which of the following are TRUE concerning adolescents? (p. 408)
   a. adolescents tend to have conflicts with their parents
   b. adolescents experience extreme mood swings
   c. adolescents may be prone to taking risks
   d. all of the above

4. Megan is a young teenager with a baby. According to the research, what other characteristics might she have? (p. 409)
   a. she is probably poor.
   b. she might not have clear career plans.
   c. her father was probably not involved in her life.
   d. all of the above

5. Episodic memory _____ and semantic memory _____ as we age. (p. 412)
   a. worsens; worsens
   b. improves; worsens
   c. worsens; improves
   d. worsens; does not change

6. Dr. Rhea Peeted wants to track the development of children over time. She proposes to interview the children at 2, 4, 6, 8, and 10 years of age. This is an example of a(n) _____ study. (p. 573)
   a. longitudinal
   b. cross sectional
   c. experimental
   d. sequential

7. Who developed the eight psychosocial stages of development? (p. 414)
   a. Freud
   b. Erikson
   c. Piaget
   d. none of the above

COMPREHENSIVE PRACTICE TEST

True/False Questions

Circle TRUE or FALSE for each of the following statements.

1.　TRUE　　FALSE　　The ovum is the largest cell in the human body. (p. 377)

2.　TRUE　　FALSE　　After twenty to twenty-five weeks of gestation, the fetus is sensitive to both sound and light. (p. 379)

3.　TRUE　　FALSE　　If the mother smokes during pregnancy, the baby might be born with fetal alcohol syndrome. (p. 380)

4.　TRUE　　FALSE　　While in the uterus, the fetus is protected from the mother's stress level. (p. 381)

5.　TRUE　　FALSE　　Early nurturing experiences can assist in the stability of temperament. (p. 383)

6.　TRUE　　FALSE　　According to Piaget, the first stage of cognitive development is preconventional. (p. 393)

7.　TRUE　　FALSE　　When evaluating Piaget's theory, it can be said that he accurately assessed the capabilities of infants. (p. 395)

8.　TRUE　　FALSE　　Bowlby dubbed the fear of being away from a primary caregiver as separation anxiety. (p. 398)

Multiple-Choice Questions

For each question, circle the best answer from the choices given.

1. Which chromosome determines the gender of the baby? (pp. 377-378)
   a. chromosome 21
   b. X
   c. Y
   d. none of the above

2. Chicken pox would be considered a _____ to a developing fetus. (p. 379)
   a. moro
   b. chemical
   c. teratogen
   d. all of the above

3. Differences in _____ between siblings can be observed at birth. (p. 383)
   a. reflexes
   b. vision
   c. temperament
   d. none of the above

4. Believing that language is acquired in part due to biological or innate reasons is consistent with: (p. 388)
   a. Behavioral views
   b. Empirical views
   c. Nativist views
   d. Skinner's view

5. The exaggerated intonation of baby talk is called: (p. 388)
   a. Interactionism
   b. Nativism
   c. Infant-Adult speech
   d. Child-directed speech

6. According to Piaget, when does a child begin fantasy play? (p. 393)
   a. during the sensorimotor period
   b. during the preoperational period
   c. during the concrete operational period
   d. during the formal operations period

7. Vygotsky's theory emphasizes the role of _____ in the development of children's cognitive abilities. (p. 397)
   a. theory of mind
   b. culture
   c. biological changes
   d. sexual identity

8. The least common type of attachment style among American babies is: (p. 399)
   a. avoidant
   b. resistant
   c. secure
   d. disorganized

9. Brendan, who is ten years old, understands reversibility. According to Piaget, Brendan is in the _____ stage of cognitive development. (p. 393)
   a. concrete operations
   b. intimacy vs. isolation
   c. preconventional
   d. formal operations

10. In Maccoby's view, _____ are the key to learning gender roles. (p. 400)
    a. peer group interactions
    b. interactions with parents
    c. hormonal influences
    d. all of the above

11. Menopause typically occurs between _____. (p. 411)
    a. thirty-five and forty-five
    b. fifty-five and sixty-five
    c. forty-five and fifty-five
    d. sixty-five and seventy-five

Short-Answer/Essay Questions

Answer the following questions in the space provided.

1. Was Piaget accurate in his description of cognitive development? _____
    _____
    _____
    _____
    _____
    _____
    _____
    _____
    _____
    _____
    _____

2. Describe the period of adolescent development. _____
    _____
    _____
    _____
    _____
    _____
    _____
    _____
    _____
    _____

3. Are there age related declines in memory? _____
    _____
    _____
    _____
    _____
    _____
    _____
    _____
    _____
    _____

When You Are Finished . . . Puzzle It Out

Across

2. Number of stages in Piaget's theory
3. Chemical that can damage a fetus
6. Developed the theory of attachment
9. Erikson's first developmental task of adulthood
13. Piaget's period from age 2–7 years
14. Emotional bond between parent and child
16. A study in which participants are followed over time
17. In Piaget's theory, an organizing mental structure

Down

1. Developed theory of moral reasoning
4. Puberty to end of teenage years
5. A fertilized ovum
7. Drop in functioning immediately before death
8. Has been reduced by sleeping on backs
10. He emphasized culture in development
11. Contained on the chromosomes in a series of "rungs"
12. They mature faster than boys
15. Developing baby from 8 weeks to birth

Puzzle created with Puzzlemaker at DiscoverySchool.com.

Chapter 10
Stress, Health, and Coping:
Dealing with Life

Before You Read . . .

Do you feel *stressed?* If so, what does this feel like physically and emotionally? In this chapter, you will learn exactly what stress is—from the physiology of it, to the sources of stress. You will learn that stress is a subjective experience and that there are certain qualities of situations (perceived controllability and predictability) that make them more or less difficult to handle. You will also read about the different areas in your life that might lead you to feel stressed including internal conflicts, hassles, and feelings of anger.

Be careful—too much stress can take a toll on your health, as you'll discover in this chapter. Immune dysfunction, cancer, heart disease, and sleep disturbances are all linked to stress. But at least there's something you can do about it. You *can* change your health-impairing behaviors and develop more effective coping strategies. You will learn about these strategies in the last section of this chapter, where you'll also read about the link between coping and social support. Mind–body interventions, gender, and culture are covered as well.

Chapter Objectives

After reading this chapter, you should be able to:

- Define stress.

- Describe the physiology of stress.

- Name common sources of stress.

- Explain how stress affects health.

- Name and describe the different types of coping strategies.

- Describe how relationships affect stress and health.

- Explain mind–body interventions.

- Describe the role of gender and culture in coping.

As You Read . . . Term Identification

Make flashcards using the following terms as you go. Use the definitions in the margins of this chapter for help. If you write the definitions in your own words, though, you will remember them better!

Activation-synthesis hypothesis
Acute stressor
Aggression
Alarm phase
Alcohol myopia
Amphetamines
Approach–approach conflict
Approach–avoidance conflict
Atherosclerosis
Avoidance–avoidance conflict
B cell
Blackout
Chronic stressor
Circadian rhythms
Crack
Depressants
Disinhibition
Emotion-focused coping
Enacted social support
Exhaustion phase
Flashback
General adaptation syndrome (GAS)
Glucocorticoids
Hallucinogen
Health psychology
Hostile attribution bias
Hostility
Hypnogogic sleep

Inhibitory conflict
Insomnia
Internal conflict
Latent content
Manifest content
Narcotic analgesic
Natural killer (NK) cell
Nocebo effect
Opiate
Perceived social support
Problem-focused coping
REM rebound
REM sleep
Resistance phase
Sleep
Sleep apnea
Social support
Stimulants
Stress
Stressor
Stress response
Substance abuse
Substance dependence
Suprachaismatic nucleus (SCN)
T cell
Thought suppression
Tolerance
Withdrawal symptoms

As You Read . . . Questions and Exercises

What Is Stress?

Stress: The Big Picture

Distinguish between **stress** and a **stressor.** _____

_____

_____

_____

_____

Provide an example from your life of each of the following types of **stressors:**

	Acute Stressor	Chronic Stressor
Physical Stressor		
Psychological Stressor		
Social Stressor		

The Biology of Stress

Describe what happens during each phase of the **general adaptation syndrome:**

Phase	Body's Response
Alarm	
Resistance	
Exhaustion	

Do you think you have a high or low _allostatic load?_ Explain your answer. _____

_____

_____

_____

_____

It's How You Think of It: Interpreting Stimuli as Stressors

Provide a personal example of a **stressor** in your life that might not be a **stressor** to someone else.

_____
_____
_____
_____
_____

Distinguish between _primary appraisal_ and _secondary appraisal._ _____
_____
_____
_____
_____
_____

Fill in the table below with examples of **stressors** that are either **controllable** or **uncontrollable,** and **predictable** or **unpredictable.** Which would be more stressful to you? Why?

Controll-ability / Predictability	Perceived as Controllable	Perceived as Uncontrollable
Predictable		
Unpredictable		

Under what circumstances is _predictability_ unlikely to be helpful in dealing with an upcoming stressor?

_____
_____
_____
_____
_____

Identify the following situations as being **approach–approach conflicts, approach–avoidance conflicts,** or **avoidance–avoidance conflicts.**

Situation	Type of Conflict
Two people you really like ask you out on a date!	
You have to take biology or chemistry, and you can't stand either one!	
You *love* the new Miata, but you can't really afford it .	
Only one graduate school accepted you, and you have nowhere else to go.	
Your mom offers you two tickets to the movies, but you have to take your sister.	
You can't decide between chocolate or vanilla ice cream.	

Sources of Stress

GO SURFING . . .

...to find out how you would score on a **Life Events Stress Test.** You can find these tests at the following Web sites:

- http://www.stresstips.com/lifeevents.htm
- http://www.success.net.au/stress_test.html

This type of test is no longer thought to be a good measure of **stress.** Why not? _____
_____
_____
_____
_____

What is meant by "daily hassles," and what are the negative effects of such hassles on a person's functioning? _____
_____
_____
_____
_____

What are some of the daily hassles in your life that create **stress?** _____

_____

_____

_____

_____

If you were the manager of a company, how would you design your office space so as to reduce your employees' **stress?** _____

_____

_____

_____

_____

As the manager of a company, what other policies could you institute to reduce **stress?**

_____

_____

_____

_____

_____

How does hostility contribute to **stress?** _____

_____

_____

_____

_____

GO SURFING . . .

...to find out if you have a **Type A personality.** Short inventories are available at the following sites:

- http://itech.fgcu.edu/cgi-bin/lchallenges/survey/typea.html
- http://stress.about.com/library/Type_A_quiz/bl_Type_A_quiz.htm

What did these surveys indicate? _____

Do you agree or disagree with the results? _____

_____

_____

Stress, Disease, and Health

The Immune System: Catching Cold

Which types of stressors are most likely to alter immune functioning? _____
_____
_____

What are the two classes of white blood cells?
- _____
- _____(which includes **natural killer cells**)

List five lines of research showing that stress can harm the immune system.

- _____
- _____
- _____
- _____
- _____

Cancer

What are the two ways in which stress can affect the growth of cancerous cells?

- _____
  _____
- _____
  _____

Heart Disease

Describe the link between **stress** and heart disease. _____
_____
_____
_____
_____

Which personal characteristics make a person more likely to suffer from heart disease?
_____
_____
_____
_____
_____

Sleep

In the chart below, indicate the following information about each stage of sleep: its length, its physical characteristics, and the associated brain activity.

	Length of Stage (at Beginning and End of Night)	Physical Characteristics	Brain Activity
Non-REM Stages			
Stage 1			
Stage 2			
Stages 3 and 4			
REM Sleep			

How do **sleep patterns** change over the lifespan? Why?

- Infancy: _____
  _____
  _____

- After 40s: _____
  _____
  _____

Sleep Deprivation: Is Less Just as Good?

GO SURFING . . .

. . .at the following sites and take the online sleep tests:

- http://712educators.about.com/od/testingsleep/index.htm

According to these tests, are you **sleep-deprived?** _____

Do you agree with the results of these tests? Why or why not? _____
_____
_____

How does **sleep deprivation** (either current or previous) affect you in each of the following areas?

- **Attention:** _____
  _____
  _____

- **Physical performance:** _____
  _____
  _____

- **Mood:** _____
  _____
  _____

- **Learning:** _____
  _____
  _____

Some governments have used sleep deprivation as a method of torture. (For more information about this topic, search the Human Rights Watch at http://www.hrw.org.) Based on these situations, as well as studies with rats, what outcome would you expect if a prisoner was not allowed to sleep for a *protracted* period of time? _____
_____
_____
_____
_____
_____
_____

Have you ever pulled an all-nighter? If so, did you experience any negative effects? _____
_____
_____
_____
_____

Do your experiences agree with the research on sleep deprivation reported in your textbook? Why
or why not? _____
_____
_____
_____
_____

The Function of Sleep

Why is **sleep** so important? In your own words, summarize the following theories:

- **Restorative theory:** _____
  _____
  _____

- **Evolutionary theory:** _____
  _____
  _____

- **Facilitating learning:** _____
  _____
  _____

Dream On

Keep a diary of your dreams for the next few days (or more). Summarize the **manifest content** of
one of your dreams: _____
_____
_____
_____
_____
_____
_____

GO SURFING . . .

. . .at one of the following "dream interpretation" sites. Use the dream dictionaries there to interpret your dreams. Do *not* pay any money to have your dream interpreted online!

- **Dream Central's Online Dream Dictionary**
  http://www.sleeps.com/dictionary/dictionary.html
- **Sleepy Bear Dream Interpretation Site**
  http://myenvoy.com/sleepybear

(Many other sites are available; just search for them!)

Offer an explanation of the **latent content** of your dream, based on the information you found online. _____

_____

_____

_____

_____

_____

_____

How else could your **dream** be explained (besides using Freud's ideas of manifest and latent content)? In your own words, summarize the following theories of the purposes of dreaming.

- **Activation-synthesis hypothesis:** _____

_____

- **Strengthening neural connections:** _____

_____

_____

Which **dream theory** does Solms's research support? Explain. _____

_____

_____

_____

_____

The Chemistry of Sleep

Complete the following table, indicating how the following **neurotransmitter** (NT) and **hormone** (H) levels change during sleep and the effects of these changes.

Chemical	Increase or Decrease?	Effects of Change
Acetylcholine (NT)		
Serotonin (NT)		
Norepinephrine (NT)		
Melatonin (H)		

Use the following word bank to complete the paragraph below.

Blind	External cues	Optic chiasm
Circadian rhythms	Internal cues	Suprachiasmatic nucleus

Daily fluctuations in responses to dark and night, called _____, control many aspects of body functioning, including blood pressure, pulse rate, body temperature, blood sugar levels, hormone levels, and metabolism. These fluctuations are guided by the _____, which is located just above the _____. The SCN produces hormones in responses to changes in light. These hormones then tell an animal when to sleep and when to wake. In the absence _____ of dark and light and _____ such as clocks, people seem to prefer a 24.9-hour cycle, not a 24-hour cycle. This is supported by research showing that even _____ people often have difficulty falling asleep at their usual times.

Describe the timing of your **circadian rhythms:** Are you a **lark** or an **owl?** _____
_____
_____
_____

How do you deal with this timing in your everyday life? _____
_____
_____
_____

Why are some people grouchy on Monday mornings? _____

_____

_____

_____

What can they do to keep from being grouchy? _____

_____

_____

_____

_____

For most people, what is the least energetic time of the day? Why? _____

_____

_____

_____

_____

Troubled Sleep

GO SURFING . . .

...at http://www.mountcarmelhealth.com/114.cfm and take the online **sleep test** there.

Does this site indicate that you may have a **sleep disorder?** If so, name and describe the disorder.

_____

_____

_____

_____

_____

Do you agree with the results of this test? Why or why not? _____

_____

_____

_____

_____

Can you think of other factors that might influence the test results? _____

_____

_____

_____

_____

Strategies for Coping

Coping Strategies: Approaches and Tactics

Identify the following coping responses as **problem-focused** or **emotion-focused**.

Coping Response	Emotion-Focused	Problem-Focused
"I refuse to feel bad about this grade—everyone else got a bad grade, too!"		
"This is a bad grade. I better buckle down and study harder for the next exam."		
"This is a bad grade. I think I'll go and talk to the teacher about how I can do better."		
Joan calls her mother and talks for hours on end about her boss, her husband, and her kids—they're driving her crazy!		

Name a situation in which you have tried each of the following **coping strategies.**

Coping Strategy	Definition	Example
Active coping		
Planning		
Instrumental social support		
Suppression of competing activities		
Restraint coping		
Emotional social support		

Coping Strategy	Definition	Example
Venting emotions		
Positive reinterpretation/growth		
Behavioral disengagement		
Mental disengagement		
Thought suppression		

Did you notice if you have a preference for certain coping strategies over others? If so, which ones? Why? Are these known to be effective coping strategies? _____

_____

_____

_____

_____

Name the factors at each of the following levels that may lead to **aggression.**

Personal Factors	Environmental Factors

In what kinds of situations are people more likely to use each of these coping strategies? _____

_____

_____

_____

_____

Drugs and Alcohol

GO SURFING . . .

. . .at http://www.alcoholscreening.org/screening/index.asp to see whether you have any substance dependencies.

Does this test reveal that you **abuse substances?** _____
_____
_____
_____
_____

Do you agree with these results? Why or why not? _____
_____
_____
_____
_____

If so, do you abuse substances *chronically?* In other words, do you have a **substance dependence?**
_____
_____
_____
_____

The two most important symptoms of substance dependence are tolerance and withdrawal. In your own words, define these terms:

- **Tolerance:** _____
  _____
  _____

- **Withdrawal:** _____
  _____
  _____

Why is alcohol characterized as a **depressant?** _____
_____
_____

Give an example of **inhibitory conflict,** other than that described in the text. _____
_____
_____
_____
_____
_____
_____

Describe the difference in how a person in a high-conflict situation would be likely to act if that person was sober and when he or she had consumed a lot of alcohol.

No Alcohol Consumed	Much Alcohol Consumed

List and describe the psychological effects of **alcohol.**

- _____
  _____
- _____
  _____
- _____
  _____
- _____
  _____
- _____
  _____
- _____
  _____
- _____
  _____

Have you ever known anyone who was an alcoholic? If so, what were the effects of his or her alcoholism? _____
_____
_____

What is alcohol myopia? _____
_____
_____

350

What are the physical and psychological problems that result from chronic alcohol abuse? _____
_____
_____

Have you ever experienced a **blackout?** Describe what it was like (or what it would be like, if you have not had this experience). _____
_____
_____

What other drugs are categorized as depressants? _____
_____
_____

Stimulants: Focus on Cocaine

Why are **stimulants** more likely to induce dependence than other drugs?
_____
_____
_____
_____
_____

Complete the following form, comparing and contrasting different aspects of using **cocaine powder** versus **crack.**

	Cocaine Powder	**Crack**
How administered		
Effects		
Dangers		

How does **cocaine** affect neurons, causing the psychological effects associated with it? _____
_____
_____

How does **cocaine,** a drug that initially produces pleasure, ultimately lead to the loss of pleasure from other sources (e.g., food and sex)? _____
_____
_____

Caffeine and **nicotine** are common stimulants. List their effects below.

Caffeine	Nicotine

What are the dangers of amphetamine and MDMA use? _____
_____
_____
_____
_____
_____

Narcotic Analgesics: Focus on Heroin

How do **narcotic analgesics** affect the brain?

- _____
  _____
  _____
- _____
  _____
  _____
  _____

What effects does **heroin** have?

- _____
- _____
- _____
- _____
- _____
- _____

Why is it so difficult for a **heroin** addict to "kick the habit"? _____
_____
_____
_____
_____

Hallucinogens: Focus on LSD

What effects does **LSD** have on users?

- _____
- _____
- _____
- _____
- _____

What are the effects of **marijuana** on users?

- _____
- _____
- _____
- _____

How do the effects of **marijuana** depend on the context in which they occur? _____
_____
_____
_____

Coping and Social Support

Describe five research findings about social support and its health benefits.

- _____
- _____
- _____
- _____

Which types of relationships lead to these benefits? _____
_____
_____
_____

Distinguish between **perceived social support** and **enacted social support.** Which is more important in buffering against stress? _____
_____
_____
_____
_____
_____
_____
_____
_____

Evaluate your **social support** network. Do you feel like you have adequate social support? Why or why not? _____

_____

_____

_____

_____

_____

_____

Mind–Body Interventions

Which mind–body interventions have you tried, or would you like to try? _____

_____

_____

_____

What are the benefits of mind–body interventions?

- _____
- _____
- _____
- _____
- _____

What is a placebo? How can it be effective? _____

_____

_____

_____

_____

_____

_____

GO SURFING . . .

at the following site and try the meditation suggested there.
- **The Skillful Meditation Project**
  http://www.meditationproject.com/Instructions.shtml

What did you experience? Do you think it worked as it was supposed to? Why or why not?

_____

_____

_____

_____

Gender, Culture, and Coping

Describe the negative and positive effects for women of having multiple roles:

Negative Effects	Positive Effects

Give an example of how culture can affect what a person perceives as a stressor._____

_____

_____

_____

Give an example of how culture can affect which coping skills are socially accepted. _____

_____

_____

_____

Looking at Levels: Voodoo Death

How might the **nocebo effect** work on a psychological level—for example, when you expect to do poorly on a test? _____

_____

_____

_____

_____

_____

_____

After You Read . . . Thinking Back

1. Why might some people perceive stress differently than others? Relate this to top-down and bottom-up processing. _____

_____

_____

_____

_____

_____

_____

_____

2. How might sleep and stress interact? Discuss. _____

_____

_____

_____

_____

_____

_____

_____

3. Use your knowledge of sensation and perception to discuss how placebos work. _____

_____

_____

_____

_____

_____

_____

_____

4. How might principles of learning be used to help individuals end substance abuse? _____

_____

_____

_____

_____

_____

_____

5. Given what you know about the functions of sleep, why might babies sleep longer and older people sleep less? (What does this mean about their brain development?) _____

_____

_____

_____

_____

_____

6. Do you think that substance abuse and substance dependence are psychological disorders? Why or why not? _____

   _____

   _____

   _____

   _____

   _____

   _____

7. Some of the substances described in this chapter can be legally prescribed as treatment for other psychological disorders (e.g., barbiturates can be prescribed to treat insomnia or anxiety). Given the potential for abuse of these substances, how effective do you think drug therapy is in treating psychological disorders? _____

   _____

   _____

   _____

   _____

   _____

   _____

After You Read . . . Thinking Ahead

1. How might group norms, such as in an office place, affect individuals' stress levels? Explain.

    _____
    _____
    _____
    _____
    _____
    _____
    _____

2. Groups sometimes influence people to abuse substances (as in peer pressure) and sometimes influence people to stop using drugs (as in Alcoholics Anonymous). Why do groups have both kinds of influence? What will determine how an individual is influenced? _____

    _____
    _____
    _____
    _____
    _____
    _____
    _____

3. How do you think stress affects relationships with others, including relationships with intimate partners? Families? Co-workers? Neighbors? _____

    _____
    _____
    _____
    _____
    _____
    _____
    _____

After You Read . . . Practice Tests

PRACTICE TEST #1

Multiple-Choice Questions

For each question, circle the best answer from the choices given.

1. According the general adaptation syndrome, the period in which the body adapts to the stressor is known as the _____ phase. (p. 427)
   a. resistance
   b. alarm
   c. reactive
   d. exhaustion

2. The emotional predicament experienced when making difficult choices is _____. (p. 432)
   a. an approach-avoidance conflict
   b. an avoidance-avoidance conflict
   c. an external conflict.
   d. an internal conflict

3. Emily's boyfriend just asked her to go on a trip to Jamaica during spring break. She is torn because her parents recently told her that they had planned a family trip to her favorite country, Greece. This is an example of _____. (p. 432)
   a. an approach-approach conflict
   b. an avoidance-avoidance conflict
   c. an external conflict
   d. an internal effect

4. According to the research, what determines whether an event will be a stressor? (p. 427)
   a. the amount of physical pain
   b. the duration of the stress
   c. the individual's perception of the event
   d. the number of people involved

5. The body's naturally produced anti-inflammatory agent(s) is/are called _____. (p. 428)
   a. endorphins and enkephalins
   b. dopamine and serotonin
   c. cortisol
   d. all of the above

6. Stage two of Selye's three-stage stress response is called _____. (p. 427)
   a. alarm
   b. exhaustion
   c. resistance
   d. coping

7. When the stress response is triggered, the brain responds to the threat through the
    _____. (p. 428)
    a. frontal lobes
    b. hippocampus
    c. hypothalamic-pituitary-adrenal axis
    d. parasympathetic nervous system

8. When you can't decide between the double-chocolate cake and the strawberry mousse pie,
    because you like them both, you are experiencing an _____ conflict. (p. 432)
    a. approach-approach
    b. avoidance-approach
    c. avoidance-avoidance
    d. approach-avoidance

PRACTICE TEST #2

Multiple-Choice Questions

For each question, circle the best answer from the choices given.

1. Which of the following statements is TRUE regarding how mental and emotional states affect the immune system? (p. 436)
   a. Elderly Chinese are more likely to die right after the Harvest Moon festival.
   b. Orthodox Jews are more likely to die right after the Harvest Moon festival.
   c. Elderly Chinese are more likely to die around the High Holy Days.
   d. none of the above

2. Stress impacts _____. (p. 435-436)
   a. the amount of time it takes wounds to heal.
   b. the functioning of NK cells.
   c. the growth of cancer.
   d. all of the above

3. An EEG displays a pattern of recording in which sleep spindles are evident. This finding is indicative of which stage of sleep? (p. 440)
   a. stage 1
   b. stage 2
   c. stage 3
   d. stage 4

4. Which two stages of sleep are referred to collectively as slow wave sleep? (p. 440)
   a. stages 2 and 3
   b. stages 3 and 4
   c. stages 1 and 3
   d. stage 4 and REM

5. John goes to a sleep clinic and has his brain waves monitored while sleeping. He has an unusually large percentage of REM sleep. Why might this be? (p. 441)
   a. Recently, John has been getting too much sleep.
   b. John must have drank too much alcohol before he fell asleep.
   c. John may have had too much coffee too late in the afternoon.
   d. John must have been sleep deprived prior this appointment.

6. How would an evolutionary psychologist explain humans' need for sleep? (p. 443)
   a. It strengthens important neural connections.
   b. It restores our bodies from the wear and tear of the day.
   c. It keeps us in bed, at a time when our vision is not very good.
   d. It increases cortisol levels.

7. The twenty-four-hour day _____. (p. 446)
   a. is largely maintained through light-dark cycles (which can be either natural or artificial)
   b. results from external aids, such as clocks
   c. is not necessarily humans' "natural" rhythm
   d. is all of the above

8. Atherosclerosis is (p. 437)
   a. the neurotransmitter involved in the stress response.
   b. the medical condition characterized by a build up of plaque in the arteries.
   c. the second phase of the stress response.
   d. the medical condition characterized by pressure in the lungs.

9. A stressor that increases the likelihood of heart disease is _____. (p. 438)
   a. Marriage
   b. Major disasters
   c. Graduate school
   d. Depression

10. Stress can cause _____. (p. 436)
    a. an increased risk of infection following an injury
    b. post-traumatic stress disorder
    c. all of the above
    d. none of the above

11. Studies that investigate the relationship between stress and the immune system typically measure _____ as an index of immune system activity. (p. 436)
    a. the number of circulating white blood cells
    b. the number of circulating red blood cells
    c. the amount of damage to white blood cells
    d. the amount of damage to red blood cells

PRACTICE TEST #3:

Multiple-Choice Questions

For each question, circle the best answer from the choices given.

1. This style of coping involves strategies that alter either the environment itself or the way in which the person and the environment interact. (p. 451)
   a. problem-focused
   b. emotion-focused
   c. decision-focused
   d. avoidance-focused

2. When someone is using a coping style that focuses on changing his or her emotional response to the stressor, he or she is using _____ coping. (p. 451)
   a. problem-focused
   b. emotion-focused
   c. decision-focused
   d. detail-focused

3. The tendency to interpret the intentions of others negatively is called _____. (p. 454)
   a. avoidant attribution bias
   b. anger bias
   c. hostile attribution bias
   d. none of the above

4. Narcissists are likely to respond to a negative evaluation of their performance on a task with _____. (p. 455)
   a. disbelief
   b. annoyance
   c. aggression
   d. none of the above

5. Alcohol use can lead to: (p. 458)

a. alcohol myopia
b. inhibitory conflict
c. increased agression
d. all of the above

6. Which of the following descriptions most accurately depicts the manner in which cocaine stimulates the nervous system? (p. 460)

a. mimicking the effect of dopamine
b. mimicking the effect norepinephrine
c. preventing the reuptake of serotonin
d. preventing the reuptake of both dopamine and norepinephrine

7. All of the following are stimulants EXCEPT: (p. 459-460)

a. Amphetamines
b. Barbiturates
c. Crack
d. Ecstasy

8. The most popular used hallucinogenic drug in America is _____. (p. 462)

a. PCP
b. LSD
c. marijuana
d. ecstasy

9. Mind-body interventions can alter_____. (p. 464)

a. heart and breathing rates
b. hormone secretion
c. brain activation
d. all of the above

10. Compared to their male counterparts, women performing multiple roles as working mothers may experience all of the following except: (p. 466)

a. more stress
b. more parental responsibilities
c. decreased feelings of self-esteem and control
d. more conflict among their different roles

COMPREHENSIVE PRACTICE TEST

True/False Questions

Circle TRUE or FALSE for each of the following statements.

1. TRUE   FALSE   Being underfed is an example of an acute stressor. (p. 427)

2. TRUE   FALSE   If the immune system is suppressed, NK cells work to prevent the spread of tumor cells. (p. 436)

3. TRUE   FALSE   Students who wrote about a traumatic experience experienced a reduction in the negative effects of stress. (p.452)

4. TRUE   FALSE   Dreams can occur in NREM stages. (p. 443)

5. TRUE   FALSE   Your "natural" circadian rhythm is exactly 24 hours long. (p. 447)

6. TRUE   FALSE   Venting is a problem-focused coping strategy. (p. 451)

7. TRUE   FALSE   Substance dependence is synonymous with substance abuse. (p. 456)

8. TRUE   FALSE   Heroin is a central nervous system depressant. (p. 461)

Multiple-Choice Questions

For each question, circle the best answer from the choices given.

1. What is the first phase of the stress response? (p. 427)
    a. exhaustion
    b. concentration
    c. alarm
    d. resistance

2. Troy just joined another club. Most likely he has _____ his allostatic load. (p. 429)
    a. increased
    b. decreased
    c. not changed
    d. none of the above

3. Perceived lack of control can lead to _____ . (p. 431)
    a. emotion-focused coping
    b. problem-focused coping
    c. hardiness
    d. learned helplessness

4. Traffic is considered _____. (p.433)
   a. a hassle
   b. an allostatic load
   c. a problem-focused coping strategy
   d. all of the above

5. Walking alone in a dark alley one night, Carrie hears footsteps behind her. Her primary appraisal of the situation will lead her to _____. (p. 430)
   a. run
   b. ask herself if she should be concerned
   c. ask herself what she can do about the situation
   d. all of the above

6. We are less likely to be stressed about uncontrollable situations if the situations are at least _____. (p. 431-432)
   a. positive
   b. predictable
   c. unexpected
   d. none of the above

7. In what way(s) can stress affect the growth of cancerous tumor cells? (p. 436-437)
   a. It can suppress the production of NK cells, which prevent the spread of tumors.
   b. It can "feed" tumors by supplying blood through the capillaries.
   c. all of the above
   d. none of the above—stress has little affect on tumor growth

8. There are a total of _____ stages of sleep. (p. 439-440)

a. three
b. four
c. five
d. six

9. It is Monday and you have determined that you need to allocate eight more hours of study to do well on an upcoming final scheduled for Friday. To fit in the study time you will have to cut back on your sleep (substituting study for sleep). Based on the research noted in your text, which of the following scenarios would reap the greatest benefits? (p. 442)

a. Cut back 2 hours of sleep each night (Monday through Thursday)
b. Cut back 2 hours of sleep on Tuesday and 3 hours of sleep on Wednesday and Thursday
c. Cut back 4 hours of sleep on Wednesday and Thursday
d. Pull an all-nighter Thursday night

10. The latent content of a dream refers to: (p. 444)

a. readily apparent content
b. content which is most memorable
c. content that is not readily apparent to the dreamer
d. content that provokes the most anxiety

11. Which of the following brain structures mediates our circadian rhythms? (p. 446)

a. pineal gland
b. pituitary gland
c. lateral geniculate nucleus
d. suprachiasmatic nucleus

12. All of the following are avoidant coping strategies except: (p. 452)

a. distraction
b. suppression of competing activities
c. behavioral disengagement
d. mental disengagement

13.   Couples who were more verbally and physically aggressive with each other were more likely to report _____ stressful events when compared to non-abusive couples. (p. 453)

a. different types of
b. the same number
c. less
d. more

14. MDMA damages neurons that release _____. (p. 460)

a. norepinephrine
b. serotonin.
c. acetylcholine
d. dopamine

15. Which of the following drugs would be most likely to produce hallucinations? (p. 462)

a. MDMA (or "e")
b. Heroin
c. Opiates
d. LSD

Short-Answer/Essay Questions

Answer the following in the space provided.

1. What is stress? _____

_____

_____

_____

_____

_____

_____

_____

_____

2. Describe the toll that sleep deprivation takes on a person's cognitive, emotional, physical health.__

_____

_____

_____

_____

_____

_____

_____

_____

3. Imagine you are a doctor and one of your patient's has problems sleeping but does not want to be prescribed any medication due to the potential adverse side effects of such medicine. Describe four nonmedicinal approaches to getting a better night's sleep that you would recommend._____

_____

_____

_____

_____

_____

_____

_____

_____

_____

_____

4. Is aggression simply a way for people with low self-esteem to feel better about themselves? Explain your answer. _____

_____

_____

_____

_____

_____

_____

_____

_____

5. What aspects of social support are most important for protecting against stress? _____

_____

_____

_____

_____

_____

_____

_____

When You Are Finished . . . Puzzle It Out

Across

1. Narcotic derived from opium poppy
4. Loss of consciousness while drunk
6. Hormone facilitating "fight or flight" response
12. A major depressant
13. Plaque build-up in arteries
15. Sleep in which the body is paralyzed
16. Repeated difficulty sleeping
17. Another name for Stage 1 sleep
18. First cognitive appraisal of stressor
19. Type of white blood cell in bone marrow

Down

2. Last phase of the GAS
3. Proposed that dreams are symbolic
5. Stimulus that disrupts equilibrium
7. Behavior intended to harm another
8. Destroys damaged or altered cells
9. First phase of the GAS
10. Most common hallucinogen
11. Disorder accompanied by snoring
13. Short-term stress
14. Person's reaction to stress
20. Symbolic meaning of a dream

Puzzle created with Puzzlemaster at DiscoverySchool.com.

Chapter 11
Psychological Disorders:
More Than Everyday Problems

Before You Read . . .

Have you ever known anyone with a psychological disorder? How did you know that he or she had a disorder? In this chapter, you will learn about some of the symptoms of psychological disorders. The chapter begins with a definition of abnormality, including explanations for what causes abnormality (at the levels of the brain, the person, and the group) and how abnormal behaviors are categorized into the major psychological disorders and personality disorders using the *Diagnostic and Statistical Manual of Mental Disorders.*

The major disorders covered in this chapter include some of the more common ones—depression, anxiety, and eating disorders—and some of the more unusual and less common ones like schizophrenia and posttraumatic stress disorder. A description and discussion of causes are provided for each disorder.

Chapter Objectives

After reading this chapter, you will be able to:

- Define abnormality.

- Explain what psychological disorders are and how they are classified and diagnosed.

- Define mood disorders and explain what causes them.

- Describe the main types of anxiety disorders, including their symptoms and causes.

- Describe the symptoms and causes of the various types of schizophrenia.

- Describe the symptoms and causes of eating disorders.

- Explain what personality disorders are.

As You Read . . . Term Identification

Make flashcards using the following terms as you go. Use the definitions in the margins of this chapter for help. If you write the definitions in your own words, though, you will remember them better!

Agoraphobia
Anorexia nervosa
Antisocial personality disorder (ASPD)
Anxiety disorders
Attributional style
Bipolar disorder
Bulimia nervosa
Compulsion
Delusions
Diathesis–stress model
Eating disorders
Generalized anxiety disorder
Hallucinations
High expressed emotion
Major depressive disorder (MDD)
Manic episode
Mood disorders

Negative symptom
Obsession
Obsessive-compulsive disorder (OCD)
Panic attack
Panic disorder
Personality disorders
Phobia
Positive symptom
Posttraumatic stress disorder (PTSD)
Psychological disorder
Psychosis
Schizophrenia
Social causation
Social phobia
Social selection
Specific phobia

As You Read . . . Questions and Exercises

Identifying Psychological Disorders: What's Abnormal?

Defining Abnormality

Provide a definition of **psychological disorder.** Be sure to use the words *distress*, *disability*, and *danger*. _____

_____

_____

_____

_____

What role does culture play in defining **psychological disorders?** _____

_____

_____

_____

_____

Explaining Abnormality

How was abnormal behavior explained . . .

In ancient Greece:
In the 17th century:
In the middle of the 20th century:

What is the *biopsychosocial model?* _____

_____

_____

_____

_____

_____

What is the **diathesis–stress model?** _____

_____

_____

_____

_____

_____

Explain some of the things that can "go wrong" at each of the following levels, which may eventually lead to a psychological disorder.

Level	What Can Go Wrong?
Brain	
Person	
Group	

Describe David Rosenhan's study and findings. _____
_____
_____
_____
_____
_____
_____

Categorizing Disorders: Is a Rose Still a Rose by Any Other Name?

The guide used to diagnose mental disorders in the United States is the _____. It is published by the _____, and is currently in the _____ edition.

List four criticisms of the *DSM:*

- _____
- _____
- _____
- _____

Axis I: An Overview of Selected Disorders

Mood Disorders

GO SURFING . . .

. . . to find out if you might have depression. Short depression inventories are available at the following sites:

- http://psychcentral.com/depquiz.htm
- http://www.allina.com/ahs/bhs.nsf/page/t_depression
- http://discoveryhealth.queendom.com/depression_abridged_access.html
- http://www.thewayup.com/newsletters/zung.htm

What did these surveys indicate? _____

Do you agree or disagree with the results? _____
_____

What are the "ABCs" that are affected by **major depressive disorder (MDD)?**
A: _____
B: _____
C: _____

How does **MDD** affect the workplace? _____
_____
_____
_____
_____
_____
_____
_____
_____
_____

GO SURFING . . .

. . .to find some of the warning signs of **suicide.** (There are lots of good sites out there.) List the signs here:

- _____
- _____
- _____
- _____
- _____
- _____
- _____
- _____
- _____

What is **dysthmia?** _____
_____
_____
_____

What is the difference between **mania** and **hypomania?** _____
_____
_____
_____
_____

Summarize the causes of **MDD** at the levels of the brain, the person, and the group.

The Brain	The Person	The Group

How do events at the different levels interact with each other? _____

_____

_____

_____

_____

Anxiety Disorders

Identify the following **psychological disorders:**

Description	Disorder
Avoidance of places where escape may be difficult if a panic attack occurs	
Fear of public embarrassment or humiliation	
Re-experiencing of a traumatic event, avoidance of stimuli, and hypervigilance	
Frequent attacks of inexplicable autonomic arousal accompanied by fear	
Persistent and intrusive thoughts accompanied by irrational behaviors	
A persistent and excessive fear focused on a specific object or situation	

GO SURFING . . .

...to find out if you might have panic disorder (or another anxiety disorder). Short self-surveys are available at the following Web sites:

- http://www.livingwithanxiety.com/anxiety-quiz.htm
- http://www.adaa.org/Public/selftest_Panic.htm
- http://www2.zoloft.com/index.asp?pageid=10

What did these surveys indicate? _____

Do you agree or disagree with the results? _____
_____
_____
_____
_____

Have you or a friend ever had a **panic attack?** If so, how would you or your friend describe it? _____
_____
_____
_____
_____

Summarize the causes of **panic disorder** at the levels of the brain, the person, and the group.

The Brain	The Person	The Group

How do events at the different levels interact with each other? _____
_____
_____
_____
_____

What is **social phobia** (or **social anxiety disorder**)? What are the symptoms? How prevalent is it? _
_____
_____
_____
_____

Do you have any **phobias?** If so . . .

GO SURFING . . .

. . .to find out the names of these **phobias.** See complete lists of phobias at the following Web sites:
- http://www.phobialist.com/reverse.html
- http://www.geocities.com/beckygretz19/weird_facts_phobias.html
- http://www.designedthinking.com/Fear/Phobias/Topics/topics.html

What do you have **phobias** of? What are the names of these **phobias?** _____
_____
_____
_____
_____
_____
_____

Summarize the causes of **phobias** at the levels of the brain, the person, and the group.

The Brain	The Person	The Group

How do events at the different levels interact with each other? _____
_____
_____
_____
_____
_____

Obsessive-Compulsive Disorder (OCD)

GO SURFING . . .

. . .to find out if you might have OCD. Short self-surveys are available at the following sites:
- http://psychcentral.com/ocdquiz.htm
- http://www.ocdaction.org.uk/ocdaction/index.asp?id=302
- http://www.bbc.co.uk/science/humanbody/mind/surveys/ocd/index.shtml

What did these surveys indicate? _____

Do you agree or disagree with the results? _____
_____

Summarize the causes of **OCD** at the levels of the brain, the person, and the group.

The Brain	The Person	The Group

How do events at the different levels interact with each other? _____
_____
_____
_____
_____
_____
_____

Posttraumatic Stress Disorder (PTSD)

The diagnosis of **PTSD** is made when three conditions are met:

- _____
  _____
- _____
  _____
- _____
  _____

Three sets of **symptoms** are persistently experienced by the person with **PTSD:**

- _____
  _____
- _____
  _____
- _____
  _____

Summarize the causes of **PTSD** at the levels of the brain, the person, and the group.

The Brain	The Person	The Group

How do events at the different levels interact with each other? _____
_____
_____
_____

Schizophrenia

GO SURFING . . .

. . .to find out if you might have **schizophrenia.** A short self-survey is available at http://psychcentral.com/quizzes/schizophrenia.htm.

Is **schizophrenia** another name for multiple personality disorder? Explain. _____
_____
_____
_____
_____

List the **positive** and **negative symptoms** of **schizophrenia.**

Positive Symptoms	Negative Symptoms

Identify the following types of **schizophrenia,** based on the descriptions:

_____ Bizarre movements, may not speak
_____ Outside of delusions, may seem normal; best prognosis
_____ Inappropriate affect and social behaviors
_____ Doesn't meet criteria for any of other subtypes

Summarize the causes of **schizophrenia** at the levels of the brain, the person, and the group.

The Brain	The Person	The Group

How do events at the different levels interact with each other? _____

_____

_____

_____

_____

Eating Disorders: You Are How You Eat?

GO SURFING . . .

...to find out if you might have an eating disorder. Short self-surveys are available at the following sites:

- http://psychcentral.com/eatingquiz.htm
- http://www.msnbc.com/modules/quizzes/eating_profiler.asp?cp1=1
- http://www.caringonline.com/eatdis/misc/edtest.htm

What did these surveys indicate? _____

Do you agree or disagree with the results? _____

_____

Which characteristic is used to distinguish between **anorexia** and **bulimia?** _____

_____

_____

_____

_____

Summarize the causes of **anorexia** and **bulimia** at the levels of the brain, the person, and the group.

Level of Brain		Level of Person		Level of Group	
Anorexia	Bulimia	Anorexia	Bulimia	Anorexia	Bulimia

Looking at Levels: Binge Eating

What is meant by the **abstinence violation effect?** How might you help a friend, at the level of the group, who you suspect has **bulimia?** _____

_____

_____

_____

_____

_____

_____

_____

_____

_____

Axis II: Focus on Personality Disorders

How are Axis II **personality disorders** different from Axis I disorders? _____

_____

_____

_____

_____

_____

_____

Name three criticisms of including **personality disorders** under Axis II (or at all) in the DSM-IV.

- _____
  _____
  _____
  _____

- _____
  _____
  _____
  _____
  _____

- _____
  _____
  _____
  _____

Look at the list of Axis II personality disorders found in the textbook. Do you know anyone who has a personality disorder, do you think? Who? Which disorder? What leads you to believe this? ____
_____
_____
_____
_____
_____
_____
_____
_____
_____
_____

List the characteristics of **antisocial personality disorder.** _____
_____
_____
_____
_____

Explain **antisocial personality disorder** at the levels of the brain, the person, and the group. Use arrows to indicate how events at the different levels may interact.

The Brain	The Person	The Group

After You Read . . . Thinking Back

1. In Chapter 6, you learned about biological preparedness. Based on this phenomenon, are there some phobias that you think are more common? Some that are less common? Why? _____
   _____
   _____
   _____
   _____
   _____

2. Sleep and circadian rhythms appear to play a role in several different psychological disorders. How? _____
   _____
   _____
   _____
   _____
   _____

3. How would you explain the amnesia associated with the dissociative disorders, given what you learned about memory in Chapter 7? _____
   _____
   _____
   _____
   _____
   _____

4. In Chapter 10, you learned about different theories of emotions. How might these theories be important in studying psychological disorders? _____
   _____
   _____
   _____
   _____
   _____

5. How can the idea of critical or sensitive periods, which you learned about in Chapter 12, be applied to the development of psychological disorders? _____
   _____
   _____
   _____
   _____

After You Read . . . Thinking Ahead

1. Different types of therapies will work differently for different disorders. Which disorders do you think could probably best be treated by trying to change someone's thoughts? By trying to change someone's behaviors? _____

_____

_____

_____

_____

_____

2. Are there any disorders for which the best that can be hoped for is that the symptoms are controlled? In other words, do you think there are some disorders for which the underlying causes cannot be treated? If so, which ones? Why these disorders? _____

_____

_____

_____

_____

_____

3. What might be the consequences of labeling a person as disordered, both at the individual level and the group level? _____

_____

_____

_____

_____

_____

4. Assume that a person moves from another culture to this one. In that previous culture, the person's behavior was not considered disordered. Here, it is. In such a case, should the person's behavior be considered a psychological disorder? What if the behavior might be considered illegal (e.g., questionable child-rearing practices)? _____

_____

_____

_____

_____

5. Some psychological disorders may pose problems in forming intimate relationships and friendships. Which disorders? What types of problems? _____

_____

_____

_____

_____

After You Read . . . Practice Tests

PRACTICE TEST #1

Multiple-Choice Questions
For each question, circle the best answer from the choices given.

1. Which of the following is NOT part of the definition of a psychological disorder? (pp. 475-476)
   a. impairment
   b. distress
   c. danger
   d. none of the above

2. Mental images so vivid that they seem real, but are not real, are called_____. (p. 476)
   a. hallucinations
   b. psychoses
   c. delusions
   d. none of the above

3. The biopsychosocial model focuses on factors at the level of the _____ as causing psychological illness. (p. 477)
   a. brain
   b. group
   c. person
   d. all of the above

4. According to the ancient Greeks, too much phlegm made people _____. (p. 477)
   a. hyper
   b. sluggish
   c. melancholic
   d. happy

5. Which of the following would be an example of a diathesis? (p. 477)
   a. an imbalance of neurotransmitter levels
   b. a natural catastrophe
   c. relationship loss
   d. culture

6. Rosenhan's (1971) study was criticized because it _____. (p. 479)
   a. did not have a control group
   b. did not randomly assign groups
   c. tried to generalize across ethnic groups
   d. was not replicated

7. Among the most common psychological disorders is _____. (p. 483)
   a. major depressive disorder
   b. obsessive-compulsive disorder
   c. panic disorder
   d. schizophrenia

8. Major depressive disorder, dysthymia, and bipolar disorder are all examples of _____ disorders. (p. 483)
   a. anxiety
   b. mood
   c. personality
   d. None of the above

9. In people with bipolar disorder, the _____ is sometimes enlarged. (p. 487)
   a. amygdala
   b. locus coeruleus
   c. hypothalamus
   d. none of the above

10. A person who experiences a period of at least one week during which an abnormally elevated, expansive, or irritable mood persists is having a _____. (p. 485)
    a. manic episode
    b. hypomanic episode
    c. dysthymic episode
    d. all of the above

PRACTICE TEST #2:

Multiple-Choice Questions

For each question, circle the best answer from the choices given.

1. A person who suffers from attacks of intense fear or discomfort, accompanied by heightened sympathetic nervous system activity, would be diagnosed with _____. (p. 491)
   a. generalized anxiety
   b. depression
   c. panic disorder
   d. agoraphobia

2. The primary difference between generalized anxiety disorder and other anxiety disorders is that generalized anxiety disorder _____. (p. 490)
   a. is not related to a specific object or situation
   b. relates to a specific object or situation
   c. refers to the anxiety experience across the lifespan
   d. all of the above

3. Phobias are normally maintained through _____. (p. 494)
   a. classical conditioning
   b. counter conditioning
   c. operant conditioning
   d. vicarious modeling

4. Which of the following is NOT an example of a compulsive behavior? (pp. 494-495)
   a. moving all your penguin figurines so that they face north
   b. using hand sanitizer so often that your hands are raw
   c. putting your own sheets on a hotel bed out of fear of germs
   d. shouting obscenities in church

5. Which of the following ways of coping would best protect someone from developing PTSD following a traumatic event? (p. 498)
   a. social support
   b. ruminating about the event
   c. using relaxation techniques after the event
   d. staying busy

6. _____ is a psychotic disorder in which the patient's affect, behavior, and thoughts are profoundly altered. (p. 499)
   a. Schizophrenia
   b. Paranoid Personality Disorder
   c. Histrionic Personality Disorder
   d. Schizotypal Personality Disorder

7. The type of schizophrenia with the best prognosis for recovery is _____. (p. 500)
   a. paranoid
   b. catatonic
   c. disorganized
   d. undifferentiated

8. Which of the following is an example of a positive symptom? (p. 500)
   a. flat affect
   b. alogia
   c. hallucinations
   d. all of the above are examples of positive symptoms

9. People with schizophrenia have enlarged _____. (p. 501)
   a. occipital lobes
   b. ventricles
   c. temporal lobes
   d. none of the above

10. An emotional style in families that are critical, hostile, and over-involved is known as
    _____. (p. 503)
    a. high expressed emotion
    b. low expressed emotion
    c. social selection
    d. negative symptom

PRACTICE TEST #3:

Multiple-Choice Questions

For each question, circle the best answer from the choices given.

1. In what ways are people with bulimia <u>always</u> different from people with anorexia? (p. 506)
   a. People with anorexia are underweight; people with bulimia are not
   b. People with bulimia binge and purge; people with anorexia do not
   c. People with anorexia stop menstruating; people with bulimia do not
   d. People with anorexia fast; people with bulimia do not.

2. _____ disorders is a category of disorders in which relatively stable personality traits are inflexible and maladaptive, causing distress or difficulty with daily functioning. (p. 511)
   a. Mood
   b. Anxiety
   c. Eating
   d. Personality

3. Someone with no guilt, conscience, or empathy for others most likely has a(n) _____ personality disorder. (p. 512)
   a. avoidant
   b. narcissistic
   c. borderline
   d. antisocial

4. Paranoid, schizoid, and schizotypal are disorders in cluster A because they involve _____.
   (p. 512)
   a. odd, eccentric behaviors
   b. emotional or dramatic behaviors
   c. anxious or fearful behaviors
   d. None of the above

5. Some researchers argue that personality disorders should not be included in the DSM because some personality disorders _____. (pp. 511-512)
   a. are too difficult to diagnose.
   b. are not significantly different than the corresponding Axis I diagnosis.
   c. are so prevalent.
   d. all of the above.

6. Which personality disorder is described by a pattern of detachment from social relationships and a narrow range of displayed emotion? (p. 512)
   a. schizoid
   b. schizotypal
   c. antisocial
   d. paranoid

7. People with antisocial personality disorder _____. (p. 514)
    a. often have a poor attachment to their caregiver during childhood
    b. may have witnessed a lack of concern for the welfare of others by peers or parents
    c. may have an underresponsive central nervous system
    d. all of the above

8. _____ personality disorder is characterized by a longstanding pattern of disregard for other people to the point of violating their rights. (pp. 513-514)
    a. Histrionic
    b. Antisocial
    c. Narcissistic
    d. Schizoid

COMPREHENSIVE PRACTICE TEST

True/False Questions

Circle TRUE or FALSE for each of the following statements.

1. TRUE   FALSE   Delusions are sensory images so vivid that they seem real. (p. 476)

2. TRUE   FALSE   Depression tends to run in families. (p. 486)

3. TRUE   FALSE   There is more known about bipolar disorder at the level of the person than depression. (p. 487)

4. TRUE   FALSE   Phoebe feels like her chest is exploding. In addition, she feels like she can't breathe and that she is about to die. Assuming that Phoebe does not have a medical problem, she is likely experiencing a mood disorder. (p. 491)

5. TRUE   FALSE   It is possible that specific phobias are learned. (p. 493)

6. TRUE   FALSE   Schizophrenia is the same as multiple personality disorder. (p. 499)

Multiple-Choice Questions

For each question, circle the best answer from the choices given.

1. The diathesis-stress model proposes that mental illnesses arise from (pp. 478-479)
   a. genetic vulnerabilities.
   b. biochemical imbalances.
   c. environmental stressors.
   d. some combination of the above.

2. Which of the following is an example of distress? (p. 475)
   a. hearing voices that no one else can hear
   b. feeling sad for long periods of time
   c. All of the above
   d. None of the above

3. For the past two weeks, Regina has felt very fatigued. She has slept almost all the time and lost a considerable amount of weight. Not even her favorite activities, such as horseback riding, can rouse her interest. Which of the following disorders does Regina probably have? (p. 483)
   a. Major depressive disorder
   b. Chronic fatigued syndrome
   c. Anorexia
   d. Dysthymia

4. How many axes are in the current version of the DSM? (p. 480)
   a. two
   b. three
   c. four
   d. five

5. Panic attacks may arise from a hypersensitivity in the _____. (p. 492)
   a. occipital lobe
   b. locus coeruleus
   c. hypothalamus
   d. heart

6. Deborah constantly complains of back pain. Her doctor cannot substantiate her claim with any medical evidence. The doctor suspects that her medical complaints are psychological in nature. According to the DSM-IV, Deborah's condition would mostly likely fall in the _____ category. (p. 481)
   a. dementia
   b. schizophrenia
   c. mood
   d. somatoform

7. Frank has been asked to present his company's proposal to a funding board in a few days. However, Frank was terrified to speak in public, and consequently quit his job to avoid what he perceived would be a great embarrassment. Most likely, Frank would be diagnosed with _____. (p. 493)
   a. social phobia
   b. generalized anxiety disorder
   c. panic disorder
   d. all of the above

8. Of the following statements, which one is TRUE regarding PTSD? (pp. 497-498)
   a. If someone is raped (regardless of gender), he or she will experience PTSD.
   b. Natural disasters are the most likely trauma that elicits PTSD.
   c. The majority of people who experience a trauma do not develop PTSD.
   d. If a person experiences flashbacks, he or she will receive a diagnosis of PTSD.

9. As children, people who later developed schizophrenia _____. (p. 503)
   a. were happier than others
   b. were more "emotionally dampened" than their peers
   c. slept more
   d. none of the above

10. Daniel has schizophrenia and remains flat in his emotional responses. In general, he fails to respond emotionally and exhibits minimal body language. He is displaying _____. (p. 500)
    a. flat affect
    b. alogia
    c. avolition
    d. delusions

11. If you have a parent with schizophrenia, the odds are you _____. (p. 501)
    a. will develop schizophrenia in your early twenties
    b. will develop schizophrenia later in life
    c. will develop schizophrenia—if you are female
    d. won't develop schizophrenia

12. A patient in the hospital sits on the edge of his bed with his arm raised straight in front of him. He never lowers his arm. Which subtype of schizophrenia does the patient most likely have? (p. 500)
    a. catatonic
    b. paranoid
    c. disorganized
    d. undifferentiated

13. An increased risk of developing anorexia occurs among women who are _____. (p. 507)
    a. depressed
    b. anxious
    c. perfectionistic
    d. conscientious

14. If a client is diagnosed with _____ personality disorder, he or she is most likely engaged in a pattern of excessive attention seeking and expression of emotion. (p. 512)
    a. paranoid
    b. histrionic
    c. borderline
    d. schizoid

15. The most studied personality disorder is _____. (p. 513)
    a. depressive personality disorder
    b. antisocial personality disorder
    c. paranoid personality disorder
    d. none of the above

Short-Answer/Essay Questions

Answer the following questions in the space provided.

1. Briefly explain the components of the diathesis-stress model. _____
   _____
   _____
   _____
   _____
   _____
   _____
   _____
   _____

2. What are some of the common misconceptions of suicide? _____
   _____
   _____
   _____
   _____
   _____
   _____
   _____
   _____

3. What are the five subtypes of specific phobias? _____
   _____
   _____
   _____
   _____
   _____
   _____
   _____
   _____

4. What are the four subtypes of schizophrenia? _____
   _____
   _____
   _____
   _____
   _____
   _____
   _____

5. Personality disorders can be broken into three clusters. What are the common symptoms of each cluster? _____
   _____
   _____
   _____
   _____
   _____
   _____
   _____

When You Are Finished . . . Puzzle It Out

Across

2. Disorder of compulsive handwasher
3. Clinicians' guide for classifying disorders
6. Recurrent thought, hard to ignore
8. Type of symptom involving the loss of functioning
12. "Fear of the marketplace"
14. Experienced by some victims of rape
15. Less intense MDD

Puzzle created with Puzzlemaker at DiscoverySchool.com.

Down

1. Mental images that seem real
3. Predisposition to a disorder
4. Eighth leading cause of death in the U.S.
5. Number of axes in DSM
7. Previously called manic-depressive disorder
9. Episode of intense fear
10. DSM axis for personality disorders
11. Fear of object that interferes with life
13. Five types of information described in DSM
15. Bizarre false beliefs

Chapter 12
Treatment:
Healing Actions, Healing Words

Before You Read . . .

Have you ever been in therapy? Was it helpful? Do you know anyone who takes Prozac or another medication to treat a psychological disorder? This chapter presents an overview of the treatment of mental disorders. The first two sections cover the principles of the most common and most studied types of therapy: insight-oriented therapies (including psychodynamic and humanistic therapies) and cognitive-behavior therapy. The origins and techniques of these therapies are described.

The next section takes a detailed look at psychopharmacology and describes the major classes of medications and their indications. You will also read about electroconvulsive therapy and transcranial magnetic stimulation in this section. Finally, the chapter explores the effectiveness of therapy and presents good information on how to pick a therapist, should you ever need one.

Chapter Objectives

After reading this chapter, you should be able to:

- Describe the focus of treatment and techniques used in psychodynamic therapy.

- Explain how client-centered therapists approach treatment.

- Describe the goals and methods of behavior and cognitive therapies.

- Explain how medications are used to treat psychological disorders.

- Describe electroconvulsive therapy, as it is used today.

- Explain what transcranial magnetic stimulation is and how it is used in treatment.

- Explain which other forms (or modalities) of treatment are used besides individual therapy.

- Discuss recent trends in psychotherapy that might affect the future of mental health care.

- List key issues you should keep in mind when reading research studies of psychotherapy.

- Describe some good ways to find a therapist.

As You Read . . . Term Identification

Make flashcards using the following terms as you go. Use the definitions in the margins of this chapter for help. If you write the definitions in your own words, though, you will remember them better!

Antipsychotic medication
Behavior modification
Behavior therapy
Benzodiazepine
Client-centered therapy
Cognitive-behavior therapy (CBT)
Cognitive distortions
Cognitive restructuring
Cognitive therapy
Dream analysis
Electroconvulsive therapy (ECT)
Exposure
Free association
Incongruence
Insight-oriented therapy
Interpersonal therapy (IPT)
Interpretation

Monoamine oxidase inhibitor (MAOI)
Outcome research
Progressive muscle relaxation
Psychoanalysis
Psychodynamic therapy
Psychoeducation
Psychopharmacology
Psychotherapy integration
Resistance
Selective serotonin reuptake inhibitor (SSRI)
Self-monitoring techniques
Serotonin/norepinephrine reuptake inhibitor (SNRI)
Stimulus control
Systematic desensitization
Tardive dyskinesia
Technical eclecticism
Token economy
Transference
Tricyclic antidepressant (TCA)

As You Read . . . Questions and Exercises

Historical Influences on Psychotherapy: Insight-Oriented Therapies

What do **insight therapies** have in common? _____

_____

_____

_____

_____

Psychodynamic Therapy: Origins in Psychoanalysis

Freud said that there are three parts to personality: the id, the ego, and the superego. How can this structure of personality create psychological disorders? _____

_____

_____

_____

_____

How did Freud say that traditional **psychoanalysis** can resolve these disorders? _____

_____

_____

_____

_____

Which techniques did Freud use during **psychoanalysis?**

- _____
- _____
- _____

Why has **psychoanalysis** declined in popularity over the last several decades?

- _____
- _____

How is **psychoanalysis** different from contemporary **psychodynamic therapy?** _____

_____

_____

_____

_____

_____

In addition to **free association** and **dream analysis,** what other technique do psychodynamic theorists use? Explain. _____

_____

_____

_____

_____

How is **transference** helpful? _____

_____

_____

_____

_____

Humanistic Therapy: Client-Centered Therapy

How does **humanistic therapy** differ from **psychodynamic therapy?** _____
_____
_____
_____
_____
_____

What do **client-centered therapists** believe is the cause of people's distressing symptoms?
_____
_____
_____
_____
_____
_____

How would **client-centered** and other humanistic therapists approach treatment? Which techniques
would they use? _____
_____
_____
_____
_____
_____

Which type of **therapist** would you prefer to see: a psychodynamic therapist or a humanistic
therapist? Why? _____
_____
_____
_____
_____
_____

GO SURFING . . .

...and make up a problem to discuss with "Eliza," an artificial intelligence program that was initially
designed to simulate a client-centered therapist. A variety of Eliza programs on the Web:
- http://www-ai.ijs.si/eliza/eliza.html
- http://www.manifestation.com/neurotoys/eliza.php3

- http://www.wilprint.com/eliza.html
- http://www.uwp.edu/academic/psychology/demos/elizaj/eliza.htm

In what ways, if any, is Eliza like a **client-centered therapist?** In what ways is she dissimilar? _____
_____
_____
_____
_____
_____
_____

Evaluating Insight-Oriented Therapies

Why are **psychodynamic therapies** so difficult to evaluate?
- _____
- _____
- _____

With which types of patients does **psychodynamic therapy** appear to work best?
- _____
- _____
- _____

What aspects of Rogers' theory have been supported by research? _____
_____
_____
_____

Cognitive-Behavior Therapy

Behavior Therapy and Its Techniques

What is the root cause of distressing symptoms, in the view of behavior therapists? _____
_____
_____

What are the ABCs of **behavior therapy?**

A: _____
B: _____
C: _____

Explain how **exposure** could be used to treat a client's anxiety. _____
_____
_____
_____
_____
_____
_____
_____

How could **exposure with response prevention** be used to treat a client's checking behavior (e.g., repetitively checking that the stove is off before leaving the house)? _____
_____
_____
_____
_____
_____
_____
_____

GO SURFING . . .

…for instructions on **progressive muscle relaxation.** Instructions are available at the following Web sites:

- https://www.amsa.org/healingthehealer/musclerelaxation.cfm
- http://www.guidetopsychology.com/pmr.htm
- http://www.depressionet.com.au/inspiration/relaxation_tips.html#060502

Ask a friend to read the instructions for **progressive muscle relaxation** aloud to you. Practice this several times over the next week. Did you notice that it made you more relaxed? _____
_____
_____
_____

Name a behavior that you would like to modify. _____
_____

How could you use classical conditioning techniques to modify this behavior? _____
_____
_____
_____

If you were a parent, how could you use operant conditioning principles to modify a child's behavior (such as preventing your son from biting other children)? _____

_____

_____

_____

_____

Do you have any problematic behavior that may benefit from **self-monitoring techniques?** If so, what are they? What information could these techniques provide you? _____

_____

_____

_____

_____

Identify the following **behavioral techniques:**

Description	Technique
Relaxation in the presence of a feared object or situation	
Making a binge eater eat, but not letting her purge	
Relaxing from head to toe	
A person with anorexia exercises only when alone; don't leave her alone!	
Rewarding a child for staying on task by giving her stickers that can later be traded for pencils or other items	

On what grounds did cognitive psychologists criticize **behavior therapy?** _____

_____

_____

_____

_____

GO SURFING . . .

...to find out how **behavior therapy** is used with children who have attention deficit hyperactivity disorder . (There are lots of good sites out there!)

Explain. _____

_____

_____

_____

_____

_____

_____

_____

_____

Cognitive Therapy and Techniques: It's the Thought That Counts

According to cognitive therapists, psychological disorders arise from _____

_____

According to Albert Ellis, three processes interfere with healthy functioning. Define each and provide an example of this process in your life.

Process	Definition	Personal Example
Self-downing		
Hostility and rage		
Low frustration tolerance		

Below are five common **cognitive distortions.** For each, give a definition and a personal example (*not* from your textbook).

Distortion	Definition	Personal Example
Dichotomous thinking		
Mental filter		
Mind reading		

Distortion	Definition	Personal Example
Catastrophic exaggeration		
Control beliefs		

Compare and contrast Albert Ellis's and Aaron Beck's theories of **cognitive therapy** in the chart below.

	Albert Ellis's Rational-Emotive Behavior Therapy (REBT)	Aaron Beck's Cognitive Therapy
Basic premise		
Associated techniques		

Using the alphabetic sequence ABCDEF, fill in the following blanks to describe how **RET** works:

Distressing feelings arise because an **A**_____, along with a person's **B**_____ lead to **C**_____. The therapist must help the client to **D**_____ the beliefs, which will lead to an **E**_____ and **F**_____ by the client.

What is **cognitive restructuring?** Can you think of a thought that you would like to restructure?

_____
_____
_____

Why is **psychoeducation** an important part of **cognitive therapy?** _____
_____
_____
_____

Cognitive-Behavior Therapy

Suppose that you wanted to develop a training program to help aggressive children develop better social skills. How could you use cognitive-behavior therapy to accomplish this goal? Name the cognitive and the behavioral components that you might include in your treatment.

- **Cognitive:** _____
  _____
  _____
  _____
  _____
  _____
  _____
  _____
  _____
  _____

- **Behavioral:** _____
  _____
  _____
  _____
  _____
  _____
  _____
  _____
  _____
  _____
  _____

Biomedical Therapies

Psychopharmacology

Complete the following table, including the names of specific **drugs** under each classification, the type(s) of disorders typically treated by each classification, and the drugs' side effects.

Classification	Specific Drugs	Disorders Treated	Side Effects
Antipsychotics (also known as neuroleptics)			
Atypical antipsychotics			

Classification	Specific Drugs	Disorders Treated	Side Effects
Tricyclic antidepressants (TCAs)			
Monoamine oxidase inhibitors (MAOIs)			
Selective serotonin reuptake inhibitors (SSRIs)			
Serotonin/norepinephrine reuptake inhibitors (SNRIs)			
Mood stabilizers			
Benzodiazepines			

Electroconvulsive Therapy

What is **ECT?** Why was it developed? _____
_____
_____
_____
_____
_____

For whom is **ECT** now appropriate? How is it administered? What are the potential side effects?
_____
_____
_____
_____
_____
_____

Would you ever have **ECT** performed on you? Why or why not? _____
_____
_____
_____
_____

Transcranial Magnetic Stimulation

What is **transcranial magnetic stimulation?** _____
_____
_____
_____
_____
_____

For whom is **transcranial magnetic stimulation** appropriate? _____
_____
_____
_____
_____
_____

How is **transcranial magnetic stimulation** different from **ECT?** _____
_____
_____
_____
_____
_____

Does **transcranial magnetic stimulation** have any advantages over **ECT?** Discuss. _____
_____
_____
_____
_____
_____

Treatment Variations and Issues

Modalities: When Two or More Isn't a Crowd

What can **group therapy** offer that **individual therapy** cannot? _____
_____
_____
_____
_____

What is the fundamental assumption of **systems therapy?** _____
_____
_____
_____

Have you ever been involved in any **group therapy,** including a **self-help group?** If so, what type? What techniques were used? Did you feel it was helpful? If so, how? _____

_____

_____

_____

_____

_____

Do you try to help yourself through **bibliotherapy** or Web-based programs? If so, describe why you use these techniques and how helpful you felt it was. _____

_____

_____

_____

_____

_____

Innovations in Psychotherapy

What is **psychotherapy integration?** _____

_____

_____

_____

_____

_____

What is **technical eclecticism?** _____

_____

_____

_____

_____

_____

What is the difference between **psychotherapy integration** and **technical eclecticism?** _____

_____

_____

_____

_____

_____

What are the benefits of using either of these integrative approaches? _____

_____

_____

_____

_____

_____

How have each of the following recent trends affected the practice of **psychotherapy?**

- **Managed care:** _____
  _____
  _____
  _____
  _____
  _____

- **Therapy protocols:** _____
  _____
  _____
  _____
  _____
  _____

- **Computer technology:** _____
  _____
  _____
  _____
  _____
  _____

Issues in Psychotherapy Research

What is **outcome research**? _____
_____
_____
_____
_____

For which two disorders is **medication** clearly the preferred form of treatment? Why?

- _____
  _____

- _____
  _____

What type of therapy would be the most **effective** at treating the following conditions?

- **Depression:** _____
- **Obsessive-compulsive disorder:** _____
- **Panic disorder:** _____
- **Specific phobias:** _____
- **Social phobia:** _____

Why is it important to understand a client's ethnic background when determining the diagnosis, process of therapy, and its goals? _____

_____
_____
_____
_____
_____

How to Pick a Psychotherapist and a Type of Therapy

What steps should you take to find a psychotherapist?

- _____
- _____
- _____
- _____
- _____

Looking at Levels: Treating Obsessive-Compulsive Disorder

How might the effectiveness of therapy be measured at the levels of the brain, the person, and the group? Draw arrows to indicate how events at the different levels might interact.

The Brain	The Person	The Group

After You Read . . . Thinking Back

1. In Chapter 1, you learned how psychological topics are studied. The effectiveness of psychological treatment is especially difficult to study. Why? _____
    _____
    _____
    _____
    _____
    _____
    _____
    _____

2. In Chapter 2, you learned about neural functioning. How does Prozac (or any of the other SSRIs) work, at the neural level? _____
    _____
    _____
    _____
    _____
    _____
    _____

3. In Chapter 10, you learned about dreaming. Does Sigmund Freud's technique of dream analysis make sense, given current knowledge about dreaming? Why or why not? _____
    _____
    _____
    _____
    _____
    _____
    _____

4. What are the principles of cognitive psychology (as discussed in Chapter 1)? How do you see these in cognitive therapy? _____
    _____
    _____
    _____
    _____
    _____
    _____

After You Read . . . Thinking Ahead

1. How might the culture affect people's views of themselves? What are the implications of this relationship for treatment purposes? Discuss. _____
   _____
   _____
   _____
   _____
   _____
   _____
   _____

2. In this chapter, you learned how therapists help clients change irrational attitudes about themselves. In Chapter 16, you will learn how advertisers and others help clients try to change attitudes about products and other people. Can you imagine some of the ways that the techniques you learned in this chapter could be applied to change stereotypes, for example? Explain. _____
   _____
   _____
   _____
   _____
   _____
   _____
   _____

3. How might Beck's common cognitive distortions lead you to think about others? How would this affect your interpersonal relationships? Explain._____
   _____
   _____
   _____
   _____
   _____
   _____

4. Can you think of situations in which family or group therapy might have negative consequences? Why might this happen? Explain. _____
   _____
   _____
   _____
   _____
   _____
   _____

5. How might culture influence a person's choice of treatment? For example, consider Ritalin, which is frequently prescribed to treat attention deficit hyperactivity disorder. How does media attention and the popularity of this drug affect others' choices? Is this good or bad? Discuss. ____

_____

_____

_____

_____

_____

_____

After You Read . . . Practice Tests

PRACTICE TEST #1

Multiple-Choice Questions

For each question, circle the best answer from the choices given.

1. Abraham believes that if he can get to the root of his problems the problems will eventually diminish. Abraham would probably endorse _____ therapy. (p. 523)
   a. insight-oriented
   b. pharmacology
   c. cognitive-behavior
   d. none of the above

2. The original insight-oriented therapy is _____. (p. 523)
   a. gestalt therapy
   b. psychoanalysis
   c. client-centered therapy
   d. integrative psychotherapy

3. The primary objective of psychoanalysis is to _____. (p. 523)
   a. medicate the patient
   b. remove mental awareness
   c. make conscious motivations that had been unconscious
   d. all of the above

4. According to Freud, when patients come to relate to their therapist as they did someone who was important in their lives, _____ is said to have taken place. (p. 525)
   a. transference
   b. insight
   c. countertransference
   d. interference

5. Carl Rogers developed _____ therapy. (p. 525)
   a. short-term psychodynamic
   b. patient-centered
   c. gestalt
   d. client-centered

6. Incongruence is a mismatch between your _____ self and your _____ self. (p. 526)
   a. real; ideal
   b. ideal; surreal
   c. surreal; ideal
   d. real; hypothesized

7.   A goal of client-centered therapy is to _____. (p. 525)
    a.   help the client uncover unconscious motivations
    b.   provide unconditional positive regard
    c.   help to change irrational thought patterns
    d.   medicate the client

8.   Eleani, a therapist, conveys positive feelings towards her client even though he is discussing the desire to beat his wife. This aspect of client-centered therapy is known as _____ . (p. 526)
    a.   genuine empathy
    b.   unconditional positive regard
    c.   interpretation
    d.   This practice is not part of client-centered therapy.

9.   The clients most likely to benefit from insight therapies _____ . (p. 527)
    a.   have affective disorders
    b.   are older
    c.   are relatively healthy, articulate people
    d.   none of the above

PRACTICE TEST #2

Multiple-Choice Questions

For each question, circle the best answer from the choices given.

1. _____ is a type of therapy that aims to change problematic behaviors and irrational thoughts and provide new, more adaptive behaviors and beliefs to replace old, maladaptive ones. (p. 582)
   a. Behavior
   b. Cognitive-behavior
   c. Psychoanalysis
   d. Client-centered

2. Which of the following techniques is NOT based on classical conditioning principles? (pp. 529, 531)
   a. systematic desensitization
   b. progressive muscle relaxation
   c. behavior modification
   d. All of the above are based on classical conditioning principles.

3. According to behavior therapy, the ABCs of behavior are_____. (p. 529)
   a. antecedents, behavior, consequences
   b. aftermath, before, changes
   c. alternatives, behaviors, criticism
   d. aftermath, background, consequences

4. Albert Ellis developed a treatment called _____. (p. 532)
   a. client-centered therapy
   b. insight-oriented therapy
   c. rational-emotive behavior therapy
   d. psychopharmacology

5. _____ is a behavior therapy technique that teaches people to be relaxed in the presence of a feared object or situation. (p. 531)
   a. Systematic desensitization
   b. Progressive muscle relaxation
   c. Habituation
   d. Behavior modification

6. Which of the following is NOT one of the processes that Ellis says interferes with healthy functioning? (pp. 532-533)
   a. thinking that you know what others are thinking of you
   b. being critical of oneself for performing poorly or being rejected
   c. being unkind to or critical of others for performing poorly
   d. blaming everyone and everything for undesirable outcomes

7. Which of the following is an example of an atypical antipsychotic medication? (p. 538)
    a. Risperdal
    b. Thorazine
    c. Haldol
    d. Dopamine

8. Selective serotonin reuptake inhibitors are used to treat _____. (p. 538)
    a. the positive symptoms of schizophrenia
    b. the negative symptoms of schizophrenia
    c. mood disorders
    d. antisocial personality disorder

9. The use of an electric current to induce a controlled brain seizure in people with certain psychological disorders is known as _____. (p. 540)
    a. electroconvulsive therapy
    b. psychopharmacology
    c. transference
    d. electronic therapy

10. A side effect of ECT is _____. (p. 540)
    a. high blood pressure
    b. tardive dykinesia
    c. TMS
    d. memory loss

PRACTICE TEST #3

Multiple-Choice Questions:

For each question, circle the best answer from the choices given.

1. _____ is type of therapy that views a client's symptoms as occurring in a larger context and holds that change in one part of the system affects the rest of the system. (p. 543)
   a. Cognitive
   b. Systems
   c. Client-centered
   d. Psychoanalysis

2. The most common theoretical orientation among family therapists is _____. (p. 543)
   a. behavioral
   b. psychodynamic
   c. client-centered
   d. systems

3. Therapy protocols are _____. (p. 545)
   a. ethical guidelines for therapists
   b. guidelines for setting up one's office and establishing fees
   c. detailed session by session manuals of how therapy should proceed
   d. descriptions of particular types of clients and the types of therapy they should receive

4. Interpersonal therapy is _____. (p. 545)
   a. a type of manual-based therapy
   b. a therapy which focuses on how issues that arise in the client's current relationships can affect mood
   c. a type of therapy developed for a research study on depression
   d. all of the above

5. Which type of treatment is most effective for panic disorder? (p. 548)
   a. CBT
   b. interpersonal therapy
   c. systematic desensitization
   d. none of the above

6. Treatment with medication can help people with schizophrenia by _____. (p. 549)
   a. providing the opportunity to learn new relationship skills
   b. making the person more socially outgoing
   c. improving the taste buds
   d. decreasing psychotic symptoms

COMPREHENSIVE PRACTICE TEST

True/False Questions

Circle TRUE or FALSE for each of the following statements.

1.   TRUE   FALSE   Psychoanalysis and client-centered are examples of insight-oriented therapies. (p. 523)

2.   TRUE   FALSE   Dr. Park, a psychologist, is beginning to relate to his client in a new way. This is known as transference. (p. 525)

3.   TRUE   FALSE   Behavior therapy is a type of insight-oriented therapy. (p. 523)

4.   TRUE   FALSE   An example of stimulus control would be a smoker not buying cigarettes. (p. 531)

5.   TRUE   FALSE   Rational-emotive behavior therapy's primary goal is to change people's unconscious behaviors. (p. 532)

6.   TRUE   FALSE   Both REBT and Beck's view of cognitive therapy always use daily records of behavioral thoughts. (pp. 532-535)

7.   TRUE   FALSE   ECT was developed for the treatment of schizophrenia. (p. 540)

8.   TRUE   FALSE   PDAs and the internet have never been incorporated into therapy. (p. 546)

Multiple-Choice Questions

For each question, circle the best answer from the choices given.

1.   Which of the following kinds of therapists would most likely say, "Tell me about your dreams." (p. 523)
     a.   client-centered
     b.   cognitive
     c.   psychodynamic
     d.   cognitive-behavioral

2.   According to Freud, which internal structure strives for immediate gratification? (p. 523)
     a.   id
     b.   ego
     c.   transference
     d.   superego

3. Which of the following is a technique used in psychodynamic therapy? (pp. 523-524)
   a. dream analysis
   b. free association
   c. interpretation
   d. all of the above

4. _____ is a type of therapy is based on well-researched learning principles that focus on changing observable, measurable behaviors. (p. 529)
   a. Electroconvulsive
   b. Behavior
   c. Cognitive-behavior
   d. Psychoanalysis

5. The "C" of behavior therapy's ABCs stands for _____. (p. 529)
   a. control
   b. consequences
   c. cognition
   d. none of the above

6. Which of the following is NOT a process that interferes with healthy functioning according to Albert Ellis? (p. 532)
   a. incongruence
   b. hostility and rage
   c. self-downing
   d. low frustration tolerance

7. Behavior therapy incorporates the ideas of _____. (pp. 530-532)
   a. classical conditioning
   b. operant conditioning
   c. social learning
   d. all of the above

8. Research that compares how effective different treatments are for symptoms of a particular disorder is called _____ research. (p. 546)
   a. systems
   b. outcome
   c. efficacy
   d. psychotherapeutic

9. _____ is a type of therapy that focuses exclusive attention on a client's thoughts rather than his or her feelings or behaviors. (p. 532)
   a. Psychoanalysis
   b. Client-centered
   c. Cognitive
   d. Cognitive-behavior

10. What is the primary focus of rational-emotive behavior therapy? (p. 534)
    a. to substitute a positive behavior for a negative one
    b. to uncover the unconscious link to the distress
    c. to empathize with the client
    d. to create more rational thoughts

11. Adam is worried that if he gets an A- in his psychology class he will get kicked out of school and end up living on the streets. Adam seems to be endorsing which type of cognitive distortion? (p. 533)
    a. mind reading
    b. catastrophic exaggeration
    c. reality appraisal
    d. mental filtering

12. Which type of treatment for depression was the first antidepressant discovered and requires users to adhere to a diet free of tyramine? (p. 538)
    a. monoamine oxidase inhibitors
    b. tricyclic antidepressants
    c. selective serotonin reuptake inhibitors
    d. serontonin/norepinephrine reuptake inhibitors

Short-Answer/Essay Questions
Answer the following questions in the space provided.

1. What are some examples of insight-oriented therapies and what makes them insight-oriented? __
   _____
   _____
   _____
   _____
   _____
   _____
   _____
   _____

2. What does ABCDEF stand for with respect to REBT? _____
   _____
   _____
   _____
   _____
   _____
   _____
   _____

3. Compare and contrast ECT and TMS. _____

    _____

    _____

    _____

    _____

    _____

    _____

    _____

    _____

4. Describe systems therapy. _____

    _____

    _____

    _____

    _____

    _____

    _____

    _____

5. Describe the focus, goals, and techniques of cognitive-behavior therapy. _____

    _____

    _____

    _____

    _____

    _____

    _____

    _____

When You Are Finished . . . Puzzle It Out

Across

3. A form of therapy
6. Examples: Prozac, Zoloft, and Paxil
7. Controlled brain seizure as treatment
11. Good therapy for panic disorder
13. Developed psychoanalysis
14. Developed rational-emotive therapy
15. Use of self-help books
16. Proposed client-centered therapy
17. First antidepressant medication
18. Therapeutic technique based on classical conditioning that relies on habituation
19. Therapy saying no person is an island

Down

1. Refusal to comply with therapist
2. Mood stabilizer used for schizophrenia
4. D in the RET therapist's ABCDEF
5. A technique used in psychoanalysis in which the patient says whatever comes to mind
8. Focus of cognitive therapy
9. Mismatch of ideal self and real self
10. Also known as support groups
12. Secondary reinforcers

Puzzle created with Puzzlemaker at DiscoverySchool.com.

Chapter 13
Social Psychology:
Meeting of the Minds

Before You Read . . .

Think of all the different ways that you interact with people every day—perhaps with a romantic partner, in groups such as classes and clubs, in the workplace, as a passerby. How do you see yourself in relationship to these people? What are your attitudes about them? How different is your behavior in different kinds of social interactions?

This chapter presents an overview of social psychology—how we think about people (social cognition) and how we interact with people (social behavior). Can we predict our behaviors from our attitudes—or is it the other way around? What happens when our attitudes and behaviors are inconsistent? Sometimes our attitudes are negative, as when we stereotype people and experience prejudice. Our attitudes arise partly from the attributions we make about our own fate and that of others.

The social behavior section of this chapter covers liking and loving relationships, the social organization of groups, and group behavior. Conformity, compliance, and obedience are discussed, as is decision making in groups. Lastly, prosocial behavior and altruism are explored—the characteristics of people who help, the people we *choose* to help, and the circumstances under which we engage in helping behavior.

Chapter Objectives

After reading this chapter, you should be able to:

- Define social psychology, social behavior, and social cognition, and explain why they are important.

- Describe attitudes and explain how they are formed.

- Define persuasion and explain why persuasion attempts work or don't work.

- Define stereotypes, and explain how they are formed and how they can lead to prejudice.

- Discuss the reasons for prejudice and describe how prejudice can be reduced.

- Define attributions and identify the various types of attributions and attributional biases.

- Identify and briefly describe the factors that affect interpersonal attractions.

- Describe the different kinds of love, and explain Sternberg's triangular model of love.

- Define the following terms: *norms, roles,* and *deindividuation.* Explain the effects on the individual's behavior of being in a group.

- Explain and differentiate between conformity and compliance, identify factors that affect them, and describe techniques that influence compliance.

- Describe Milgram's studies on obedience.

- Describe the factors involved in group decision making, including social loafing and social facilitation.

- Describe the factors that affect prosocial behavior and bystander intervention.

As You Read . . . Term Identification

Make flashcards using the following terms as you go. Use the definitions in the margins of this chapter for help. If you write the definitions in your own words, though, you will remember them better!

Altruism
Attitude
Attribution
Attributional bias
Belief in a just world
Bystander effect
Cognitive dissonance
Companionate love
Compliance
Conformity
Correspondence bias
Deindividuation
Diffusion of responsibility
Door-in-the-face technique
External attribution
Foot-in-the-door technique
Group
Group polarization
Groupthink
Ingroup

Internal attribution
Lowball technique
Mere exposure effect
Norm
Obedience
Outgroup
Passionate love
Persuasion
Prejudice
Prosocial behavior
Recategorization
Role
Self-serving bias
Social cognition
Social cognitive neuroscience
Social facilitation
Social loafing
Social psychology
Stereotype
Triangular model of love

As You Read . . . Questions and Exercises

Social Cognition: Thinking About People

Attitudes and Behavior: Feeling and Doing

What are the three components of **attitudes?** Name and describe them.

- _____
  _____
- _____
  _____
- _____
  _____

Can you think of a time when **attitudes** affected what information you processed about a specific event? (This example may be a time for which you and someone else have very different memories.) Describe this situation. _____
_____
_____
_____
_____

Attitudes are more likely to affect behavior when the **attitudes** are . . .

- _____
- _____
- _____
- _____
- _____

Think of an example from your life when your behavior affected your **attitude** about something. Why might this have occurred? _____
_____
_____
_____
_____
_____

What is **cognitive dissonance?** _____
_____
_____
_____
_____
_____

Explain the two theories of **cognitive dissonance.**

- _____
  _____
  _____
  _____

- _____
  _____
  _____
  _____
  _____

What are four different ways by which we may try to decrease **cognitive dissonance?**

- _____
  _____
  _____

- _____
  _____
  _____
  _____

- _____
  _____
  _____

- _____
  _____
  _____
  _____

Which factors will increase the likelihood of **persuading** someone?

- _____
- _____
- _____
- _____
- _____
- _____

What are the four common obstacles to **persuasion?**

- _____
  _____

- _____
  _____

- _____
  _____

- _____
  _____

Explain the **social cognitive neuroscience** approach to social cognition. _____

_____

_____

_____

_____

What have social cognitive neuroscientists found about **cognitive dissonance?** _____

_____

_____

_____

_____

_____

_____

Stereotypes: Seen One, Seen 'Em All

Why do we **stereotype** people? _____

_____

_____

What errors do we make when **stereotyping** people? _____

_____

_____

_____

_____

What is the relationship between **stereotyping** and **prejudice?** _____

_____

_____

_____

_____

GO SURFING...

...at http://www.understandingprejudice.org/demos/ and take the following tests:
- The Baseline Survey.
- The Slide Tour of Prejudice

- Ambivalent Sexism Questionnaire.
- Slavery and the U.S. Presidents.
- What's Your Native IQ?
- Test Yourself for Hidden Biases.
- The Baseline Survey, to see if your thinking has changed.

Describe the results of the tests here. _____
_____
_____
_____
_____
_____
_____
_____

Prejudice can stem from emotions in two ways:

- _____
  _____

- _____
  _____
  _____

Give an example of how **prejudice** has primed your behavior. _____
_____
_____
_____
_____

Explain how each of the following processes may contribute to the development and maintenance of **prejudice:**

Process	Explanation
Competition for scarce resources	
Social categorization and ingroup bias	
Social learning	

Briefly explain the two methods of **decreasing prejudice:**

- _____
  _____
  _____

- _____
  _____
  _____

What conditions increase the likelihood that increased contact will decrease **prejudice?**

- _____
  _____
- _____
  _____

Attributions: Making Sense of Events

In the table below, indicate the types of statements you might make about something good or bad that happened to you, assuming you make internal or external attributions.

Situation	Type of Attribution	
	Internal	External
You ace a test.		
You fail a test.		

GO SURFING . . .

...at http://discoveryhealth.queendom.com/access_lc.html and take the Locus of Control and **Attributional Style** test.

What kind of **attributional style** do you have? Explain. _____
_____
_____
_____
_____
_____
_____
_____

Suppose that you receive a rude e-mail from someone you thought was a friend. Using Kelley's **theory of causal attribution,** under what circumstances would you think that the rude e-mail was a result of your friend's personality? List them.

- _____
- _____
- _____

Under what circumstances would you think that this rude e-mail was a result of a situation that your friend was in? List them.

- _____
- _____
- _____

What comment might a person make if using the **correspondence bias (fundamental attribution error)** in the following situations?

Situation	Comment
A woman is raped.	
A waitress forgets an order.	
A homeless person asks for money.	
A man confesses to a crime.	

According to the **self-serving bias,** what types of attributions (internal/external) do you make in the following situations?

Situation	Type of Attribution
You get a good grade on an exam, despite the fact that you didn't study very hard.	
Your roommate gets a good grade on an exam, despite the fact that he didn't study very hard.	
You get a bad grade on an exam, despite the fact that you studied very hard.	
Your roommate gets a bad grade on an exam, despite the fact that he studied very hard.	

GO SURFING . . .

...at http://www.erzwiss.uni-halle.de/gliederung/paed/ppsych/segbjw.pdf and take the Belief in a Just World Scale. What was your score? _____ (The higher your score, the more you believe in a just world.)

How does **belief in a just world** lead to blaming the victim? _____

_____

_____

_____

_____

Social Behavior: Interacting with People

Relationships: Having a Date, Having a Partner

What are the three factors that influence us to like someone else?

- _____
- _____
- _____

What are the three dimensions of love, according to Robert Sternberg's **triangular model of love?** Briefly explain each.

- _____
  _____
- _____
  _____
- _____
  _____

Think of the last romantic relationship you were in. Were you high or low on each of the three dimensions?

- _____
- _____
- _____

Briefly describe the three major **attachment styles.**

- _____
  _____

- _____
  _____

- _____
  _____

GO SURFING . . .

...at http://www.web-research-design.net/cgi-bin/crq/crq.pl and take the Attachment Style Questionnaire.

According to this questionnaire, what type of **attachment** do you have now? _____
_____
_____

Do you agree or disagree with these results? Why? _____
_____
_____

Fill in the table to show the interaction between **attachment** and **love relationships.** Also, indicate the percentage of Americans who fall into each category.

Attachment Type	Relationship Type	Percentage of Americans
Secure		
Avoidant		
Anxious–ambivalent		

In the table below, list the characteristics that men and women find attractive, according to the evolutionary theory of mate selection.

Characteristics That Men Find Attractive	Characteristics That Women Find Attractive

Describe two lines of research that suggest that **mate selection** is about more than **natural selection.**

- _____

- _____

Social Organization: Group Rules, Group Roles

What four characteristics define a **group?**

- _____
- _____
- _____
- _____

What is **deindividuation?** Does it explain violence in anonymous crowds? Why or why not? _____
_____
_____
_____
_____
_____
_____
_____

What are some of the **norms** at your school? _____
_____
_____
_____

Think of a group (either formal or informal) in which you are involved. Who are the different people in that group? What **role** (either formal or informal) does each person play?

Person	Role

Describe the Stanford Prison Experiment. _____

_____

_____

_____

_____

_____

_____

_____

_____

_____

_____

Yielding to Others: Going Along with the Group

What factors increase and decrease the likelihood that individuals will **conform** to a group standard or opinion?_____

_____

_____

_____

_____

_____

Conformity is a change in behavior brought about by _____, whereas **compliance** is a change in behavior brought about by _____.

What are the six principles underlying effective **compliance?**

- _____
- _____
- _____
- _____
- _____
- _____

Which of the preceding principles underlies the following **compliance** techniques?

- **Foot-in-the-door:** _____
- **Lowball:** _____
- **Door-in-the-face:** _____

Identify which of the above techniques is described below:

Compliance Scenario	Technique
Your roommate asks you to drive her home—three states away! You say "no," but then agree to drive her to the airport—it's only one hour away.	
Your roommate asks you if she can borrow your notes from last week when she was sick. You agree and then find yourself giving her your notes every week!	
You agree to buy a car for $15,000 (telling yourself you'll spend no more than that), but then end up driving away with a $20,000 car because you want the "extras" that didn't come with the $15,000 price tag.	

In Milgram's study, what percentage of people obeyed instructions to give the highest level of shock under the following conditions?

Condition	Percentage
Milgram's original study	
"Teacher" participant sets the voltage level	
College student gives the order	
Two authority figures disagree with each other	
"Teacher" holds electrode to "learner's" skin	
Commands are given over the phone	

Performance in Groups: Working Together

What are two rules that determine which side in an argument will "win"?

- _____
  _____
- _____
  _____
  _____

What is **group polarization?** _____
_____
_____
_____
_____

What are two reasons for **group polarization,** and when does each occur?

- _____
  _____
- _____
  _____
  _____

When is **groupthink** more likely to occur?

- _____
- _____
- _____
- _____

How does the **heterogeneity** of the group affect group communication? _____
_____
_____
_____

How can the negative effects of **heterogeneity** be reduced?

- _____
- _____
- _____

Describe a situation in which you or someone else engaged in **social loafing.** _____
_____
_____
_____
_____

Have you ever experienced **social facilitation?** Describe that experience. _____
_____
_____
_____
_____
_____

Have you worked on a group project yet? Which of the group processes described in the chapter have you observed? Was social loafing or social facilitation present? Did your group have to reach a decision about something? How did the decision come about? _____
_____
_____
_____
_____
_____

Helping Behavior: Helping Others

In the table below, list the characteristics of the helper, the person being helped, and the situation that increase the likelihood of **prosocial behavior.**

Characteristics of the Helper	Characteristics of the Person Being Helped	Characteristics of the Situation

According to Darley and Latane, which factors are likely to increase **bystander intervention?** Which factors are likely to decrease bystander intervention?

Factors Increasing Bystander Intervention	Factors Decreasing Bystander Intervention

Looking at Levels: Cults

Are the factors that influence cult behavior similar to the factors that influence the behavior of students who rush a fraternity? Explain how a fraternity can exert so much power over inductees, at the levels of the brain, the person, and the group. Draw arrows to indicate how events at the different levels may interact.

The Brain	The Person	The Group

After You Read . . . Thinking Back

1. In Chapter 1, you learned about the ethics of psychological research. Would Milgram's study be allowed today? Why or why not? _____
   _____
   _____
   _____
   _____
   _____
   _____
   _____
   _____
   _____

2. In Chapter 7, you learned that cognition can affect emotion. In Chapter 5, you learned that emotion can affect cognition (e.g., memory). How are both of those themes reflected in this chapter? _____
   _____
   _____
   _____
   _____
   _____
   _____
   _____
   _____
   _____

3. In Chapter 9, you learned about the tasks of adulthood. Which tasks would be met by having a partner? Why are these tasks important? _____
   _____
   _____
   _____
   _____
   _____
   _____
   _____
   _____
   _____

4. How are stereotypes similar to and different from prototypes, which you learned about in Chapter 6? _____
   _____
   _____
   _____
   _____
   _____
   _____
   _____

After You Read . . . Practice Tests

PRACTICE TEST #1

Multiple-Choice Questions

For each question, circle the best answer from the choices given.

1. An attitude is often considered a _____. (p. 561)
   a. feeling
   b. belief
   c. predisposition to behave in a certain way
   d. all of the above

2. When an attitude and a behavior, or two attitudes, are inconsistent with one another, the resulting feeling is called _____. (p. 563)
   a. conflict of conformity
   b. attitudinal conflict
   c. cognitive dissonance
   d. all of the above

3. Persuasion would be most likely to occur when the person being persuaded _____. (p. 566)
   a. has high self esteem
   b. feels fearful because of the message
   c. is paying full attention to the message
   d. all of the above are equally likely to persuade a person

4. Which of the following would NOT decrease prejudice? (p. 569)
   a. a competition for resources
   b. recategorization
   c. working toward a shared goal
   d. a jigsaw classroom

5. When your friend is late meeting you, you say to yourself, "Joel is just a chronically late person—I should have known," this is making a(n) _____ attribution. (p. 573)
   a. situational
   b. outgroup
   c. ingroup
   d. internal

6. The area of social psychology that focuses on how people perceive their social worlds and how they attend to, store, remember, and use information about other people and the social world is known as _____. (p. 561)
   a. cognition
   b. social psychology
   c. social cognition
   d. sociology

PRACTICE TEST #2

Multiple-Choice Questions

For each question, circle the best answer from the choices given.

1. Repeated contact with a person typically leads to _____. (p. 577)
    a. decreased liking for that person
    b. no change in feelings for that person
    c. increased liking for that person
    d. feelings of love for that person

2. According to Sternberg, only _____ love has passion, intimacy, and commitment. (p. 578)
    a. compassionate
    b. agape
    c. consummate
    d. reciprocal

3. David Buss argued that women most prefer men who _____. (p. 579)
    a. are attractive
    b. are faithful
    c. have good "pedigree"
    d. have good earning potential

4. Which of the following statements about conformity is FALSE? (p. 585)
    a. Rates of conformity have remained constant over the past several decades.
    b. Rates of conformity are higher in collectivist cultures.
    c. Men and women conform at the same rates.
    d. Conformity is higher for more difficult tasks.

5. Making a ridiculously large request, followed by a more reasonable smaller request, is called the _____ technique. (p. 586)
    a. foot-in-the-door
    b. door-in-the-face
    c. lowball
    d. big-and-then-little

6. Which of the following factors played a role in the Stanford Prison Experiment? (p. 582-583)
    a. obedience
    b. norms
    c. roles
    d. all of the above

7. Asch's classic line experiment demonstrates _____ social influence. (p. 586)
    a. informational
    b. normative
    c. support
    d. compliance

8. Who conducted the most famous study on obedience? (p. 587)
   a. Freud
   b. Cialdini
   c. Milgram
   d. Asch

COMPREHENSIVE PRACTICE TEST

True/False Questions

Circle TRUE or FALSE for each of the following statements.

1.   TRUE   FALSE   An attitude is more likely to affect behavior when the attitude is chaotic and unstable. (p. 562)

2.   TRUE   FALSE   When we change our attitude to reduce cognitive dissonance, we are using indirect strategies. (p. 564)

3.   TRUE   FALSE   The jigsaw classroom is a method of reducing prejudice through interdependence. (pp. 572-573)

4.   TRUE   FALSE   The "belief in a just world" attribution is when you attribute your failures to the external world. (p. 575)

5.   TRUE   FALSE   Sternberg's triangular model of love poses that love has three dimensions: passion, intimacy, and infatuation. (p. 578)

6.   TRUE   FALSE   Groupthink has been used to explain NASA's disastrous *Challenger* launch.

Multiple-Choice Questions

For each question, circle the best answer from the choices given.

1. Which of the following minimizes cognitive dissonance? (pp. 564-565)
   a. We change our attitudes.
   b. We change our behaviors.
   c. We trivialize the inconsistency between the two attitudes (or attitude and behavior).
   d. all of the above

2. According to the self-serving bias, we tend to attribute our successes to _____ causes and our failures to _____ causes. (p. 573)
   a. internal; internal
   b. external; external
   c. internal; external
   d. none of the above

3. In Milgram's original experiment, _____ percent of the participants shocked the confederate with the highest voltage. (p. 587)
   a. 15
   b. 45
   c. 65
   d. 85

4. According to evolutionary theory, men look for women who _____. (p. 579)
   a. are independent and self-supporting.
   b. are dependent upon them for support.
   c. appear "fertile" by having a well-proportioned body and symmetrical features.
   d. all of the above

5. According to Darley and Latane, bystander intervention occurs when _____. (pp. 591-594)
   a. an emergency is noticed by the bystander.
   b. the bystander assumes some responsibility to intervene.
   c. the bystander is motivated to help.
   d. all of the above must occur.

6. According to the belief in a just world, _____. (p. 575)
   a. chance plays a major role in what happens to people
   b. a divine being intercedes on the behalf of all people
   c. just behavior is punished
   d. people deserve what they get, and get what they deserve

7. Another name for the change in attitude that results from simply becoming familiar with something is known as _____. (p. 565)
   a. self-perception
   b. the self-fulfilling prophecy
   c. the mere exposure effect
   d. passionate love

8. What is a limitation of the Robber's Cave experiment? (p. 570)
   a. the study only used Caucasians
   b. the study only used males
   c. the study only use children
   d. all of the above

9. _____ is a means of reducing prejudice by shifting the categories of "us" and "them" so that the two groups are no longer distinct entities. (p. 571)
   a. Recategorization
   b. Discrimination
   c. Stereotype
   d. none of the above

10. Further studies extended Milgram's original study. Which of the following was NOT an extension of the original study? (pp. 587-588)
   a. Women in the same situation also complied.
   b. Children in a similar situation also complied.
   c. College students in a situation where another college student gave them the order.
   d. A study had the female experimenter ask the male participant on a date first.

11. In group situations, when someone works harder than he or she would alone, it is known as
    _____ . (p. 590)
    a. social loafing
    b. social facilitation
    c. sofa surfing
    d. responsibility shifting

12. The Kitty Genovese story and the Darley and Latene (1968) study exemplify the _____
    effect. (pp. 593)
    a. prosocial
    b. bystander
    c. cost
    d. altruism

13. A local realtor is advertising homes for a very reduced price. When you approach the realtor
    about buying one of the houses, he tells you that they are no longer available for the much
    reduced price, but they are available for a reduced price. The realtor is attempting to the
    _____ technique of compliance. (p. 565)
    a. lowball
    b. door-in-the-face
    c. foot-in-the-door
    d. lower-the-price

14. According to Sternberg, which of the following is a dimension of love? (p. 578)
    a. exposure
    b. timing
    c. appearance
    d. none of the above

Short-Answer/Essay Questions
Answer the following questions in the space provided.

1. The contact hypothesis suggests that prejudice can be decreased due to what? _____
   _____
   _____
   _____
   _____
   _____
   _____
   _____
   _____
   _____

2. What is an attributional bias? Provide an example of a type of attributional bias. _____

    _____

    _____

    _____

    _____

    _____

    _____

    _____

    _____

    _____

3. Describe the triangular model of love. _____

    _____

    _____

    _____

    _____

    _____

    _____

    _____

    _____

    _____

4. Describe the classic compliance techniques and why they are effective. _____

    _____

    _____

    _____

    _____

    _____

    _____

    _____

    _____

    _____

After You Are Done . . . Puzzle It Out

Across

4. Belief about people in a category
5. Conducted famous obedience studies
9. Most common attachment style
10. Rules that govern group members
12. Difference between two conflicting attitudes
13. One's own group
14. Behavior change due to request
17. Attribution that cause is self
19. Intimacy, passion, and

_____
20. Attempts to change attitudes

Down

1. Loss of sense of self
2. Kitty _____
3. Behavior that benefits others
6. Liking something familiar
7. Compliance with an order
8. Behavior change to group norms
11. Triangular theory of love author
15. Negative attitude toward outgroup members
16. Motivation to help another person
18. Explanation for the cause of an event

Puzzle created with Puzzlemaker at DiscoverySchool.com.

GRADE AID STUDY GUIDE ANSWER KEY TO PRACTICE TESTS

Chapter 1 Psychology

What Kind of Psychologist Are You?
A = psychodynamic
B = behaviorism
C = cognitive psychology
D = humanism
E = evolutionary psychology

Practice Test 1:
1. d
2. d
3. c
4. a
5. a
6. b
7. c
8. c
9. a
10. d
11. d
12. d
13. c

Practice Test 2:
1. d
2. d
3. a
4. b
5. d
6. a
7. d
8. b
9. b
10. d

Practice Test 3:
1. d
2. c
3. d
4. c
5. a
6. a

7. b
8. a
9. a
10. b
11. a
12. a
13. a
14. d
15. d

Comprehensive Practice Test:
True/False Questions:
1. F
2. T
3. F
4. F
5. T
6. T
7. T
8. F
9. T
10. F
11. F
12. T
13. T

Multiple-Choice Questions:
1. a
2. b
3. a
4. d
5. d
6. c
7. a
8. d
9. d
10. d
11. a
12. c
13. c
14. c
15. d
16. a
17. d
18. a
19. b
20. d
21. a

22. d
23. a
24. d

Short-Answer Questions:

1. Structuralism; describe rules that determine how sensations and feelings contribute to the development of mental structures. The primary method used to test theories was introspection, or self-reports.
page ref: 11 - 12

2. Both schools of psychology emphasize Darwin's theory of natural selection. Each attempts to address the similar question of why we do what we do. Evolutionary psychology, however, proposes that certain cognitive processes are ingrained in us because at one point in time such thinking increased our chances of survival. One other obvious difference is that functionalism predates evolutionary psychology.
page ref: 12 - 13; 18 - 19

3. preparing and delivering lectures; attending a committee meeting; conducting research; office hours
page ref: 24

4. Specifying a problem; Observing events; Forming a hypothesis; Testing the hypothesis; Formulating a theory; and Testing a theory.
page ref: 38 - 41

5. Correlation describes a relationship between two variables. If there is a relationship, there may be either a positive or negative relationship. A positive relationship occurs when positive changes in one variable are accompanied by positive changes in another like height and weight. A negative relationship occurs when on one variable there are positive changes but negative changes on the other variable.
page ref: 44

6. Surveys may be limited in value by the following: people may not be able to accurately report on some subject matter; people may not provide honest answers; some people may not respond at all; wording of surveys may inadvertently affect results.
page ref: 43 - 44

7. Independent variable is the variable the experimenter manipulates (e.g., amount of sugar); dependent variable is the variable that is measured (e.g., problems solved); experimental condition or group receives the level of the independent variable thought to affect performance (e.g., no sleep) whereas control condition or group does receives or is exposed to something other than this (e.g., eight hours of sleep). Note that one may have more than one experimental condition or group.
page ref: 45 - 47

8. Samples and populations are related to one another. Both may be used for research purposes. Samples, however, are subsets of a given population. For example, students in your class represent a sample of students at your university. Populations are composed of every potential individual for a given research project. Populations are normally hard to study therefore samples are used.

page ref: 59 - 60

9. Yes; based on the limited information, participants may encounter physical harm. It is most likely that the benefits of the research will not outweigh the risks. However, if the benefits can be shown to outweigh the risks then an IRB may in fact allow the research.
page ref: 29 – 30

Chapter 2 The Biology of Mind and Behavior

Practice Test 1:
1. d
2. a
3. d
4. c
5. a
6. d
7. d
8. a
9. d

Practice Test 2:
1. b
2. a
3. d
4. d
5. d
6. c
7. c
8. d

Practice Test 3:
1. b
2. a
3. a
4. d
5. b
6. c
7. a
8. c
9. c
10. b

Comprehensive Practice Test:
True/False Questions:
1. F
2. T
3. F

Practice Tests

4. F
5. F
6. T

Multiple-Choice Questions
1. d
2. d
3. d
4. a
5. a
6. d
7. c
8. a
9. c
10. d
11. c
12. c
13. b
14. c

Short-Answer/Essay Questions:
1. The passage of an electrical signal along the axon implies that an action potential has arisen. When this occurs, Sodium channels open allowing sodium ions to briefly enter. After the sodium channels close, potassium channels briefly open and potassium ions exit. This is then followed by the exact opposite occurrence. Sodium pumps push sodium ions out with potassium ions being drawn inside. This sequence occurs sequentially down the axon.
page ref: 54-55

2. Parkinson's patients most likely have lowered levels of dopamine. To help restore dopamine levels L-Dopa can be prescribed.
page ref: 57, 59

3. The peripheral nervous system is divided into the sensory-somatic nervous system and the autonomic nervous system. The sensory-somatic nervous system is responsible for transmitting sensory input to the central nervous system. It is also responsible for directing voluntary movement. The autonomic nervous system regulates involuntarily bodily activities such as heart rate and breathing rate. It is further subdivided into the parasympathetic and sympathetic divisions.
page ref: 61-63

4. The lobes are the occipital, parietal, temporal, and frontal lobes. The frontal lobe is clearly different in our brains relative to the brain of monkeys.
page ref: 64-65

5. Plasticity is defined as the brain's ability to be molded by experience. Four circumstances in which this clearly evident include the following: during infancy and childhood when the brain is shaped by interactions with the environment; when the body changes, such as losing a limb in an extreme case, so that the sensory input changes; when we learn something new or store new information; and as

compensation after brain damage.
page ref: 86

Chapter 3 Sensation and Perception

Practice Test 1:
1. b
2. c
3. c
4. d
5. d
6. d
7. a
8. a
9. d

Practice Test 2:
1. d
2. a
3. b
4. a
5. c
6. b
7. d
8. d
9. d

Practice Test 3:
1. d
2. b
3. b
4. a
5. b
6. d
7. b
8. a
9. d
10. d

Comprehensive Practice Test:
True/False Questions:
1. F
2. T
3. T
4. F
5. T
6. T

7. F

Multiple-Choice Questions:
1. d
2. c
3. a
4. c
5. d
6. d
7. c
8. a
9. c
10. d
11. a
12. c
13. b

Short-Answer/Essay Questions:
1. First, receptors must transduce physical energy into neural impulses. This process is basically the process of sensation. Perception takes place in two phases: First, the neural impulses are organized into coherent units and second, the information is identified in terms of "what" and "where."
page ref: 100-101

2. The light first strikes the cornea where it is refracted or focused. Next, light travels through the pupil which is governed by the iris depending on how well lit an area is. Light then strikes the lens where it is further focused onto the last major structure, the retina where the rods and cones are located.
page ref: 104

3. Failure to replicate effects of both ESP and PK; No neurological basis, or brain mechanism, has been implicated for such abilities; No physical basis has been ascertained as the basis for such abilities (e.g., light for vision, sound waves for audition); Alternative explanations may account for such abilities or may not be easily ruled out.
page ref: 136-137

Chapter 4 Learning

Practice Test 1:
1. d
2. c
3. a
4. d
5. a
6. c
7. d
8. d

Practice Test 2:
1. c
2. b
3. d
4. b
5. c
6. b
7. a
8. c
9. d

Practice Test 3:
1. a
2. d
3. c
4. b
5. c
6. a
7. d
8. b
9. d

Comprehensive Practice Test:
True/False Questions:
1. T
2. F
3. F
4. T
5. F
6. F
7. T
8. T

Multiple-Choice Questions:
1. a
2. b
3. d
4. c
5. c
6. b
7. b
8. d
9. c
10. d
11. b
12. c
13. b

14. a

Short-Answer/Essay Questions:
1. Learning is defined as a relatively long-term change in behavior that results from experience. Nonassociative learning is the simplest form and occurs when repeated exposure to a stimulus alters an organism's responsiveness. Associative learning involves relating one object or event with another object or event.
page ref: 145

2. Using a fixed ratio schedule involves providing reinforcement after a fixed number of responses. Using a variable ratio schedule involves providing reinforcement after a variable ratio of responses. Using fixed interval schedule involves providing reinforcement for a response emitted after a fixed interval of time. Using a variable interval schedule involves providing reinforcement for a response emitted after a variable interval of time. Examples should be consistent with the definitions.
page ref:168-171

3. The more attention paid to the model the more likely one will learn from the model. Therefore, the following characteristics have been demonstrated as being beneficial in observational learning: expert, good looking, high status, and socially powerful.
page ref: 179

4. Observational learning is learning that occurs by watching others. Therefore, if children watch TV they will undoubtedly watch others doing various things. This occurs through a process of modeling, learning new behaviors through observing others. If the models are performing "negative" behaviors then children can learn these acts. On the other hand, if the models are performing "positive" behaviors then children can learn more positive behaviors. An example of a show that promotes children's behavior in a positive manner is any show that consists of nonviolent behavior along with prosocial behavior, such as Sesame Street, Mister Roger's Neighborhood, or Barney.
page ref: 178-180

Chapter 5 Memory

Practice Test 1:
1. e
2. a
3. d
4. c
5. e
6. a
7. c
8. b
9. d
10. b

Practice Test 2:
1. a

2. a
3. d
4. c
5. b
6. a
7. b
8. b

Practice Test 3:
1. a
2. b
3. b
4. d
5. c
6. b
7. a
8. a

Comprehensive Practice Test:
True/False Questions:
1. F
2. F
3. F
4. F
5. T
6. F
7. F
8. F

Multiple-Choice Questions:
1. c
2. b
3. d
4. c
5. d
6. b
7. d
8. c
9. c
10. b
11. d
12. c
13. e
14. e

Short-Answer/Essay Questions:
1. First, STM only specified one process (rehearsal) operating on stored information while WM postulates several processes that interpret and transform information more generally. Second, WM

more finely characterizes how information is stored in memory with distinct stores for verbally produced sounds (the articulatory loop) and visual and spatial information (the visuospatial sketchpad). Third, the theory of WM includes a function for planning, reasoning, and problem solving, called the central executive, which operates on information from one or the other stores. These additional components make WM an advancement over earlier theories of STM.
page ref.: 189-190

2. Evidence for different types of memory stores comes from brain imaging and brain damage studies. In these studies, semantic and episodic memory recall activated different sides of the frontal lobe, suggesting that they are distinct types of stores. Also, brain damage can impair some types of memories while leaving others intact. For example, patients with brain damage may lose their episodic memories, while their semantic memories are intact.
page ref.: 198, 215

3. The more directly the memory is involved in controlling behavior, the less likely they will need to be reconsolidated. For example, avoidance learning, such as an animal escaping shock, results in memories that do not need to be consolidated. Also, if the memories have been effectively stored for a long amount of time, then reconsolidation is not necessary. Other factors, such as the nature of the task can affect the need for reconsolidation as well.
page ref.: 192-193

4. Memories are not stored in whole units, but rather in small pieces that are fleshed out during recall. Successful recall depends on retrieving the right fragment that will allow the reconstruction of the memory. Good memory cues direct you to key fragments that in turn allow you to reconstruct the memory. Like good clues, they narrow down the possibilities of the correct memory from other memories that are similar to the one you wish to recall.
page ref.: 206-208

5. One reason that people forget information is that the information was not properly encoded, known as an encoding failure. Information must be encoded into the system before it can be recalled. Also, the information you are trying to recall may be highly similar to other information, and therefore difficult to single out and retrieve. Also, if the information is not well organized in memory it will be difficult to retrieve. Interference from other information can cause temporary forgetting. Finally, damage to the brain can cause forgetting in the case of amnesia.
page ref.: 212-215

Chapter 6 Language, Thinking, and Intelligence

Practice Test 1:
1. b
2. c
3. b
4. d
5. b
6. b
7. d

8. a
9. a
10. c
11. d
12. a

Practice Test 2:
1. a
2. a
3. d
4. b
5. c
6. d
7. b
8. a
9. a
10. b
11. a
12. b
13. d
14. b
15 a
16. d
17. c

Practice Test 3:
1. b
2. b
3. a
4. d
5. b
6. b
7. c
8. a
9. a
10 b
11. d
12. b
13. c

Comprehensive Practice Test:
True/False Questions:
1. T
2. T
3. F
4. F
5. F
6. T

7. F
8. T
9. T
10. F
11. T

Multiple-Choice Questions:
1. c
2. a
3. a
4. b
5. c
6. b
7. b
8. c
9. a
10. b
11. a
12. c
13. c
14. c
15. b

Short- Answer/Essay Questions:
1. Mental imagery has been found to have distinct dimensions like those of perception, such as spatial extent, limited size, and grain. Brain damage to the occipital lobe, which is vital for visual perception, can affect imagery, suggesting that both processes use at least some of the same brain areas. Also, when participants are shown three-dimensional looking objects in various degrees of rotation, and then asked to verify if they are the same object, the time to verify rotated objects is linearly related to the degree of rotation between the objects (it takes longer to verify the more rotated object) suggesting that these processes have similar limitations.
page ref.: 239

2. To use a heuristic, you would look in the places where you normally leave your notes. For example, you would look in the places that normally have your notes. In this way, you would not be looking in every place you had been, but only in a subset of those places. This method would be quicker than looking everywhere, but you might not find your notes. Using an algorithm, you would methodically look everywhere you had been since last having your notes. This would eventually guarantee a solution, but might take more time.
page ref.: 244

3. The major challenge is to represent the problem correctly. Next, you must stay focused on the actual problem. Also, you need to be flexible in how you see and approach the problem to prevent functional fixedness and mental sets. Finally, if you do get stuck, walk away from the problem and come back to it with a fresh mind.
page ref.: 246

4. Intelligence testing has been around at least since the days of Binet and Simon between 1904 and 1911 when they devised a test to look for relatively slow learners. Binet and Simon defined intelligence by comparing a child's mental age with their chronological age. Terman revised the Binet-Simon test, now called the Stanford-Binet, and expanded its use to adults. Wechsler created the modern intelligence test which is divided into verbal and performance subtests.
page ref: 253-255

5. Carroll found that relations among test scores were neatly structured into a three-strata hierarchy. Most modern researchers accept a hierarchical model of intelligence, but many disagree as to the arrangement of that hierarchy. For example, Horn and his colleagues argue that fluid and crystallized intelligence belong at the top instead of g, and other researchers believe that the tiers can be further reduced.
page ref: 259-260

6. Sternberg believes that intelligence has three distinct components. Analytic intelligence is book smarts, practical intelligence is knowing how to do things, and creative intelligence is being able to solve novel problems. He is criticized for not having data that strongly support his theory, and for arguing that creativity is a separate type of intelligence rather than a use of other types of intelligence.
page ref: 263-264

Chapter 7 Emotion and Motivation

Practice Test 1:
1. c
2. b
3. c
4. a
5. c
6. c
7. b
8. d

Practice Test 2:
1. b
2. a
3. a
4. b
5. c
6. c
7. b

Practice Test 3:
1. a
2. d
3. c

4. b
5. c
6. b

Comprehensive Practice Test:
True/False Questions:
1. F
2. T
3. F
4. T
5. T
6. T
7. F
8. T

Multiple-Choice Questions:
1. d
2. c
3. c
4. c
5. b
6. d
7. b
8. b
9. b
10. d
11. c
12. b
13. c

Short-Answer/Essay Questions:
1. Answer must include that James-Lange theory suggests that emotions occur after physical arousal and the interpretation of that arousal, while cognitive theory suggests that in addition to physical arousal, the context of the situation is included in an interpretation.
page ref: 292-293

2. Answer must include discussion of what the text refers to as "emotional reflex," the idea that fear is classically conditioned, that it interacts with mental processes and the actual role of the amygdale.
page ref: 297

3. Answer must include a brief discussion of any of the following: difficulty controlling emotions as a possible source of violent aggression, consequences of suppressing overt behavior, and the interactions between emotions and cognition.
page ref: 301-302

4. Answer must include the idea that repeated attempts to change something – if met with failure, may result in giving up.
page ref: 310

5. Answer must include a.) men and women are similar in bodily reactions to sex, b.) women respond more slowly – but stay aroused longer than men, c.) women's ability to have multiple orgasms and men's refractory period, d.) "size doesn't matter."
page ref: 321

Chapter 8 Personality

Practice Test 1:
1. c
2. c
3. b
4. c
5. a
6. b
7. d
8. b
9. c

Practice Test 2:
1. c
2. b
3. d
4. b
5. a
6. c
7. a

Practice Test 3:
1. c
2. b
3. d
4. c
5. c
6. b
7. a
8. d

Comprehensive Practice Test:
True/False Questions:
1. T
2. F
3. F
4. T
5. T
6. T

7. F
8. T

Multiple-Choice Questions:
1. b
2. c
3. a
4. c
5. c
6. a
7. d
8. d
9. c
10. d
11. b
12. a
13. b

Short-Answer/Essay Questions:
1. Answer must include the idea that denial involves actual refusal to accept a concept or situation, while rationalization involves justification of actions or ideas in order to make them acceptable to the self.
page ref: 337

2. Answer must include the idea that fewer traits means that they are less predictive of specific behavior.
page ref: 344

3. Answer must include definition of *reactive,* such as the intensity of a response and the time delay before response.
page ref: 350

4. Answer must address the variability between residences of twins and the similarities and preferably include an example of how this might be a problem.
page ref: 355

5. Answer should include an understanding of self-control versus influence by others and environmental situations. It should also include an explanation of the level of personal responsibility accepted by individuals with differing loci.
page ref: 360

6. Answer should address the focus of personal motivation by individuals in each type of culture, with individualist societies being centered on personal desires and achievements, while collective cultures focus on the well-being of the group – whether family, company or society.
page ref: 366

Chapter 9 Psychology Over the Life Span

Practice Test 1:

1. a
2. d
3. c
4. a
5. d
6. a
7. b
8. c

Practice Test 2:

1. d
2. b
3. d
4. b
5. c
6. a
7. d
8. a
9 c
10. d
11. a
12. c

Practice Test 3:

1. a
2. a
3. d
4. d
5. d
6. a
7. b

Comprehensive Practice Test:
True/False Questions:

1. T
2. T
3. F
4. F
5. T
6. F
7. F
8. T

Multiple-Choice Questions:
1. c
2. d
3. c
4. d
5. c
6. b
7. b
8. d
9. a
10. a
11. c

Short-Answer/Essay Questions:
1. There are parts of Piaget's theory that have been supported. For example, he was correct in describing the qualitative shifts in performance of specific tasks. Other aspects of his theory have not been support in the recent research. For example, his timing of formal operations has not been supported.
page ref: 395-396

2. The period of adolescent development is characterized by the appearance of sexual characteristics. It begins with puberty. It is period when adolescents tend to have conflicts with their parents, may be prone to take risks, and experience extreme mood swings.
page ref: 404-409

3. Semantic memory, implicit memory, and the storing of new episodic memories remain intact into very old age. The elderly have difficulty when they must recall specific episodic memories due to frontal lobe impairment, which is also responsible for difficulties the elderly have with tasks involving working memory.
page ref: 412-413

Chapter 10 Stress, Health, and Coping

Practice Test 1:
1. a
2. d
3. a
4. c
5. c.
6. c
7. d
8. a

Practice Test 2:
1. a

2. d
3. b
4. a
5. d
6. c
7. d
8. b
9. d
10. c
11. a

Practice Test 3:
1. a
2. b
3. a
4. c
5. d
6. d
7. b
8. c
9. d
10. c

Comprehensive Practice Test:
True/False Questions:
1. T
2. F
3. T
4. T
5. F
6. F
7. F
8. T

Multiple-Choice Questions:
1. c
2. a
3. d
4. a
5. b
6. d
7. c
8. c
9. a
10. c
11. d
12. b
13. d

14. b
15. d

Short-Answer/Essay Questions:
1. It is a general term for the myriad of bodily and psychological responses to an event, object, etc. that alters your body's equilibrium.
page ref: 427

2. Sleep deprivation adversely affects cognitive, emotional, physical health. People are less likely sustain attention, learn and remember information when sleep deprived. People are also more likely to be irritable when sleep deprived. And, sleep deprivation can also weaken one's immune system.
page ref: 441-442

3. Develop a routine sleeping schedule for every day of the week which provides the person with 8 hours of sleep. By routine, the person should stick to the time he or she goes to bed and awakes each day. Insure that one's bedroom area is free from potentially distracting sources providing one with an environment conducive to sleep. In the evening, avoid ingesting substances considered to be stimulants. If possible incorporate meditation or deep relaxation techniques into one's lifestyle which has many benefits of which an important one is decreasing levels of stress.
page ref: 448

4. No, people with unstable high self-esteem are more likely to use aggression.
page ref: 455

5. A variety of supportive relationships. In addition, research has shown that it is generally perceived support, not enacted support, that provides the buffer against stress.
page ref: 463

Chapter 11 Psychological Disorders

Practice Test 1:
1. d
2. a
3. d
4. b
5. a
6. a
7. a
8. b
9. a
10. a

Practice Test 2:
1. c
2. a
3. c

4. d
5. a
6. a
7. a
8. c
9. b
10. a

Practice Test 3:
1. a
2. d
3. d
4. a
5. b
6. a
7. d
8. b

Comprehensive Practice Test:
True/False Questions:
1. F
2. T
3. F
4. F
5. T
6. F

Multiple-Choice Questions:
1. d
2. c
3. a
4. d
5. b
6. d
7. a
8. c
9. b
10. a
11. d
12. a
13. c
14. b
15. b

Short-Answer/Essay Questions:
1. It is a way of understanding the development of a psychological disorder, in which a predisposition to a given disorder (diathesis) and specific factors (stress) combine to trigger the onset of the disorder.
page ref: 477-478

2. If you talk about it, you won't really do it. People who attempt suicide are "crazy." Someone determined to commit suicide can't be stopped. People who commit suicide weren't willing to seek help. Talking about suicide could give someone the idea, so you shouldn't talk or ask about it.
page ref: 485

3. Animal fears, blood-injection-injury fears, natural environment fears, situations fears, miscellaneous fears
page ref: 493

4. Paranoid, disorganized, catatonic, and undifferentiated
page ref: 500

5.   Cluster A – odd, eccentric behaviors
         Cluster B – emotional or dramatic behaviors
         Cluster C – anxious or fearful behaviors or symptoms
page ref: 511-512

Chapter 12 Treatment

Practice Test 1:
1. a
2. b
3. c
4. a
5. d
6. a
7 b
8. b
9. c

Practice Test 2:
1. b
2. c
3. a
4. c
5. a
6. a
7. a
8. c

9. a
10. d

Practice Test 3:
1. b
2. d
3. c
4. d
5. a
6. d

Comprehensive Practice Test:
True/False Questions:
1. T
2. F
3. F
4. T
5. F
6. F
7. T
8. F

Multiple-Choice Questions:
1. c
2. a
3. d
4. b
5. b
6. a
7. d
8. c
9. c
10. d
11. b
12. a

Short-Answer/Essay Questions:
1. Psychoanalysis, client-centered
page ref: 523

2. Activating event, beliefs, consequences, dispute, effect, further action
page ref: 534

3. ECT is a controlled brain seizure and has been utilized for a number of years. ECT was developed for use with schizophrenia, but it has been used primarily with depression. TMS transmits high-intensity magnetism to the brain in short bursts lasting 100-200 microseconds. It does not require hospitalization like ECT. TMS is considered experimental. TMS and ECT have been shown to be equally effective.

page ref: 540-544

4. Systems therapy is a type of therapy that views a client's symptoms as occurring in a larger context, or styste (such as the family or subculture), and holds that a change in one part of the system affects the rest of the system. The client is the "identified patient," but the system is considered the "patient" that is to be treated.
page ref: 543

5. Behavioral techniques such as relaxation, exposure, or behavior modification, focus on changing maladaptive behavior, its antecedents, or its consequences. Cognitive techniques such as cognitive restructuring or role playing, focus un changing dysfunctional unrealistic thoughts to more realistic ones and recognizing the relationships between thoughts, feelings, and behaviors.
page ref: 536

Chapter 13 Social Psychology

Practice Test 1:
1. d
2. c
3. b
4. a
5. d
6. c

Practice Test 2:
1. c
2. c
3. d
4. a
5. b
6. d
7. b
8. c

Comprehensive Practice Test:
True/False Questions:
1. F
2. F
3. T
4. F
5. F
6. T

Multiple-Choice Questions:
1. d
2. c
3. c

4. c
5. d
6. d
7. c
8. d
9. a
10. d
11. b
12. b
13. a
14. d

Short-Answer/Essay Questions

1. Both groups becoming more aware of the similarities between the groups. Evidence being presented that alters stereotypes. Shattering the illusion that the outgroup is homogenous.
page ref: 571

2. A cognitive shortcut for determining attribution that generally occurs outside of conscious awareness. Correspondence, self-serving, belief in a just world
page ref: 573

3. It is comprised of three dimensions: passion, intimacy, and commitment. Different mixes of these dimensions give rise to seven types of love. For example, the presence of all three dimensions is consummate love while the presence of just commitment is empty love.
page ref: 578

4. The foot-in-the-door technique consists of achieving compliance by beginning with an insignificant request, followed by a larger request. This is effective because people want to seem consistent. The lowball technique consist of getting someone to make an agreement and then increasing the cost of that agreement, also effective because people want to seem committed or consistent. The door-in-the-face technique begins with a very large request and then, when it is denied as expected, a smaller request for what is actually desired. This is effective because of the reciprocity principle.
page ref: 586-587

GRADE AID STUDY GUIDE ANSWER KEY
TO CRISS-CROSS PUZZLES

Chapter 1 Criss-Cross Puzzle

Across
5. James
7. Correlation
9. Sampling bias
12. Data
15. Clinical
16. Skinner
17. Hypothesis
18. Sample
19. Reliability
20. Population
21. Wundt

Down
1. Replication
2. Dependent
3. Darwin.
4. Gestalt
6. Meta-analysis
8. Operational
9. Survey
10. Freud
13. Applied
14. Introspection

Chapter 2 Criss-Cross Puzzle

Across
5. Genotype
10. Dendrite
11. SSRI
12. Gyri
13. Lesion
14. CNS
15. Hippocampus
17. Thalamus
20. Glial cells

Down
1. Reflex
2. Lobes
3. Synapse
4. Negative
6. Heritability
7. Myelin
8. Neuron
9. Pruning
16. Plasticity
18. Amygdala
19. Mutation

Chapter 3 Criss-Cross Puzzle

Across
1. After image
3. Blindspot
4. Astigmatism
5. Loudness
9. Tastebuds
12. Attention
14. Pheromones
15. Popout
17. Kinesthetic

Down
2. Ganglion cells
6. Figure
7. Bias
8. Fovea
10. Endorphins
11. Rods
13. Topdown
14. Pitch
16. Pupil

Chapter 4 Criss-Cross Puzzle

Across

2. Shaping
5. Positive
7. Extinction
11. Law of Effect
14. Amygdala
16. Skinner
17. Operant
19. Tolman
20. Pavlov

Down

1. Habituation
3. Avoidance
4. Bandura
6. UCS
8. Latent
9. Partial
10. Phobia
12. Classical
13. Ratio
15. Albert
18. Insight

Chapter 5 Criss-Cross Puzzle

Across

3. Luria
4. Cues
6. Rehearsal
10. Chunk
11. Recognition
13. Habit
14. STM
16. Mnemonic

Down

1. Amnesia
2. Flashbulb
5. Ebbinghaus
7. Storage
8. Consolidation
9. Retrieval
12. Code
15. Decay
16. Method of loci
17. Episodic

Chapter 6 Criss-Cross Puzzle

Across

3. Adoption
4. Prodigy
5. Working
6. Fluid
8. Test bias
13. Algorithm
16. Two
17. Telegraphic speech
19. Syntax

Down

1. Empiricism
2. Factoral analysis
7. Spearman
8. Testosterone
9. Semantics
10. Gardner
11. Creativity
12. Norming
14. Gifted
15. Heuristic
18. Phoneme

Chapter 7 Criss-Cross Puzzle

Across
1. Homeostasis
7. Incentive
9. Drive
12. Maslow
17. Estrogens
18. Approach
20. Implicit

Down
2. Obesity
3. Self-actualization
4. Display rules
5. Androgens
6. Need
8. LeDoux
10. Ekman
11. Insulin
13. Bisexual
14. Want
15. Polygraph
16. Set point
19. Six

Chapter 8 Criss-Cross Puzzle

Across
2. Bandura
3. Self-efficacy
8. Expectancies
12. Eysenck
13. Rogers
14. Five
17. Firstborn
18. Three
19. Freud

Down
1. Projective test
3. Superego
4. Psychoticism
5. Secure
6. Maslow
7. Repression
9. Personality
10. Activity
11. Inhibition
15. MISTRA
16. Collectivist

Chapter 9 Criss-Cross Puzzle

Across
2. Four
3. Teratogen
6. Bowlby
9. Intimacy
13. Preoperational
14. Attacj,emt
16. Longitudinal
17. Schema

Down
1. Kohlberg
4. Adolescence
5. Zygote
7. Terminal decline
8. SIDS
10. Vygotsky
11. Genes
12. Girls
15. Fetus

Chapter 10 Criss-Cross Puzzle

Across
1. Opiate
4. Black out
6. Cortisol
12. Alcohol
13. Atheroschlerosis
15. REM
16. Insomnia
17. Hypnogogic
18. Primary
19. B Cell

Down
2. Exhaustion
3. Freud
5. Stressor
7. Aggression
8. NK cells
9. Alarm
10. Marijuana
11. Sleep Apnea
13. Acute
14. Coping
20. Latent

Chapter 11 Criss-Cross Puzzle

Across
2. OCD
3. DSM
6. Obsession
8. Negative
12. Agoraphobia
14. PTSD
15. Dysthymia

Down
1. Hallucinations
3. Diathesis
4. Suicide
5. Five
7. Bipolar
9. Panic Attack
10. Two
11. Phobia
13. Axes
15. Delusions

Chapter 12 Criss-Cross Puzzle

Across
3. Modality
6. SSRI
7. ECT
11. Cognitive
13. Freud
14. Ellis
15. Bibliotherapy
16. Proposed client-centered therapy
17. MAOI
18. Exposure
19. Systems

Down
1. Reistance
2. Lithium
4. Dispute
5. Free association
8. Thoughts
9. Incongruence
10. Self-help groups
12. Tokens

Chapter 13 Criss-Cross Puzzle

Across

4. Stereotype
5. Milgram
9. Secure
10. Norms
12. Dissonance
13. In-group
14. Compliance
17. Internal
19. Commitment
20. Persuasion

Down

1. Deindividuation
2. Genovese
3. Prosocial
6. Mere exposure effect
7. Obedience
8. Conformity
11. Sternberg
15. Prejudice
16. Altruism
. 18. Attribution

NOTES

NOTES

NOTES

NOTES

NOTES